Happy Hiking

Happy Hiking

Falling In Love on the Appalachian Trail

Emily M. Leonard

FIRST PAPERBACK EDITION

Edited by Elaine Starner

Cover and Interior Design by Berge Design
Inspiration from photos taken by Bruce Leonard, Emily Leonard, and Stephanie Harvie

Photos by: Bruce Leonard, Andrew Bement, James Fetig, Karl Berger,
Liz Wojcicki, Stephanie Harvie, Emily Leonard and several unknown AT hikers

Summary: *Happy Hiking* is a biographical story about Emily Leonard's 2015 Appalachian Trail thru-hike.

ISBN 978-1-7361568-0-3 (paperback bw)
ISBN 978-1-7361568-2-7 (paperback color)
ISBN 978-1-7361568-1-0 (ebook)

Other titles written by the author are
Black Bear's Adventure
Black Bear's Adventure Companion Guide

The author can be reached through her website EmilysEscapades.com

Some names have been changed to protect the privacy of the individuals.

Printed in the United States of America

Dear Mom and Dad,

Mom, thanks for giving me life. The Lord took you from us way too soon, but not before you could teach me the importance of faith, to appreciate life to its fullest, and that joy comes from the inside. You were always happy even though times were not always great. I may not have listened to your advice when you were here, but I sure do now!

Dad, thanks for teaching me how to work hard, even when I didn't want to. You taught me to do the best that I can and that if it is worth doing, it is worth doing right; to never give up, no matter how tough it gets; and when you stop loving what you're doing, it is time to quit. I am sorry for not completing my book before you went to be with Mom.

Contents

Prologue

Sleep came fast. The best yet, but soon after drifting away, I awoke in a panic. Without stirring, I screamed, "OH MY GOSH! BRUCE, THERE'S AN ANIMAL ON MY LEG! I CAN FEEL ITS FUR ON THE BACK OF MY ANKLE! I DON'T DARE MOVE! WHAT DO I DO?"

I was in a deep, peaceful sleep, then abruptly awakened by something furry rubbing back and forth against my exposed skin. Alarmed and frightened as thoughts filled my sleepy, terrified brain, I tried discerning the danger. Was it some carnivorous creature looking for a midnight snack, or worse? I was frozen in fear. What if I was sprayed by a skunk? Okay, maybe being scented by Pepe Le Pew wasn't as threatening as having my leg gnawed off. But when you are terrified and you have no clue where you are, your reasoning skills are non-existent. My mind raced as horrendous scenarios played out in split seconds.

I began to wonder if I was cut out to hike 2,200 miles solo. What was I thinking? I grew up in the woods, hunting and fishing, but had never been there alone. Had I embarked on an adventure that was doomed to fail?

It is truly amazing how the brain works. I went from fear of death to fearing I would have to admit defeat. I am still not sure which was more terrifying.

APPAL
WILDERN
DAWSON
BOARD OF
GEORGIA
ASSOC
PPALACHIAN
REATION S
REI
XPLORER PO
SCOUTS OF

1

Road Trip

Good-bye parties were thrown, hugs and kisses shared, and the car packed. A year and a half of planning had gone by faster than expected. It was time to leave my current safe and comfortable life. The preparation was complete. Most of my to-dos were done. Unfinished items would have to wait.

The excitement was such a rush I could barely contain myself. It reminded me of our road trips when we were first married. Bruce's job required lots of travel. In the beginning, I had the luxury of joining him on the road. Later, kids, work, life, and responsibilities put a stop to all those adventures.

At 7:00am on March 7, 2015, we pulled out of our garage in Lowell, Maine. Our destination was Georgia. It was below freezing, with 2 feet of snow on the lawn and 3 feet of ice on the lake. With the GPS programmed and our Subaru Outback stuffed, we headed south. Unlike our earlier road trips, this one would end with me on a journey without Bruce.

First stop was 35 miles down the road. We needed to pick up my hiking partners, Andrew and his service dog, Mozzie, a duo I had met at work. Andrew needed a ride to the terminus and my family wanted me to have a hiking partner.

Andrew, a quiet young man in his thirties, was a retired Marine. Mozzie, his one-year-old black German-shepherd mix of 88 pounds and still growing, was more of a clown than a dog. While he was on command, you wouldn't even know he was in the room. But in play time, watch out! He was everywhere and such a goofball. He made our duo a trio of hiking fun.

I suppose a normal husband would have been jealous of his wife taking off for a six-month adventure with a strange, handsome man. But not my guy. We were all about trust—and far from normal.

Andrew filled in the gaps for me. Bruce was my master planner. Andrew specialized in high tech, an expertise hubby and I were both lacking. He had all the cool navigation and weather apps on his iPhone. I did own the newest and biggest iPhone but did not have the know-how. I could take pictures with it!

More hugs, kisses, and good-byes with Dana, Andrew's wife, and we were once again headed south. Dana wasn't quite as excited about us leaving as we were. Why would she be? She was being left alone.

We were all happy little travelers, even Mozzie. Bruce and I took turns driving and shotgun. Andrew and Mozzie enjoyed being chauffeured. Uneventful, but nonetheless a long day. Hours behind the windshield tend to make a person a little brain dead and lifeless, no matter how good the company or scenery. We were glad to be at our destination.

To split the drive in half, we stopped at the Aloft Hotel in Winchester, Virginia, a pet-friendly place. Our days of long-distance driving through the night were over. No catnapping in the car at rest areas on this trip. We wanted to be fresh and strong for our first steps on the trail.

We shared a room with two queen beds. Upon check-in, we were asked if we'd like to borrow a dog bed. Of course, we did. But apparently it did not meet the Moz's standards. He must have known in a couple days he'd be sleeping on the ground. That night it was Bruce and I in one bed and Mozzie and Andrew in the other. Then it was Bruce, Mozzie, and I in one and Andrew solo.

Throughout the short night, I didn't know if I would wake to Bruce snoring in my ear or Mozzie's fur tickling my nose. Mozzie took full advantage of pillow surfing from one bed to the other at his desire. Smart dog. As long as Andrew stayed where he belonged, all was good.

We were up and ready early with a complimentary to-go breakfast from the hotel's bistro. Another 594 miles behind the windshield filled our day's agenda. Our final destination was Amicalola Falls State Park and Lodge, the unofficial start of the Appalachian Trail for a northbound hike.

The southern terminus of the AT is the peak of Springer Mountain, and there are two ways to get there. The easier of the two is USFS 42, a dirt road to Springer Mountain parking lot. This road is passable by most vehicles except during prolonged bad weather. From the parking lot, thru-hikers must hike south one mile uphill to reach the peak of Springer Mountain, then retrace their steps, passing through the parking lot to continue north. We chose to start at the second option, the Amicalola Falls approach trail, located in Amicalola Falls State Park.

The main attraction in the 829-acre park is Amicalola Falls; at a height of 729 feet, it is the tallest waterfall east of the Mississippi River. The park's name comes from Cherokee language meaning "tumbling waters." An 8.8-mile blue-blazed trail from Amicalola Falls Lodge leads to the top of Springer Mountain. This route takes hikers up 700-plus steps by the cascading falls, adding an extra day to their hike. What's one more day, when we were planning to be gone for six months? I had come all this way, and I wanted to see everything I possibly could.

After two days on the road, we were greeted by our very own personal welcoming committee, Jimmy, I Believe, Owl Bear, Cozy, Bison, Mom, and Dad. I Believe, Owl Bear, Cozy, and Bison had hiked the trail in 2014, supported by Jimmy. I had followed I Believe on *Trail Journals* and met them when they reached Maine.

The meet and greet was quick due to the welcome center closing soon. We registered, then weighed our packs, so we wouldn't have to do that task in the morning. An extra-early start was planned. We had 10 minutes to do our tasks before the welcome center's doors were locked.

Andrew and I claimed hiker numbers 304 and 303. Several thousand hikers attempt a thru-hike of the 2,189.2 miles, but on average, only one in four hikers complete the mammoth journey. And of that twenty-five percent who complete the trail, about 25 percent of those hikers are female. If you ask the hate stalker on my blog, the stats were stacked against me.

Accommodations at the lodge were simple, with a stunning westerly view of a mountain range that seemed to go on forever. Bruce and I would be sharing our room again with Andrew and Mozzie and also Mom and Dad. The room featured two double beds on the main level and one in the loft. Mozzie and Andrew took the loft; there would be no surfing tonight.

There was much to be done before lights out. We needed to transition from road trip to hiking. Once settled in, we checked and rechecked our food and gear. Then we gathered in the dining room to chitchat with our greeting committee.

Two beautiful, warm, sunny days set our moods high. We continued soaking up the golden rays in the cool mountain air as we watched the sun drop behind the horizon like the curtain closing at the end of an act. Andrew and Mozzie climbed the ladder to their bunk, and Mom, Dad, Bruce, and I crawled into our beds.

It may have been bedtime, but my brain was far from tired. I couldn't believe that the next day the adventure would begin.

It was March 8, 2015. Not quite 18 months before on September 30, 2013, I had received a simple text from my dear friend Sharon. It was an ordinary, no-thrills day at home. I was chin deep in a pile of paperwork, medical bills to be exact. Nothing serious, just organizing and keeping track of our health spending account. "I just love paperwork" is a phrase you will never hear from my lips.

I was on my side of the office while Bruce was on his side. He was actually working and earning a living. We concentrated silently on our own tasks. He has the luxury of working from home when not on the road traveling. The silence was broken by the designated text tone for Sharon. Usually my phone is on do-not-disturb when I am working in the office with Bruce, but I had forgotten to do it that day. The sound of the incoming text excited me for a couple reasons: First, I hardly ever receive text messages, and second, because I knew it was Sharon. All the text said was, "Do you want to hike the AT?"

A year prior to this, I would have found this question to be out of character for her, but lately, adventure had become her thing. We had already completed an introductory rock-climbing class over in North Conway, New Hampshire, that spring. When she invited me to join her on that adventure, I said "Sure!" I never fessed up about my fear of heights until we were strapped in and climbing the face of a ledge. So much for an introductory class! I would hate to see the class titled "intermediate." I did not want my fear to keep me from experiencing something new.

After I read her text, without saying a word, I handed my phone over to Bruce to read. He didn't even look up from his work and replied, "I think you should do it." In one minute, I went from not even a conscious thought of the Appalachian Trail to a thru-hiker in the making.

Over the next several days, Sharon and I texted back and forth as we discussed our excitement about our future adventure, our fears, and our doubts if we could even accomplish such a journey. After all, neither one of us had any backpacking experience.

A few days later, Bruce and I watched a National Geographic documentary about the Appalachian Trail. It was a short film showing the beauty of the trail in all her glory and how it came to be. Benton MacKaye was the visionary behind the Appalachian Trail. I won't bore you with the historical facts of how the trail began. That information can be found at the Appalachian Trail Conservancy, also known as the ATC.

Of course, all the footage was the AT at her best. Who wouldn't want to escape the clutches of reality for the peace and serenity of the wilderness by entering into the charming embrace of the oldest mountain range in the world? I was hooked.

Unfortunately, after several months of planning and growing excitement, it appeared I would be hiking alone. Sharon's plans changed unexpectedly, and she was unable to go. My family was very grateful when I found Andrew.

APPALACHIAN
GEORGIA APPALACHIAN TRAIL CLUB

2

Day One

Daybreak came and with it, a new scene. Gone was the warmth of the sun. It was replaced with fog, rain, and temperatures that had us questioning our gear choices. Drizzly weather would not delay our start, though.

There is a saying on the trail: "No Rain, No Pain, No Maine!" But did it really need to start on our first day? Couldn't the rain and pain have waited until we were more trail strong? Nope! Why put off until tomorrow what can be done today?

It was just enough to make us realize this wasn't going to be all sunshine and happy faces. If we wanted that, we could have stayed home and watched the Travel Channel.

Though still full from supper, we couldn't pass up the all-you-can-eat (AYCE) breakfast buffet before strapping on our packs and hitting the trail. It would be several days before we could have real food again. The extra-full tummy made it hard to carry my pack.

Since we had tweaked our packs one last time, we decided to get another weight measurement before officially starting. My pack weighed in at a solid 34 pounds, four more than I wanted. Andrew's topped the scales at a whopping 48 pounds.

We proceeded to the archway and the sign pointing us to the approach trail. The Appalachian Trail is marked by white blazes, two inches wide by six inches long, painted on trees, fence posts, rocks, buildings, and any other surface along the trail for hikers to easily see which way to go. The approach trail and most side trails are blue blazed.

Mom and Dad took our photos under the arch. It was 9:20am. We said good-bye to our welcoming and farewell crew. We were off. It wasn't the bright and early start I had planned on, but that turned out to be a good thing. The drizzle we woke to had stopped, and the morning mountain chill had warmed.

Bruce's initial plan was to hike to the terminus with us, camp out for the night, then hike north the one mile to the Springer Mountain parking lot where Jimmy would meet him for a shuttle back to the car. But USFS 42 was in poor shape. There had been record amounts of snow for the whole East Coast that season, making travel on USFS 42 questionable for any non-4-wheel-drive vehicle. Bruce decided to hike up with us, camp with us for the night, then in the morning, hike back down the same way we had come up.

The view as we climbed the 700-plus steps passing the waterfall was breathtaking and impressive, but at the same time exhausting. We had to stop several times to catch our breath, and that was just the start. Beginning elevation was 1,800 feet, the falls were at 2,216 feet, and our day would end at 3,782 feet. We could have started at the parking lot at 3,350 feet and only climbed 432 feet. But no, someone was determined to only hike in one direction, no backtracking or flip-flopping for her!

As the day progressed, the southern sun warmed the air and dried the night rains, leaving little trace of dampness. The only thing remaining wet were our sweaty backs and feet. It was hot for us Yankees. We had gone from winter to summer quicker than a hiker can down a hamburger. We weren't complaining, but we weren't too happy, either.

The first water source was at Black Gap Shelter, 7.3 miles from the arch. It was 0.1 mile east of the trail, according to *The A.T. Guide* by David "Awol" Miller. The spring was down a steep side trail and barely a trickle. This was the first of many disappointing water sources. But it was water.

We took a long lunch break at Black Gap. The shelter was empty, although a trail maintenance crew was working on the privy out back.

Those five men and women volunteered their time fixing whatever needed to be done on their section of trail. Their dedication to preservation of the trail is incredible.

Since we were alone and it was only mid-day, we took the liberty of spreading out inside the shelter for some R&R, lunch, and a catnap. The forest was quiet and peaceful except for the occasional rustle of dry leaves disturbed by a gentle breeze. We didn't even hear the work crew, who were working several yards behind the shelter. It was a most enjoyable nap away from the hustle and bustle of town, work, and people. I was doing just what I wanted to do on this adventure. I was hoping this would be a trail practice I would do frequently.

Nap time was over. We needed to make the final 482-foot elevation push over 1.5 miles to Springer Mountain and the true start of our thru-hike. Not a tough climb by any means, but we were already hot, tired, and worn from the approach trail and our lack of fitness.

Just as we were heading out to finish the day, the trail maintenance crew were finishing up their duties. One of the crew was carrying a large tent abandoned by a previous hiker. We asked if this was normal and their response was "Absolutely!" They informed us that inexperienced hikers often overpack, then leave things along the trail and at shelters. In fact, one man commented that this particular crew donates what they find to a local Boy Scout troop and are able to keep them well stocked in good gear, just from what others leave behind. Great for the scout troop, but not so pleasant for the souls who have to pack out what others discard.

Leave No Trace (LNT) is a 7-principle outdoor code of ethics. Anyone participating in the wild should adhere to this code. Principle #3 is "Dispose of waste properly," or "If you pack it in, pack it out."

At 3:30pm, we arrived at the plaque marking the summit of Springer Mountain. It read "Appalachian Trail Georgia to Maine. A footpath for those who seek fellowship with the wilderness. 1934 The Georgia Appalachian Club."

We took turns posing next to the metal monument attached to the rock, documenting proof that we really were there—just in case anyone back home had any doubts. This marked mile zero and the first white blaze.

Every year, the distance between Springer Mountain and Katahdin, the mountain in Maine marking the northern terminus of the AT, changes due to trail reroutes, acquisition of land, and a host of other reasons. Ninety-nine percent of the original trail has been rerouted. In 2015, the total distance was 2,189.2 miles.

After our informal photo shoot, we put our packs back on for the last time of the day and took our first steps on the Appalachian Trail as we passed our first white blaze. Only 4,999,999 steps to go. Little did we know how important that white mark would become.

The shelter was only .1 mile from the peak and already three-quarters full, but that was okay. We had planned on tenting. We found two spots roughed out by previous hikers. LNT principle #2: Travel and camp on durable surfaces. To help minimize the wear and tear of the shelter areas and along the trail, it is recommended to tent in already established sites. This helps to prevent erosion and maintains the integrity of the outdoor experience.

Andrew used a bivy bag underneath a tarp. A bivy is a waterproof sack you put your sleeping bag and sleeping pad in. I set up both my tents, the Cuben Fiber tarp tent with enclosure from Hyperlite Mountain Gear (HMG) and my Hubba Hubba™ nylon self-standing tent from Mountain Safety Research (MSR). I wanted to see which one I liked better. This would be the first time I had set up either one outside. Back home, winter had prevented any real situation practice set-ups. Both were two-person shelters. Bruce and I decided to sleep in the Hubba Hubba and store our gear in the Hyperlite.

It took me awhile to set up camp. I would not let hubby help me since he would not be with me on the trail most of the time. I had in my mind what I wanted to do, but perception is sometimes far from reality. Once our tents were erected, it was time to think about food.

The temperature was dropping with the sun and the rain was returning. It was barely a drizzle, but wet is wet and at 3,700 feet, wet is cold. When the sun set, little did we know it would be the last time we would see it for several days.

Dinner took longer than anticipated. Again, I had in my mind what to do, but my plans never included having Bruce with me. At one point while I was sorting our food—his, mine, mine, mine, his—he thought my other bag of food was free game. Wrong! He had been grazing for a while on my gluten-free stash that was supposed to last me five days!

When our kids were babies, I would prep the kiddos' food, and if Bruce was near, I would hand him the dish, snack, or whatever munchie I had just fixed. I would then ask him to give it to whichever child it was intended for. I would prep the next one, turn around, and see baby number one still waiting to eat and Bruce holding an empty dish, often saying, "That was tasty." It was a good thing my "hiker hunger" had not yet kicked in, or else I would have been one very hungry hiker those first few days.

While we were finishing our dinner of dehydrated meals cooked with my Jetboil, Sisu joined us for a chat. "Sisu" was a trail name used by Jim Fetig, who was a volunteer ridge-runner for the state of Georgia. He also volunteered at the ATC headquarters in Harpers Ferry. Ridge-runners help to educate hikers along the trail, making sure everyone is following good hiker etiquette.

He noticed my two tents, so I explained to him I wasn't sure which tent to use. He said, "I always tell hikers when they consider what gear to use, to ask themselves just one question and the answer to that question will help them with their choices. That question is: Are you here to camp or are you here to hike? Choose the gear that will help you have a successful hike."

That was some of the best advice I heard. Whenever I stopped in town and thought about picking up something new or changing something out, I would keep that in mind.

Andrew and Mozzie were tucked away under their tarp; it looked cozy but way too rustic and unprotected for me. I liked the idea of being a minimalist more than actually being one. Bruce and I zippered ourselves inside my Hubba Hubba and were settling in for the night just as the rain began to dance on the tent's fly.

It was comfy inside our little abode despite the dropping temperatures and increasing precipitation. Before long, my eyelids were drooping, then closed completely. I was falling into a nice sleep when hubby decided nature called and he needed to answer it sooner rather than later. So off to the privy we went together.

I didn't go with him because he needed a bodyguard. Rather, since I was disturbed from my slumber, I too needed to tinkle. It was so foggy, we could hardly discern the trail to the privy and actually got disoriented. My headlamp and his flashlight barely cut through the cloud that had closed in on the mountain. The ground was coated in a slippery, slimy mud, making it a challenge to remain upright. We were giggling like two teenagers out past curfew.

We made it to the outhouse and took turns, ladies first, what a gentleman. The space was quite roomy and airy, not what you might typically think for outdoor plumbing. Most people conjure up a vision of Laura Ingalls on *Little House on the Prairie* in her long dress. Across the yard she ran, holding on to her bonnet with one hand and reaching for the door with a crescent moon window with the other. That was not the case for most privies on the Appalachian Trail. This structure did have a roof, but the walls only stretched from knee to shoulder height with a half door held closed with a hook and eye. With all that ventilation, one would think the aroma wafting up from the depths wouldn't have been too bad. One could only hope.

It was my turn to hold the lights just so, not to blind the squatter, yet not cast too much light that would put him on exhibition. All of a sudden, it hit me like a vortex, sucking the air out of my lungs. How could he have produced such a horrible smell from what little food we had eaten that day? Oh, that's right, he ate half my bag. I couldn't breathe! I thought I was going to gag and eventually puke!

Then, to make matters worse, his privy skills were not up to par. "I need more t-paper. I got some on my hands," he reported. Oh my gosh! That's just too much information!

Now I was in hysterics. I couldn't stop laughing. With every inhale, I thought my stomach contents would erupt. It was a struggle between laughing gasps and holding down barf. He was on his own; I wasn't helping. I had all I could do to not drop the light while keeping my dinner down.

Bruce finally cleaned up—enough. When we reached the tent, I grabbed the needed supplies of water, soap, wipes, and antibacterial lotion. Once I deemed him safe and germ free, he was allowed back into the tent. It was the first day on the trail, and Bruce had already gone over budget of my gluten-free food and hygiene supplies. What a beginning.

After our late evening comedy act, we were soon back to snuggling in our tent and off to sleep—only to be awakened by a little field mouse who desperately wanted to seek shelter inside with us or find a snack. But he was out of luck, since our food bags were safely hung. He scurried from one side of the tent screen to the other; back and forth he went until we finally scared him away.

Some element was keeping us from sleeping. First it was the bathroom break, then the mouse, then rain on the tent. Or maybe it was the simplicity of the trip so far. We had nothing to do except think about the moment and each other.

As much as we wanted to sleep, we kept chatting about nothing, snuggled, and stole kisses. Who were we? Had we fallen down some rabbit hole to an earlier time when all we had to worry about was finishing a term paper or homework after a date? As we reminisced, I couldn't help thinking about how we had met.

Midway through college, I had been partially educated and I could see my degree at the end of the road. In a couple more years or a few at my pace, I would be marching across the 50-yard line of the University of Maine's football field with a degree in teaching and coaching, my first major accomplishment of my simple life. But those couple years left me heartbroken and alone. I had loved and lost and thought I was doomed forever. Maybe I was meant for a religious life.

I decided to put all my efforts into studying. (Huh, that was a novel thought, since I was at college!) If it was meant to be, that "someone" would find his way to me. I was so hoping religious life was not my calling.

On a warm November night in 1987, I went to a hockey game on campus with my friend, Tonya. At the time, our men on ice were a top-ranked team. Cheering on the Black Bears as they defeated yet another team was everyone's weekend highlight. Unfortunately, that night we came away with an unusual loss.

It was a Saturday, and the night was young. When the third period was over, we were not ready to call it a night. Off to Bangor we drove to drown the loss in music and dance. We didn't even bother to change or fancy ourselves up.

At the establishment, it didn't take me long to set my eyes on a handsome prince. He was tall, well built, with short, curly hair and blue eyes. And that smile, wow! I didn't wait to be approached; I initiated first contact.

I was raised with four brothers and two sisters. My sisters were too girly, so we didn't hang out. My older brothers taught me everything I needed to survive, like how to hunt, fish, drive motorcycles, and fight. At least, that's what they said was all I needed to make it. Yup, fight. Coyness was not in my behavior code of ethics. They said I needed to protect myself in case they weren't around to do so. They never mentioned how to be nice. I guess that was Mom's and the church's job.

Even though I lacked in natural beauty, I was very confident and outgoing, at times maybe even a bit confrontational, a trait that is not too appealing. *I don't care,* I would just say to myself; but it would have been fun to say out loud, "You don't know what you are missing."

That night I did not have to be confrontational. I played it calm and cool and asked Prince Charming to dance. He said, "Yes." Before I knew it, he was escorting me to the dance floor. He placed his arm around my waist and nestled it on the small of my back ever so gently as we walked to the dance floor. Oh, how I turned to mush! I could hardly keep from melting into the floor. As I write this, I still get those warm and tingling feelings.

We polished the dance floor through many songs, chitchatting as the music blocked all consciousness of anything around us. It was just Prince Charming and I, twirling around like Jennifer Grey and Patrick Swayze in *Dirty Dancing.* That's what it felt like. I am sure it looked more like Pinocchio and Geppetto, tangled in string.

The establishment may have been chem-free, but the man of my dreams was not. He was inebriated just enough to be slightly silly. After several pieces of music, a slow song came on and ended our dance number. He decided he needed a beverage—or that was his excuse. I read it as "She is good enough to dance with but not good enough to get close to." And the beverage offer was just a courtesy to get out of a close encounter. He went to the bar, and I joined my friend.

Tonya was surrounded by young studs desperately trying to make advances on her and then myself. They wanted to dance, but I declined. My stomach was still doing somersaults over the guy who had just stolen my heart. I politely told them I needed to rest and that my knee was hurting. True fact. I had injured it earlier in the week playing soccer.

Bruce ended up being ditched by his buddies, so he needed a ride home. Lucky for him, his house was on our way back to campus. If I had been driving, wherever he lived would have been the way I was going. The ride gave us time to talk a little more. I guess he wasn't actually getting out of a dance and he really did need a drink because we set up to meet the next night. Why do us women read into situations? We have a difficult time taking things at face value. We always feel there is an ulterior motive.

While I had been dancing with Bruce, Tonya had met his roommate. They were Maine Maritime Academy students, and we were UMaine coeds. Funny how things work out. So a double date was set for the following evening, and we were going to meet at Alfond Arena. They liked hockey and we had access to tickets. I guess that made us pretty good catches.

The next night couldn't come fast enough. But this time, my friend and I did fancy ourselves up. Tonya had been a beauty queen back in her home state and was a pro at the girl thing. I, on the other hand, needed more attention. My "dressing up" usually involved a sports-team uniform that was already coordinated for me.

My toughest challenge was taming my locks. I had medium-length hair that was extremely curly and frizzy. In high school, my soccer coach used to call me Brillo Pad. He even wrote in my yearbook, "Frizz..." How I used to hate that hair!

Today, I would love to have it back. It took me a long time to learn to work with what I have, and now that I don't have it, I want it back. Life is like that! We take things for granted on a daily basis, and it isn't until we are without that something, that we see just how blessed we were to have it. It can be something as trivial as untamed hair or something more valuable like our spouses, families, and friends.

Tonya worked wonders on my hair. I couldn't wait for the hands on the clock to tell me it was time to go watch UMaine hockey—and, more importantly, to see Prince Charming.

I was there with my brother Mark. When Bruce arrived with his friends, I said, "Hi Bruce, it's nice to see you again."

He looked a little puzzled, and said, "How do you know my name?" It was at that point I realized he didn't recognize me. It was awkward. I was feeling a little sad inside because I had all those gooshy feelings for him, but it seemed there was nothing in return. It took him a few minutes to realize I was the girl from the previous night.

To reassure him, in my non-confrontational way I said, "YOU DON'T EVEN RECOGNIZE ME, DO YOU?" Maybe it wasn't so polite. All I could think was *How drunk was he last night?*

I was shocked and couldn't believe it when he actually said, "No!"

It took me several years to learn the lesson from that night. I originally went to the club "as is." The next night I was trying to be someone I wasn't, and where did it get me? So often we try to be someone else—and it doesn't work. We are who we are. That's not to say one shouldn't improve or work to be a better person. We just need to be ourselves at heart. To do anything else is not fair to ourselves.

Bruce and I started dating seriously right after the second night. Since we attended different schools, we only saw each other sporadically. We did rack up the minutes on our phone bills, though. There was no such thing as unlimited calling plans back in the 80s. When we were together, we had nothing but fun. Sometimes we went out dancing, and sometimes we would just hang out at my apartment, where I cooked and we watched TV. It didn't matter what we did as long as we did it together.

Once we were married, over time, we spent less and less time together. Not because we didn't want to, but because responsibilities got in the way. We didn't even realize we were growing complacent. Just like a frog placed in hot water will jump right out, but when it is placed in cool water and the heat is slowly turned up, the frog doesn't even know it is being boiled alive. It just enjoys the bath until it is no longer alive.

But that first night on the trail, slip-sliding in the mud, gagging on rotting odors, and dealing with hygiene failures was just as fun as those first dates. It would have been easy to get upset, but what fun would that have been?

Sleep eventually came, as those warm, tingly feelings burned through the insulation covering our hearts caused by years of complacency.

3

Rain

We woke to more rain. It poured all night, slowing our start. I am an early bird. If the sun is up, I want to be up. If the sun is down, I am also. Only day two, and beginnings were already slow, mostly because it didn't even start to get light until 7:00am.

In the Northeast, morning rays tickle the horizon about 5:30am in early March. Down south, daybreak is more like a teenager dreading a school morning. This confused the heck out of me. My physical being said, "It's time to rise." But my brain insisted on no such thing, since darkness still dominated.

We woke to a drizzle, ate breakfast in a drizzle, broke camp in a drizzle, and said good-byes in a drizzle. Bruce was headed back down the approach trail. He had only joined us for the one overnight, which was probably a good thing. I wasn't sure I had enough food or supplies for him for the next five days. Besides, he had to go back to work. One of us had to bring in the dough. Might as well be him. He is much better at it than I am.

After more hugs and kisses—from me, not Andrew—Bruce headed back to the car to catch a flight. Andrew, Mozzie, and I headed north in the rain.

Despite the depletion of food rations consumed by Bruce and my decision to ditch a few miscellaneous items back at our room, my pack felt heavy. At least, it was not as weighty as if I had chosen to carry the rain-soaked Hubba Hubba tent. I was glad we had brought both options. It gave me a chance to see how each performed with last night's rain. Both had kept their contents dry, but the Cuben Fiber tent didn't absorb any moisture and had less condensation buildup. The Hubba Hubba nylon free-standing tent offered easy setup with more headroom but retained moisture, making it heavier and harder to pack. The winner was the Echo II tarp tent by Hyperlite Mountain Gear, and the Hubba Hubba went back down the mountain with Bruce.

We started hiking at 9:30am. Later, Bruce recalled that he thought we never were going to leave. It was a three-hour delay from my preferred start time. I learned very quickly that Andrew was not a morning person.

It rained all day. The first full day on the trail was wet. The only benefit was that it made water sources plentiful, unlike the day before. There is nothing like the taste of an ice cold, fresh mountain spring.

I can't recall many trail details those first few days except that we were dirty and I could have planted a veggie garden under my nails.

We hiked roughly eight miles in five hours. Just a little better than 1.5 mph. Not really that bad, considering it was only our second day of hiking and we had sloppy conditions. The trip had already produced an IT band issue for Andrew and two blisters for me, one on my left heel and one on my right fourth toe. Great, still three days and 23.6 miles until we reached Neel Gap.

The Gap would be our first scheduled stop back in "civilization," where Bruce, Jimmy, and I Believe would check to see how we were doing. Andrew had already mentioned a few times that he might consider going home when we arrived there. I hoped not. I felt safe with Andrew, and Mozzie was so much fun to be around. I had not planned on having hiking partners, but now that I had them, I didn't want to give them up.

Hawk Mountain Shelter was full. Hikers flooded the trail, preventing any chance of feeling alone or scared—or of enjoying welcomed solitude. Excitement decorated the conversations, even with the rain.

We were in the honeymoon stage of our grand adventures. Hell probably could have cast its wrath upon us, and we would have been glad it was warm.

Bumpy, a fellow hiker, made friends with us. He was a quiet gentleman in his sixties. He liked Andrew and joined him at his tarp tent for an evening chat. Hidden in my abode, journaling, I overheard their conversation. Andrew shared with Bumpy that he might go home at Neel Gap. Bumpy commented to Andrew that he should stay on the trail because it would be good for him, and having a nice, feisty hiking partner would help. Yeah, my head swelled just a tad.

Day 3 and the honeymoon was over. We hiked to Gooch Mountain Shelter, only a 7.7-mile day. It was one of ups and downs. The trail was smooth, following a ridge. One side of the trail sloped up while the other side dropped, with the 24-inch trail sculpted out. The incline or decline switched from left to right as switchbacks carved their way along the mountainside. The day's elevation started at 3,209 feet and ended at 2,821 feet, never dipping below 2,619 feet. It would have been a nice, easy stroll if it had not been for the rain.

Mother Nature cried all day and shed her last tears as we reached the shelter. The gray and gloom stifled my desire to take photos. Setting up the tent and cooking in the rain were even less desirable tasks that needed to be done. I didn't mind hiking in the rain, but it made everything else miserable. Add the cool mountain temperatures, and I was not a happy hiker.

I had to keep reminding myself that it was my choice to be out there and I could leave anytime I wanted. Well, almost anytime. First, I would need to hike to a road crossing.

But leaving was not a choice. I was committed. I am not a quitter. When I start something, I like to finish it. That doesn't always happen, and when I leave something unfinished, it drives me batty. One thing I did to help increase the odds of my success on this thru-hike was to be accountable not just to myself, but to others. It's easy to give up when you are the only one holding yourself accountable, so, I had told everyone—and I mean everyone—I was going to hike the Appalachian Trail.

I figured the more people I told, the harder it would be to back out. I had two schools committed to following me, grades 4 and 5 at All

Saints Catholic School in Bangor, Maine, and Enfield Station School 5th graders in Enfield, Maine. They were two schools I was associated with as a teacher/coach, and our sons had attended those schools.

Once I began telling people about my plans, I was met with a wide range of responses. Most were very positive and very encouraging. I had little negativity about my abilities presented to my face. Who knew what was said when I wasn't present! I could tell by their responses and body language who believed in me and who didn't.

Just like starting a new job, new hobby, new relationship, or marriage, the honeymoon phase is exciting. It's fun, and one is blind to the nitty-gritty annoyances of that job, hobby, or other person. In fact, what we think are cute nuances in the beginning often become irritations after a while.

Hiking was the same. Instead of taking months or years to discover the honeymoon was over, it took a short 72 hours. But just like all my other new quests, I took my newest adventure seriously and worked to bring joy back into what I was doing. It wasn't a one-time fix. I had to repeat this mindset often. It wasn't because I was having a terrible time on the trail. I would simply forget why I was out there. I let the little things get in the way of the bigger picture. I kept asking myself, "Is my 'why' big enough?"

It's easy to quit when you reach a certain point. It's much harder to persevere. But when you persist and work through the struggles, whether you are long-distance hiking, tackling a project, or bringing spice back to your relationship, it is always worth doing. The honeymoon never has to be over. It is just a choice.

Life is full of choices, and those choices can yield positive outcomes bringing us joy or yield consequences associated with great pain and anguish. Sometimes results are not apparent at first; instead, they are accumulative: one decision after another decision, built upon the previous, producing either a positive or negative experience. A series of good choices over time begets great things. And a chain of poor choices yields unwanted results. We are a product of our decisions whether we want to admit it or not.

If I was to have a successful hike, I knew I needed to make a choice to not let the rain bother me or I needed to just go home. It would be a decision I would have to make over and over again.

I was sleeping in my tent again. I thought I might like shelter life, but we usually left late in the morning and by the time we arrived at the end of the day, the shelters filled up. My chosen tent with its big-ticketed price tag did not provide adequate head room to spend hours in waiting out the rain. My short, five-foot-three inches of vertical dimension couldn't even sit up without cocking my head to one side. I was already thinking I needed a third tent.

I had decided against the Hubba Hubba because it weighed too much when wet. But it was fast and easy to pitch. So I thought the Hubba, MSR's single version of the same tent would be perfect. That purchase would have to wait, though. Bruce may have cut into my food budget, but I had already spent our rainy-day fund on the two tents I already owned.

To make matters worse, my sleeping pad and sleeping bag were failing me in the comfort department. I had chosen a 3/4-length version of a blow-up pad to save on weight and space. I really was trying to be a minimalist and learn to make do.

My mummy sleeping bag was too small, or I was too fat. Either way, I couldn't move around in it. My fear of being restricted often causes panic attacks. Back at Springer Mountain, I had mentioned to Sisu that I hated my mummy sleeping bag because of my issue with confined spaces. He joked and said I would learn to love it like a spouse. I doubted that.

So here we were on the night of day 3, and I was not liking my gear, I had two more blisters, and Andrew was still thinking about leaving the trail. And it was raining, AGAIN!

The hike from Gooch Mountain Shelter to Lance Creek camping area was beautiful. Day 4 was cloudy but rain-free, and a warm breeze helped to dry the sweat. In the few short days on the trail, we had learned being wet was just part of the deal. It was caused either by rain, sweat, or sometimes both at the same time.

We welcomed the sunshine as the sweat soaked our clothes. The wind helped reverse the effects of the sun on our backs. The rain-free day gave us a chance to dry out our soaked boots and gear. Several times we were able to stop to air and powder our feet. This was crucial to getting the blister party on my feet down to a dull roar. At one point, we even took a long lunch break complete with a nap, my favorite.

Just under two miles into the day's hike, we crested Ramrock Mountain at 3,266 feet. It was our first real view of the journey. I cried. Andrew let me have my moment. It wasn't full-out crocodile tears, just a little sentimental sniffle and a single teardrop. I am not a big waterworks emotional crybaby. I don't really cry at sad events or even when friends or family die. I am sad; I just don't show it.

I am more of an action-packed-movie gal who enjoys thrillers like the *Bourne* movies and *24* series with Jack Bower. The *Saw* movies were awesome! Just don't kill the dog. I am more apt to cry at that and at happy times like weddings or in that day's case, a spectacular view. It's warped, I know, but what can I say?

We experienced our first trail magic, twice that day. A hiker named Neema was in the woods where the trail crossed a dirt road. She had a canopy set up, covering her outdoor camp kitchen, serving hot and cold beverages and a variety of foods. We helped ourselves to a drink as Neema cooked breakfast. Enjoying the hot cocoa and snacks, the three of us, Mozzie, Andrew, and myself, posed for a photo that would be added to the Class of 2015 *Hiker Yearbook*.

Later in the day, right about lunchtime, we exited the woods and found Tick-Tock, a bearded old chap who was cooking up hot dogs. The large picnic table was filled with everything you could think of from donuts, fruit juice, ham, bologna, condiments, and more. The table was so full that I couldn't even see everything. Tick-Tock entertained us with conversation as we rested. When it was time to head on, we thanked him kindly for his generosity and I took one piece of bologna to go.

We were starting to recognize the other hikers in our bubble. A hiking bubble is a group of hikers who tend to end up at the same places, give or take a few days. It's the people you see consistently on the trail at any given time. We were in a very large bubble.

Early March is a popular time for hikers to begin a northbound thru-hike, making our bubble quite big. After four days in the woods and meeting up at shelters or campsites, faces were becoming familiar. There were a lot of people on the trail. I saw about thirty new faces a day. But a few started to stand out. Here is an excerpt from my journal, briefly describing some of the original hikers I came in contact with in those first few days.

Doug - looks like Buck from *Band of Brothers*
Kiwi - from New Zealand
Bumpy - old man we met at Amicalola Lodge breakfast
* Nome - looks like Santa Claus, really nice
Girl & Guy Couple - both quiet, he smiles a lot.
Andrew & Armaeus - guy and his Doberman
Ian - world religion major taking a semester off.
GA Tech Student - hiking with friends for spring break. Nice kid. Hurt his knee so they had to get off trail.
Shrek and Donkey - Justin and his dog Lila. From Maine.

Shrek was a big, burly, tattooed dude. Our first meeting was not a good one. He let his dog, Donkey, run free. She was a cute little thing and harmless, but it is wise to take precautions with strange animals on the trail. The trail not only changes people but it can also have an impact on dogs. It is common for a loving family pet to become hostile. Dogs also get tired and sore.

At that first greeting, Lila came running up to greet Mozzie, who was on leash. Andrew held out his hiking stick to prevent any possible dog-to-dog contact and said to Shrek, "Do you mind?"

Shrek looked like he could rip us to shreds with a flick of his wrist. But he was very polite. He called Lila back and said nothing in return. The next time we saw them, Shrek completely ignored us. But with each encounter over the beginning days, the friction eased. The dogs became best friends, and we discovered what a great guy Shrek was—and hopefully he thought the same of us.

After the fourth day of hiking, home for the night became a designated campsite near Lance Creek. There was no shelter and barely a creek. Where had all the rain drained? There was only a trickle of runoff, which made collecting water for dinner and the next day laborious.

Hikers were already occupying the spots close to the trail, so we followed an old, leafed, overgrown road farther off the trail from the other tenters. Andrew and I each claimed our own piece of real estate, giving each other plenty of space so we could decompress alone. With a perfectly pitched tent, I set out to collect water.

Two others set up in the vicinity of Andrew; I was about fifty yards away, all by myself. A solo hiker came through, looking for a spot. He was a strange one, dressed head to toe in camouflage, carrying a small, rough-looking pack. He dropped his load and set up his tarp a little too close for comfort.

His tarp was also camouflage, and he strung it out using guy lines to trees and weighted it with rocks. He then buried the edges with leaves. His whole setup was at the most twelve inches off the ground. Now that was primitive camping. I would have been impressed—if I wasn't so scared of him.

I took my dinner over to where Andrew was and asked if he minded if I moved closer to him. I didn't want to be near Rambo. Andrew prejudged the hiker, and so did the other two hikers. They all had the same uneasy feeling.

Once my tent was repositioned, we went from acres of privacy to crowded condominiums, where our own guy lines almost crossed. But I felt safe. I found out later the hiker's name was Finn. He was a nice guy, and we eventually became Facebook friends. To this day, I still have not told him how he freaked me out the first time I saw him.

There are four Finns in the Class of 2015 Hiker Yearbook, so if you think you know him, you have a one-in-four chance of being right. Or a 75 percent chance of being wrong. Either way, don't tell him our secret.

The freaky feeling continued. I woke to the thunderous sound of a single aircraft with huge bright lights skimming the treetops. I immediately thought of the UFO shows where a redneck southerner with missing teeth tells of his encounter with an unidentified flying object in the night sky. I thought to myself, jokingly, *It's actually true*! The next day, I asked if anyone else saw or heard the mysterious fly-over. I was the only one. How could they have missed it? It was just over the treetops and the lights were so bright and the noise deafening.

Friday the 13th. I should have known then why the day was so miserable. But it never entered my mind. I didn't even realize the date until just now as I am reviewing my journal. It started raining about fifteen minutes into the day, and it continued that way until the end of the day's hike. We began with warm temps, but as we climbed up Blood Mountain at over 4,400-feet elevation, the warmth evaporated and was replaced by cold rain.

Blood Mountain was all hyped up by many of the other hikers. It is the highest peak in Georgia on the Appalachian Trail and the sixth tallest mountain in the state. According to Wikipedia, Blood Mountain is the high point of the Apalachicola River watershed via the Chattahoochee River, making it the highest point of any land draining to the state of Florida.

Most hikers were worried about the hike up the mountain and how difficult it was going to be. Other than the misery of the rain and cold, when we reached the top, Andrew and I thought, "So this is it?" If it wasn't for the sign and survey marker designating the summit, we wouldn't have even known we were at the top. We didn't think it was that difficult of a climb. And with the rain and clouds obscuring any possible view, we didn't realize we had hiked so high.

The guidebook stated there was cell service at the top of the mountain and it was advisable to call Blood Mountain Cabins for a reservation, especially in bad weather, since they fill up quickly.

Mountain Crossing, an outfitter, also had bunks available, but it was first-come-first-serve. We didn't know what we were doing. Bruce, Jimmy, and I Believe were going to meet us, but we didn't have any details. If it wasn't for this fact, I could have stayed at the top in the shelter, although it wasn't very inviting.

Blood Mountain Shelter was originally built in the 1930s, using local stone. It is primitive and creepy looking with its paneless windows and graffiti, not to mention the history behind the area. There are different stories on how the mountain got its name. The possibilities range from the red lichen growing near the summit, to a bloody battle between the Cherokee and Creek Native Americans. Also, in 2008, a young female hiker went missing on a nearby trail, and later a man confessed to her murder.

The weather was miserable, and I just wanted to get out of the rain. As I passed the decrepit shelter, I didn't really give serious thought to staying there. I gave it a fleeting glance and continued on for the 2.4-mile descent into Neel Gap, where our chariot would be waiting.

I had made our call at the summit. According to the voice on the phone, the climb down would take thirty minutes to an hour and a half, depending on one's fitness level and the weather. I was fairly fit, but it was raining. I estimated it would take me 45 minutes.

Ten minutes into the downslope, my left knee started giving me trouble. Fifteen minutes in, it was screaming at me. It had not bothered me at all so far. And out of nowhere, I became a hobbling hiker. I had to limp the rest of the way down, taking the downhill steps leading with my left, then followed by the right. It was so slow and cold. My pace was not fast enough to keep my body warm. The physical pain was only made worse by the mental pain I was suffering.

Another hiker had caught up to me. I called him Bottles because he carried three aluminum bottles attached to the outside of his pack. They swayed freely and clanged annoyingly like some giant wind gong. I never saw them full. Bottles and I had flip-flopped a few times over the last several days. I thought I had seen the last of him when he was struggling to climb up Blood Mountain earlier as I passed him with ease. But with my failing knee, he now caught up to me and actually gained the advantage. Not that hiking was a race. I was just trying to distance myself from the annoying sound.

I don't like irritating sounds. I thought it was just a pet peeve. It's actually a syndrome called misophonia. I had proof for my family and friends that I wasn't crazy—I had scored a seven out of ten in severity on an online self-testing.

I had been able to use avoidance tactics and hike ahead of Bottles, which prevented me from losing my mind from the *clang, clang, clang* of bottles swaying with his side-to-side stride.

I didn't get that either. He seemed to need a lesson in physics. Not that I am a scholar in that field. I have a mathematical handicap, but this guy was wasting so much energy with his side-to-side momentum. Hadn't he heard of Sir Isaac Newton? He tired me out, just watching him. At times, I so wanted to help Bottles with another law of motion—an object in motion stays in motion until acted upon by an outside force. I wanted to be that force! With one little push, I could have helped him down the mountain and the wind gong would be gone.

With only one good knee, my pace slowed, and I was now forced to listen to the noise most of the way down the mountain. Thank goodness he had to stop and rest. I was able to pass him, freeing myself from the mental pain once again. I never saw or heard him after that.

An hour and a half after I took my first step from the summit, I arrived at Mountain Crossing, Neel Gap, Georgia. I was more than a little off on my estimated arrival time. This is the first milestone for thru-hikers.

Mountain Crossing is a full-service outfitter, and the Appalachian Trail passes right through it. They offer a range of services catering to hikers, including a pack shakedown where they will go through your pack and tell you what you really need and what you should ship home—another service they gladly do for a small fee.

Twenty to thirty percent of hikers choose to leave the trail here. Some people call them quitters, some call them smart. I say, hike your own hike. I was wondering if Andrew had decided to end his hike.

He and Mozzie were already at Mountain Crossing. He had offered to stay back and hike with me, since my knee hurt so badly; but I knew I'd be okay. No sense all of us suffering in the terrible weather.

The trail leads under a stone archway connecting to the outfitter. It is here where I found my two very unhappy, soggy, and slightly hypothermic hiking partners. The blog I was writing, hosted by The *Bangor Daily News* may have been titled "Happy Hiking," but I was far from a happy hiker at that moment. The three of us looked like shivering, drowning rats. And there was no chariot waiting for us. It would be another thirty minutes before it arrived.

I was able to make contact with our support crew, Jimmy, I Believe, and Bruce. Hubby wasn't landing in Atlanta until 4:30pm and still had to make the drive over. It was 1:30pm. Andrew and I took rotations watching our gear and going into the store to warm up.

It wasn't long before Jimmy and I Believe pulled up. We felt bad that we were so wet and dirty, but they were all too accustomed to hiker grime. They protected the seats with towels, and we climbed in.

4

Neel Gap

What a relief to be out of the rain, cold, and woods. A few minutes in the truck warmed us back to humanity. Jimmy and I Believe drove us south to Gainesville, Georgia, while Bruce drove north from Atlanta.

Soon into the ride, I received an unexpected text from Bruce. Service was limited, at best, in the mountains. The text said, "You just sent an SOS signal from your device."

No, I didn't! My InReach® tracker was in the back of the truck. Between the hills and valleys, I managed to reach hubby, who informed me an InReach dispatcher had attempted to notify him. They called his parents next. Mom answered, and the dispatcher told her I had just sent an emergency request signal. My poor mother-in-law! She was worried enough that I was out there on the trail.

Jimmy quickly pulled the truck over so I could retrieve my device. Apparently, when I threw my bag in the back, it landed on the SOS button. I learned there are different ways to send a signal. Usually it is a two-step process to prevent accidental alerts. Another way to activate SOS is to press and hold the button. The weight of my pack did just that!

I couldn't see the small screen to navigate a cancellation. I handed the device back to Andrew, my personal techie, while I googled DeLorme's support number. Andrew was able to hit the correct series of buttons to cancel the SOS request. After the initial panic and we were once again driving away, Jimmy said, "Wouldn't they notice you were okay since you were moving so fast, probably in a vehicle driving away?"

"But how would they have known I hadn't been abducted and we were speeding away never to be found again?" was my reply. We all laughed. In retrospect, it was reassuring to know how quick the response time would be in case there was a real need.

Both vehicles drove into the parking lot of the hotel simultaneously. We could not have timed it more perfectly. Our trail angels delivered us safely into the hands of Bruce. They headed back to Neel Gap to help other hikers, and we proceeded to shake off the last five days of misery. We would reconnect with Jimmy and I Believe the next day; they had invited us to spend the next night at their cabin. Our focus turned to appreciating the amenities of indoor plumbing, food that didn't have to be rehydrated, and a soft bed.

Time for a zero day. Hikers have a language all their own. It's easy to learn but strange at first. A zero day is just that, a day with no hiking. A nero day is one of low miles ("nearly zero") relative to what a hiker's average has been. By March 14, we had 5 days of hiking, 31.7 AT miles, and 8.8 miles on the approach trail logged in our journals. A slow, wet, and rainy start.

Even with the rain, I was enjoying the trip—except for the descent down into Neel Gap. Andrew, not so much. Our zero day allowed us to rest and recuperate. At the hotel, Bruce washed our dirty clothes. All we had to do was repack our food from our re-supply boxes.

Bruce was so incredible. Not that he wasn't already. But he made everything seem so simple, from planning the road trip down, to making sure we got off on the right foot, to checking in on our well-being after the first section. It may have seemed easy, but it was no simple task. He still had to work and do his own travel logistics. Not only did he provide drop-off, pick-up, and maid service for us, he was keeping the funds coming in as well.

Our first zero day was about R&R, keeping warm, and visiting with Jimmy and I Believe.

I had known I Believe and her husband, Jimmy, less than a year. I met them in 2014. I found I Believe on *Trail Journals*, choosing her from the hundreds of hikers in the class of 2014 because I liked her trail name, I Believe. It was positive and self-affirming with a touch of faith that spoke success. Jimmy was supporting her along the way, like Bruce was planning to do for me.

I had reached out to I Believe through her *Trail Journals* blog and offered to help once they reached Maine. Jimmy took me up on my offer, and I had the privilege of meeting them in western Maine, just after the Bigelows near Flagstaff Lake.

Jimmy and I parked where the trail dumped out onto Long Falls Dam Road, and we eagerly waited for I Believe and Owl Bear, her hiking buddy, to show up. As Jimmy and I sat in camp chairs, getting to know each other, we met a few other hikers as they appeared from the woods. They were shocked to see people sitting at the trailhead. The area was desolate, the road less traveled.

I can still remember the name of the first thru-hiker I met; his name was Turbo. He sported a bright orange shirt and his head was topped with a pile of dreads sprouting out of his ponytail and flopping in all directions, like Thing 1 and Thing 2 from Dr. Seuss's *Cat in the Hat*.

Then came triple crowners, an older couple who had already hiked the AT, the Pacific Crest Trail, and the Continental Divide Trail. This was their second time on the AT. My thought was, *They must be crazy to do that!* Turbo looked strong and healthy, but these two looked worn and beaten. I had worried then about how I would look at that point in my hike the next year. Would I be full of energy and robust or look like I was ready for the grave? Age wise, I fell somewhere in the middle, between Turbo and the triple crowners, so I figured that's where I'd be physically as well. I vowed then to make sure I didn't overdo it when I was on the trail myself.

As Jimmy and I waited for I Believe and Owl Bear, I was able to provide my first trail magic for hikers. Trail magic is the generosity of strangers, and it appears in all sorts of forms—from free food, beverages, and supplies left in coolers and containers along the trail, to rides and even stays at private homes. It appears like magic when hikers least expect it and are in most need of it. That day, I earned my Trail Angel wings. (I made up that term. Since trail magic is provided by trail angels and angels have wings, I thought it was a cute phrase.)

But one stalker on my *Trail Journal* post didn't find the humor in it. He actually went on a long harangue about trail angels and trail magic and blah, blah, blah. Some people are way too serious. I learned to use the delete feature when I would receive negative feedback on my site. One person even had the gall to tell me my odds of completing the thru-hike were less than 50 percent. How on God's green earth could he tell that just by my posts? He didn't know me. DELETE!

When it comes to your goals and dreams, don't let the stupidity of others drag you down. Eliminate the negativity. Just hit Delete. If you can't hit Delete, make sure you are adding more self-affirming value and positive affirmations to offset the garbage.

The trail magic I provided as we waited for I Believe and Owl Bear was homemade donuts, freshly picked apples, and Moxie. We all have had homemade donuts and fresh apples, but have you ever had a Moxie? It was one of the first bottled soft drinks and originally made in Maine for medicinal purposes. Moxie drinkers love it, and if you don't drink it, it's because you hate it. Most of the time, there is no gray area.

I happen to be addicted to the stuff. We literally cannot keep it in the house because I have no control. Just the crisp, ca-chure sound it makes as you twist open a bottle or pop the top of a can sends me salivating. I don't know what's in it, and I don't want to know. I love to introduce Moxie virgins to this "Distinctively Different" taste. As I shared this with the hikers, most of them liked it. But as I learned on my own hike, long-distance hikers will enjoy eating or drinking just about anything.

It was getting late. I Believe and Owl Bear had not appeared from the woods yet, so Jimmy led the way four miles to an awesome campground on Flagstaff Lake. We claimed a beautiful spot nestled among tall pines, with a fire pit overlooking the water. I built a fire. Yes, I could do that. I may have been a camping novice, but that didn't mean I was absent of backcountry skills.

Once camp was set, Jimmy went back to the trailhead to wait for our hikers. I tended the fire that was warming the homemade chicken potpie and dessert. I wanted to spoil my new hiking friends.

It wasn't long before Jimmy was back with I Believe and Owl Bear. I was so excited to meet I Believe! I had been following her blog as she traveled north from Georgia to Maine, and I was finally going to put a face to the words in her journal. I felt like I was meeting a movie star. In less than a year, I would also have family, friends, and strangers living vicariously through me as I hiked the Appalachian Trail. It was all becoming so surreal.

Relief came when I saw I Believe. She looked fantastic, strong, fit, and happy, not at all like the triple crowners—and she was even older than that couple.

Once Bruce saw that Andrew and I were in good hands, he headed south to Florida. That afternoon, Jimmy and I Believe drove Andrew and I a few hundred feet back to the outfitters. We didn't want to walk, even though it was probably shorter than the distance across a Super Walmart's parking lot.

Andrew picked up a single hiking pole. I tried purchasing some Tyvek to use as a ground cloth for taking breaks. They wanted $10 for a small piece, so I skipped it. I Believe overheard my request and offered to give me hers from her 2014 hike.

While we were in the store, a voice called out, "Are you Black Bear? Is that really you?"

Black Bear was my chosen trail name. Many long-distance hikers use trail names for a host of reasons. Some use it for anonymity; others, because they are escaping the real world for a change—so why not use a different name? But I would guess that the main reason hikers use trail names is because it is fun. Usually a hiker earns a trail name by doing something repeatedly or something stupid. A hiker who stumbles might earn the trail name of Trip or Stumbles. A fast hiker might become Turbo. A hiker called Gasbag—well, you can guess that one.

I had chosen my own trail name for two reasons: one, I like to be in control; I wasn't going to wait for someone else to give me a name. And two, I was afraid of what name I might earn because I can do and say some pretty stupid stuff.

I chose Black Bear, a name full of symbolism for me. The most obvious reason, for those who know me, is that I went to the University of Maine, and our mascot is a black bear, and once a Black Bear, always a Black Bear. Then I learned that the first live black bear to be used as a mascot at a UMaine football game was a motherless cub found on Katahdin—and it was in the same year I was born, 1966. To all of those connections, add the fact that black bears and I have a lot in common: we are grouchy when hungry, protective of our families, like to sleep in winter, and are just so adorable. The trail name "Black Bear" was a perfect fit for me.

"Yes, I am Black Bear," was my reply to the young hiker. "How did you know?"

It's a small world. Here I was, over 1,200 miles from home, and someone recognized me from a photo in a newspaper article that was in *The Lincoln News*, my local paper. Her mom was from my area and had noticed the article about my upcoming hike and sent it to her daughter who was also hiking. A star is born.

That evening, Jimmy and I Believe cooked up a giant pot of jambalaya. The spice was just right to warm us from the inside out. Their generosity exceeded all conceivable expectations, from the shuttle service out of the cold, to letting us stay in their cabin with a hot meal for supper and breakfast the next day. My humble trail magic for them the year before paled in comparison to what these almost-strangers did for us.

Appreciation and gratitude filled my heart, but a hint of sadness tainted my emotions. Our youngest son's nineteenth birthday was that day. This would be the first time I had missed one of the kids' special days. I had pre-planned a birthday wish for Patrick on my *Happy Hiking blog*. I knew my hike would cause me to miss all of my family's birthdays, so I was proactive and posted messages to them in advance.

I was glad I had the foresight to do so, because service was not reliable at so many places on the trail.

The next day was Bruce's birthday. Double whammy. First week on the trail, and I missed two important days. Those weren't the only special events I would miss back home.

Life happens. We are forced to make decisions or choices. Sometimes those decisions are hard and sometimes they are easy, as in this case. Missing a birthday or two in the grand scheme of things would not cause our world to end. Sometimes, one has to make a choice between doing something good or doing something great.

It was also Jimmy's birthday, so I was at least able to celebrate with him that morning before we headed back out on the trail.

In the next section, Andrew and I would cross a state line and pass the 100-mile mark, the first of many such milestones. But this day we focused on lucky number seven. It was the seventh day of our journey when we headed out of Neel Gap.

I know it wasn't luck but rather more of a blessing to finally have sunshine. Four out of the first five days had been rainy, and the fifth day was cloudy, with every night ending in rain as we slept. But on day 7, March 15, it was beautiful.

The day began with a huge breakfast cooked by Jimmy and I Believe. We left the cabin by 8:00am, warm, dry, and full—a great way to start another section. Our goal was Low Gap Shelter, eleven and a half miles away, with the day's elevation never dipping below 3,000 feet.

With favorable weather and fairly easy terrain, it was a pleasant hike, despite still dealing with severe knee and metatarsal pain. It took me forever to hike the distance because I had to stop and rest my knee and feet often. There was no real injury to either, just pain caused by overuse.

My knee pain was intermittent. I had injured it playing soccer back in college. This hike was supposed to be about new adventures, but I kept thinking about the past—first, those warm feelings when I first fell in love with Bruce, and now my knee injury.

When my knee flared up while descending Blood Mountain, all I could think about was the Ring Dance at Bruce's college, Maine Maritime Academy. The dance was a big deal, with a wonderful ceremony rich in tradition. As in all merchant marine academies across the country, students (known as midshipmen) at Maine Maritime are not allowed to wear their college rings until they have completed their junior year of studies and training. Decked out in dress-blue uniforms and ball gowns, the midshipmen walk through an arch of sabers. Their dates wear the class rings on ribbons around their necks until the point in the ceremony when the rings are dipped in water from the Seven Seas and then presented to the midshipmen. It is to be a reminder of their hard work at the academy and future lives at sea.

I was quite happy to be Bruce's date for this special event.

Again, I needed to call upon my girly-girl friends to help me fancy up for this occasion. One friend loaned me a dress, and Tonya once again helped in taming the curls into yet another beautiful coiffure. I was hoping that Bruce would recognize me this time!

On the morning of the dance, I had an indoor soccer game. Usually this would be just another contest I would participate in and all would be fine. But this particular match brought concern from my family, friends, and Bruce. The only ones not worried were my dad and myself.

Before Bruce and I first met, remember, I had injured my knee. The doctor assured me the injury was probably a fluke, and after several weeks of therapy, I was told I was good to go. On examination, everything in my knee looked and acted fine. A little more therapy and strength training, and I would be good to score more goals. That diagnosis lasted twenty minutes into the next game.

Believing I was invincible, I committed to play in a soccer game the morning of the dance. Sometimes, a can-do attitude and stubbornness are needed in life to endure challenges that seem impossible. Couple that with faith in God to help overcome Vegas-style odds, and one is sure to come out on top. I needed that partnership many times on the trail.

But that weekend, my hardheadedness proved to be a downfall. And fall I did. With ten minutes left in the game, I went to kick the ball, and for some reason, my plant leg did not hold my weight. I heard a very loud pop, then fell. By the time I was helped off the court, my knee and leg had swollen to twice their normal size. All I could think about was how disappointed Bruce was going to be.

That evening, I arrived with Tonya at Maine Maritime where our dates met us. I had ditched the full leg-length immobilizing knee brace for my own ace wrap that was hidden by my dress. But I could not disguise the brown, ugly crutches.

I expected the worst. When Bruce saw me, he said nothing. He hugged me and told me I looked really nice. I could have cried. He was being so kind, even though I knew he must have been disappointed. He taught me so much that night about kindness. I realized just how selfish I had been to play in that game. All I had thought about was playing—I'd never considered the possible consequences.

Our decisions affect others. Sometimes, it is in little, undetectable ways, and at other times, effects are more obvious. It became quite apparent to me that my life now involved more than just me. I needed to be aware of how my actions impacted others. Especially the person I loved.

The night continued, and when it came time for the ceremonial part of the evening with presentation of the rings to the midshipmen, I was able to ditch the crutches and use Bruce as my support. Ever since that night, I have been relying on him and vice-versa.

But was I taking advantage of him again on this hike? I hoped not.

Most of the time, my knee was pain free and served me well. Every once in a while, it would yell, "Hey, remember me? I don't want to do that today!" And I would be forced to slow down, step methodically, and take caution until the aggravated joint calmed down.

The metatarsals on both feet were another story. They'd start hurting an hour or two into the hike each morning. The soreness in my feet had been present ever since I had bilateral bunion surgery fifteen years before. The surgery corrected my left bunion but resulted in an infection, bone spur, a terrible scar, and both feet having intense metatarsal pain when I use them for prolonged periods of time. Not good if long-distance anything is the activity of choice.

I first noticed it on our family bike ride from Fort Kent, at the top of Maine, to Kittery, the southern tip of the state. Toward the end of each day's ride, I would get a severe burning sensation on the bottom of my feet that would radiate to the toes. I eventually had to stop and undress my feet so they could rest and calm down.

After that bike ride, the issue continued on my daily walks with our dog and on any day hikes. I put up with the pain. But now, out on the Appalachian Trail, the pain grew more intense, even with the footpads suggested by my doctor. The only thing that helped was to stop walking and rest. This would allow me another hour or so without pain. I would continue hiking, then the pain would start up again, and I would repeat the process several times a day.

The longer the day, the more miles, or the faster I hiked, the sooner the pain would start and the more intense it would be. Ironically, difficult uphill terrain or soggy conditions produced less pain. I learned to embrace the physical challenge of the inclines and even the wet and rainy trail because it was more comfortable on my feet.

I had no backpacking experience. But I did have years and years of athletic experience. This AT hike was different from any other activity I had ever done, but the lessons were similar. Both depended not necessarily on how smart or fit I was or how great my gear was. What mattered was how well I could learn from each situation. So far, my body told me to slow down when it hurt. My mind told me to chill when I got panicky. The trail was teaching me to adapt.

The trail was also teaching me to face my fears. I had never been one to step out of my comfort zone. I excelled at what I knew I was good at and seldom ventured away from my strengths—the fear and discomfort of failure was too great. I was slowly eliminating that bad habit, first with my rock-climbing excursion with Sharon and then by accepting a job in retail.

I had no fears with any other form of employment in my teaching/coaching roles. But my first job ever in retail was another story. In my new job, I was scared.

It had been awhile since I was gainfully employed. I needed an income to help pay for my hiking gear for the AT hike. My niece Stephanie worked for L.L.Bean and suggested I apply at the outlet store close to my home. She thought it would be a good fit since I liked people and have a knack for serving others. It's a gift I particularly enjoy doing and receive great satisfaction out of doing so.

But starting that new job had me on pins and needles. Let's just say I was a little more than challenged in the math department, to say the least. I was petrified to run the cash register. In the interview, I let my store manager know this. I held no reservations in telling her so. I was hoping I would be eased into the position, as she explained would happen. Besides, how would they dare put someone who confessed such weaknesses at the front of their business? Especially L.L.Bean, a company that takes pride in their customer satisfaction.

I shared a new-employee orientation with four other more-deserving souls, then spent the next shift observing the lead on duty (LOD) at the register. What? Up front already? I wanted to stay in the back and sort stuff. That's what I am good at. Or put me on the sales floor, helping customers find what they need—I am really good at that! Please, please, please don't make me touch that machine!

Observing was pretty much a waste of time for me. I do not retain much by just watching. After watching two or three transactions, I was gone into some other mental zone. I am not much of a bystander; hands-on is more my learning style.

The computers crashed. I didn't do it. But I did secretly rejoice in that fact. So after the start of the shift, I was able to hit the sales floor and help the customers. Phew! Saved by a technological glitch!

Next shift, back to the front I went to observe. But not for long. There is a saying, "Careful for what you wish for." I got my hands-on training!

My LOD, Sue, stepped aside and said, "There, now you log in."

"Yikes!" I didn't remember my password or half the multiple steps needed to make just one sales transaction. There were so many screens to navigate through. How was I ever going to remember each one? And then there were returns, the never-ending line of returns.

The only thing that saved me was that I was a very experienced L.L.Bean shopper so I knew what the process was from the other side of the counter. Also, my LODs were all very helpful and patient. My transactions were painstakingly slow for my customers. It took me forever to process and hone in on all the information on the screen. Most of it was irrelevant for normal transactions. But that was an oxymoron. The "normal transaction" only existed in the training guide. There was too much info on the screen, but when a more challenging transaction needed to be conducted, that information did come in handy.

I will always remember the advice my assistant manager, Carlie, gave me when I was lost in screen-information overload. She calmly said, "No worries. Just remember, all the information you need is always right in front of you. It just takes a little searching. Don't be afraid to look and push buttons."

My friendly and fun personality combined with great management and patient customers made the transition from domestic engineer to sales representative easier. By the end of the third shift, I was flying solo behind the world famous L.L.Bean counter—still scared to death. I was like a duck. Calm and cool on top, and paddling like the dickens underneath. I had only wanted to be a floor rep or back-of-house personnel. But I faced my fears head on and tackled them. There was no going back. I needed this skill several times on the Appalachian Trail—tackling my fears, that is, not running the register!

I did not come out completely unscathed as cashier, nor on the trail. After about six or seven shifts, Carlie approached me and said, "Oh, Emily, we have an Emmie-ism." Emmie-ism is a term I shared with my co-workers that my family had coined to describe something silly or stupid I may have done. Yeah, it happens. It happens so frequently that it needed its own term. I am my own entertainment and apparently that of others, too.

I am a very hard worker, reliable, and trustworthy, but I can also be a little bit "blonde." Yup. No political correctness here. I fit the stereotype. When my manager approached me and said what she said, all I could think was, *What did I do now?*

She laughed and informed me I had made a mistake returning an item for a customer. It was an item from Lands' End, a different catalog store! She may have been laughing, but I was horrified. My worst fears had come to fruition. I had made a grave error involving the loss of someone else's money, taking back an item that was clearly not even our product! Obviously, not so clear for me.

To top it all off, I was apparently not done making mistakes even a year later.

I had decided to go back seasonally as a Cashier Goddess at Christmas time, I didn't even charge a lady for a $200 jacket. Thank goodness, she was honest and brought it back in for me to ring up. My LOD, Linda, was standing right next to me. After I fixed my error, my customer left. Linda said to me, "Glad to see I am not the only one who has done that." She didn't need to share that with me, but she did, and it was her way of letting me know it happens to all of us. I worked with some great leadership. Is it any wonder I went back to my old job?

You are probably wondering what all this has to do with hiking the AT. Plenty! In life, we will have fears and we will make mistakes, just like I did at learning the job of cashier and taking wrong turns on the trail. We must stand up to our fears if we ever want to grow, learn, and overcome. Those fears still may come to fruition—they often will—but with perseverance, guidance, and a lot of humor, we can overcome and do things we never thought we could.

Learn to not let fear guide you. There is a difference between life-threatening fear and crippling fear. It's good to be afraid of that cliff and not get too close to the edge. It's good to get that funny feeling in the pit of your stomach in certain situations or around certain people. But it's the fear that grounds us to our comfort zone that we must overcome in order to experience life as we never have before.

I could have panicked when I made that return error. Or thrown in the towel and quit with the excuse that it was too embarrassing, I'm not good enough, I can't run the cash register. But I didn't. I persevered, and that season, I won the Visa Card Application challenge for our store. We shouldn't dwell on our weaknesses, but sometimes when we work hard enough on them, they become our strengths.

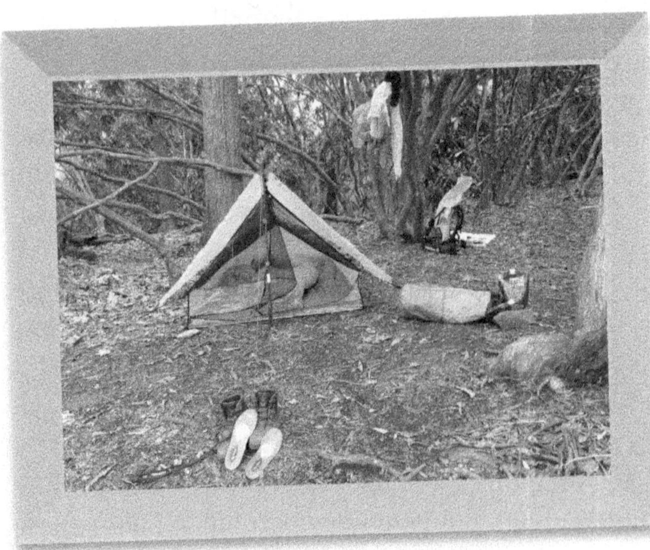

5

Adjustments

Andrew began using the trail name "Gilligan." I then renamed Mozzie "Skipper." The wonderful thing about trail names is you do not have to accept one that has been bestowed upon you, as in this case.

Gilligan's name derived from working at a summer Girl Scout camp during his youth. Everyone had camp names, so he had chosen Gilligan—being the only male, he felt stranded on an island. I added that you can't have Gilligan without Skipper, so I named Mozzie Skipper. Andrew did not go along with this.

They arrived at Low Gap Shelter way ahead of me. My pain once again slowed my arrival. I arrived about 4:00pm. Eleven and a half miles made our longest day yet. I was happy with the increase in daily mileage even if it was only at a 1.5 mph pace. It was still lucky day number 7 to me, filled with sunshine and trail magic.

Two ladies from Illinois provided a cookout for hikers at the Appalachian Trail crossing of GA 348. Even though we had our fill at breakfast, we were not going to turn down any free food. I had my first hot dog in over fifteen years. I felt like I had just fallen off the wagon. It tasted so good.

The day also brought a hint of spring. I saw my first flower, a small, four-petaled purple flower with a yellow center. I've called them forget-me-nots for years, but Google says they are bluets. In season, they can carpet an area with hundreds of thousands of blooms, but there was just one solitary silhouette for my pleasure. It truly was a lucky—more like blessed—day on the trail.

As we continued on the path toward Franklin, North Carolina, we had relatively good weather with decent terrain. My aches and pains were even beginning to wane a little. We were settling into our own routines. I liked mornings, and Gilligan preferred sleeping in.

One morning I was up and packed by 7:00am. We were camped at Rocky Mountain campsite. The wind had blown down my tent while I was getting ready in the morning. Instead of adjusting the stakes and retreating to the comforts of my space to wait for sunrise, I packed up.

Gilligan was not as eager to greet the day. I was ready by 7:00am, but neither the sun nor Gilligan were awake. Not excited to venture on my first solo dark hike, I waited. And waited. And waited. By the time Gilligan was ready, it was 8:30am and I was freezing. The 4,000 feet of elevation combined with wind had my bones doing more than just rattling. But I was too afraid to hike out alone. There is that fear issue again.

When we finally set out for the day, Gilligan and Skipper took off and left me behind. I was so mad—furious, actually. I had waited around for him for an hour and a half.

It was at this point that I decided if I was going to hike alone, I might as well leave when I wanted to, scared or not. Once my pity-party was over, I got my attitude right and had a great hike. Nowhere had we signed an allegiance to be on the same schedule.

Andrew and I met up a few times for breaks or a snack. It was then I discovered that is what I really enjoyed most. Hiking alone stimulates the senses and lets the soul decompress. Then, meeting up for breaks gives one something to look forward to after being alone. The end of the day provided comradery that was welcomed after a long day's hike.

Another life lesson learned on the trail: When things don't go our way or as planned, our first instinct is to get mad, frustrated, or maybe even hostile. But most of the time, if we step back, breathe, adjust our attitude, and take the emotion out of the situation, we are apt to find it isn't nearly as bad as we thought. And in most cases, it turns out to be better than we could have imagined.

The first two weeks on the trail, I developed my hiking rhythm. Packing up. Hiking. Resting. Eating. Collecting water. Filtering water. Camping. Repeat. With that rhythm came education. I learned what I really needed, what I didn't need, my likes, and dislikes. I learned I was definitely on the trail to hike and not to camp. Evenings in the shelters or in the company of other hikers was enjoyable also. It was a huge part of the experience. I met some really wonderful friends on the trail.

One of my favorite things to do at the end of the day was to retreat to my sleeping bag and listen to the other hikers discuss their days. My only regret is that I didn't record all the awesome stories I heard.

As long as I had my tent, sleeping bag, and bare necessities, I was good. I went through my pack and made a note of what I really needed and what I didn't. Since I was already on the minimalist side, I tweaked and looked for those extra ounces that didn't seem like much but added up when combined.

For example, I pared down to one extra pair of socks instead of four. Plastic baggies replaced plastic containers for vitamins and pain relievers. One pair of extra batteries instead of two. No spare undies; going commando if needed never hurt anyone! It was actually quite comfy. Who decided we needed underwear anyway? Sorry, Grammie, it's just way better to be free. And if I get into an accident, I don't have to worry about wearing dirty panties if I am not wearing any.

As soon as I had decided I was going to do this hike, I started journaling and making a list of the gear I was sure I would be needing. I was inexperienced. The first five items were tampons—yup, that was first on my list—followed by flashlight, ball cap with a light, clothing with bright colors, and a note to consider getting a short haircut. I had read that long hair increased your chances of picking up ticks, my numero uno fear on the trail.

Looking back at that list, I think it is funny where my thoughts were pre-hike. That's all I could come up with for an initial list for a six-month hike in the woods? Boy, did I have a lot to learn.

I love lists and my journal was full of them. I used bullets more often than actual paragraphs to record my journey. It was quicker and used less paper. Every gram counts in a thru-hiker's pack. Post-hike, reading my notes made me realize just how much I had learned and how I made adjustments.

Adjustments were made even before I set out on the hike. Only one of those initial five items made the cut. I actually grew out my hair and wore black most of the time. I did not carry a flashlight but used a headlamp instead. I nixed the ball cap with a light; there was no room for duplicate items. The only item of the original five that made it into my pack was the feminine hygiene products. More on that later.

The more I confronted, the more I had to learn. For the first two weeks, my learning curve looked like an infinite positive linear regression graph on a mathematician's quest to find the answer to the universe. (Thanks to my engineering husband and son. They helped me with these terms. I invoked their brains so I could sound smart. They said, "You only sound confusing.")

Here are a few of those lessons learned.

- How to hike
- How to use bear cables
- How to throw a line for my food bag
- How to tie off my food bag line
- How to dry my clothes while wearing them
- How to sleep on slanted ground
- How to pitch my tarp tent for rain; when it's windy
- How much water to carry (never enough)
- How to prevent blisters
- How to bandage a blister if previous prevention didn't work
- How to filter water (properly)
- How to collect water from a shallow source
- How to load my pack efficiently
- How to put on my pack efficiently without hurting my arms or back
- How to pack in the rain. I learned that fast.

These are not the only things I learned on my hike, but they were what I learned right off the start. Another list I created included my likes and dislikes

Likes:

- Hiking
- The sun on my face
- The views
- Rhododendron forests
- Cold mountain water to drink
- Camp time with other hikers
- Gilligan and Mozzie
- Trail Magic
- The simplicity of nature

It was a good thing I liked hiking since I had over 2,100 miles to go. Whenever anyone asked me what I liked most about my journey, I responded, "The hike." I didn't care if it was raining, windy, cold, sunny, hot, or buggy. I liked hiking. Nothing else mattered. When I was moving, everything was great. I loved the changes of terrain. I liked the way the trail transformed from a thick forest to an open mountaintop. Or how it meandered through a rhododendron tunnel whose leaves were dormant, hanging toward the ground, waiting for spring to wake them up. As the path carved its way along a ridge, it brought new surprises with each switchback.

But when I stopped, it was a different story. Most things were annoying to me when I was stationary.

Dislikes:

- Clanging bottles
- Being cold and wet at the same time
- Biting insects (I already knew that)
- Wind
- My tent
- Having to go pee at night
- Late sunrise
- Early sunset
- Waiting

I wrote a whole paragraph on Bottles, the annoying hiker with aluminum bottles attached to the outside of his pack. My oldest brother, John, was worried about my safety on the trail and offered to gift me a handgun. Bottles was lucky I did not let John buy me that equalizer he so wanted me to carry. I just may have gone postal on him. Not really, but the noise did drive me insane. Google "misophonia" and you will have an idea of how it bothered me.

Besides irritating noises, having to go pee in the middle of night in the wilderness is also quite bothersome. It's bad enough when you are at home. Out in the woods at night when it is cold, rainy, or scary, is even worse. Many nights I would lie awake with a full bladder, putting off the task until morning when it was time to pack up.

Several of my male hiking friends carried an extra-wide-mouthed sport drink bottle designated for their nightly nature call. I didn't dare to try it. I dreaded the thought of poor aim. External plumbing, I am sure, makes the task easier.

If the weather was bad, I stopped drinking after 5:00pm. I'd hydrate in the morning. This was not wise. Your body needs water. And it will tell you so, as I learned later on.

The last list I wrote in my journal was about what not to do as a hiker. The first major no-no was when I set off my emergency device accidentally. I learned to be ever vigilant after that. I wished I could say that it only happened once.

The outdoor code of ethics found at LNT.org sums up nicely what not to do. I just wished everyone on the trail knew the code. One evening, I was collecting my water from a very small stream that trickled along the forest floor, playing hide-n-go-seek in the leaves and rocks. The water source was no more than two inches at its deepest point, making collection very challenging. The process was slow and tedious. Another hiker, forgetting what he learned in kindergarten about waiting and taking turns, jumped upstream of me and started digging out a deeper spot, thinking this would make the process go more quickly. Not only did he turn the clean spring into a muddy, leaf-filled pool, it contaminated everything downstream. So it is a big no-no to mess with the water supply when others are using it. Principle #7: Be considerate of other visitors.

Proper etiquette in the woods is to dispose of your food waste properly. That's Principle #3. Part of that means disposing of food waste away from your sleeping area, or better yet, pack it out. Another hiker had part of it correct. She ate and then disposed of her leftover food and the water she used to clean her dishes away from her tent. She even brushed her teeth a distance away from where she was sleeping. What she failed to do was to keep a safe distance from my tent. She was about forty yards from her own place but only about ten feet from my spot and another hiker's spot. I was not impressed. I was still carrying my polite ways from back home and kept quiet.

For the most part, hikers were very considerate of each other. But just as in the real world, there will always be that one bad apple or two. It wouldn't be until much later in the hike that I would learn to speak my piece without reservation. Nicely, of course. No one likes to be told what to do, but sometimes it must be done.

After the honeymoon stage came the adjustment stage: learning and adapting to trail life. Learning to fix my attitude when things didn't go as planned or go my way was a huge adjustment. Learning my gear, what worked, what didn't, my likes, dislikes, the weather, and how to prevent and/or heal from injuries, all helped me grow and enjoy what I was doing.

The biggest challenge of all—and one of the most rewarding at times—was dealing with all the people. There were so many hikers out there. It wasn't nearly as secluded or deserted as one would think.

A quick 6.5-mile nero day brought us to Dick's Creek on day 9. The hike tortured my knee and feet. The inclines and terrain were the toughest so far. Working out the kinks, unfavorable weather, and the frustration of hiking someone else's hike had my attitude in the dumpster.

People were waiting for me at Dick's Creek—or so I thought. Gilligan and I had met two section hikers whose car was waiting at the parking area, and they offered to give us a ride to the hostel where we were staying that night.

At some point in the day, everyone passed me. I tried to catch up. I did not rest as much as I needed to. Just as I exited the woods, I saw the couple crossing the road into the parking lot. They had just arrived and were not waiting for me after all.

Then I realized Gilligan was nowhere to be found. Fifteen minutes later, he and Mozzie came strolling off the trail. I asked how I had passed him, and he said they had taken a side trail to see the view. I remembered seeing the sign for that trail and view. Someone had even carved the word Epic into it. I skipped it, thinking I would be holding up the crew. Another lesson learned: Hike your own hike.

We stayed at Top of Georgia (TOG) Hostel, a simple place with a friendly staff. For a small fee, you got a bunkbed, laundry done separately from other hikers', and breakfast. They also provided hospital scrubs to wear while your clothes were being washed.

Gilligan and I happened to receive matching outfits. We were styling as we took the shuttle into Hiawassee for supper and resupply. We looked more like escapees from *One Flew over the Cuckoo's Nest.* Rumor has it the nearby town thinks the hostel runs a cult and allows their members to go to town in their garments. We were not sipping any Kool-Aid at the Top of Georgia, but they did offer pizza and a breakfast.

Bunks were in two different areas, one for hikers with pets and one for hikers without pets. We had Mozzie, so we were in the doghouse called the Wolf Den. Another hiker and her dog, Potato Wedge, shared our room. The dog was a cute mutt but could be temperamental. His owner was also cute but ditzy. Her name was also Emily, a fact that made me cringe. After meeting her, I took great pains not to let people know my real name in fear they would think I was her. Stories travel faster than hikers on the trail—a fact I learned all too well later on.

After our jaunt into town in our cult uniforms, we went back to our bunkhouse, only to be greeted by Potato Wedge, who didn't think we should be allowed in. He tangled himself around the bedpost he was tied to. Miss Potato Wedge was nowhere to be found. I usually never approach a strange dog, but since we had met earlier on the trail, I was banking on his bark being all show. Gilligan had his hands full with Mozzie, so I helped free the pooch, for which he was grateful.

This would be my first introduction to a hostel. The closest experience I've had to hostel life would have to be hunting camp. My brothers and dad owned a small, rustic camp in the middle of the woods. There was a kitchen, a mudroom, and a bunk room that slept eleven. The differences between camp and TOG were that at TOG, everyone was a stranger and there was power and plumbing.

Peace and quiet would have been nice! "Hiker midnight" is considered to be about 7:30pm, but it was well after that when two more weary souls joined our pack. Only humans, though; we had enough dogs for the night. On the outside, these two may have had manlike qualities, but the noises that came from within while they slept bordered on monstrous.

At one point, I couldn't sleep and went next door to the other room, which housed the bathroom. I realized our room was quiet compared to the racket that was coming from the other bunkhouse, so I returned to my less-noisy bedroom and tried to drown out the sound with ear plugs.

The next morning, I met Bionic Woman, a hiker who was an amputee. Her story was incredible. She was an outdoor enthusiast and had taken a bad rock-climbing fall, resulting in the loss of one leg from the knee down. She was hiking the trail in hopes of regaining strength and confidence to go back to her job as a ski instructor.

She was getting off the trail for a bit due to an infection caused by her prosthetic. Later, I was told someone had stolen her wallet and all her money, not at TOG but someplace else. Shrek, a fellow hiker, fixed her broken crutch with a broom handle to get her by until she was able to get back to the hospital. Her journey was highlighted in the *AT Journeys* magazine in 2016. What an incredible story! My metatarsals no longer hurt so much.

We were back at it the next day, but not for long. We only hiked four and a half miles to Plum Orchard Gap Shelter. The reason for the short hike: RAIN! Gilligan hated hiking in the rain. I don't like camping in the rain; I wanted to keep going. But it was a good idea to stop. The rain kept pouring down, and the temperature also dropped.

Stopping early gave us a chance to dry our clothes before sleeping. If we would have continued, we might not have been able to dry off.

This would be our first night in a shelter. It was a cozy, three-level structure. The first level was topped off shoulder height with the second level. There was enough room on the lower level to sit up in your sleeping bag, but not to stand. Same was true for the second level. The third level was accessed by a ladder and created a ceiling for the picnic table area. It formed a place to wait out the rain.

We claimed a spot on the lower level close to one wall, Mozzie and Gilligan, then me. I made my sleeping area with my ground cloth first, then blew up my pad, and finished with my sleeping bag. I did not change into my dry clothes right away. Instead, I zipped up my Gore-Tex rain jacket and put on my stocking cap and hood to conserve what body heat I was producing. I didn't just sit, either; I walked around in the shelter the best I could. With my body heat captured in my breathable Gore-Tex, I was able to dry out my shirt and sports bra. My pants even dried. Once I was no longer soaked, I changed into my wool base layer for the night, stuffed my hiking attire into my sleeping bag, and crawled in to keep warm for the rest of the afternoon.

The soggy conditions brought in lots of hikers. Thirteen of us sought refuge from the elements under the tri-level structure. Besides us three amigos, there was Lunch Lady, a lady my age. Midnight, a disabled veteran in his 50's, who went AWOL from a VA clinic, added to the mix of company. Shrek and Donkey took up residence for the night as well. There were two college kids and three other hikers I don't remember.

Lunch Lady, Midnight, and I were keeping warm by bag dancing. Bag dancing was my term for the ridiculous activity we chose to keep busy as the rain kept us cooped up in the shelter. Shrek was playing music, and we were in our sleeping bags, sitting up against the back wall, swaying and moving to the soundtracks. It served two purposes—kept us warm and kept us entertained, since it was way too early to go to bed, even for me.

During the dance party, two new faces showed up. Walking Man and Karl, a father-son duo from Boothbay, Maine, walked up to the shelter. We all shared a quick greeting, and, in a flash, Karl striped off his wet coat and shirt. I looked at Lunch Lady and she looked at me, both with approval of the eye candy. It was our own little glimpse of a PG-rated Playgirl magazine. Being the polite 40-somethings that we were, we did not stare. It's funny how we stopped noticing the rain.

That night, I slept well, despite how cold it was. At one point, I woke up and could hear and feel Gilligan shivering. I felt really bad for him. It was the mother bear coming out. Not wanting him to be cold or too proud to ask for warmth, I said I was really cold, and could I scoot over? Without waiting for a reply, I did, and I also reached out, putting my arm around him. I wasn't cold, and I thought I was helping. Apparently not! I don't remember what he said, if anything, but my comforting act was not welcomed! Oops. Sorry, Andrew. As they say, "No good deed goes unpunished."

Even with a good night's sleep, we had a slow start the next day. We didn't get out until 10:00am and were done hiking by 2:50pm. We hiked a mere 7.3 miles, again in the pouring rain. Muskrat Shelter would be our stop for the night. What a dump! I wanted to continue, but Gilligan was done. He found no joy in the rain.

So far, by day 11 on the trail, we had completed a mere 81 miles. Only two days were our miles in double digits, and we had already spent three nights in a real bed under a real roof. Due to our slow pace, Bruce told me later that he was planning on having Thanksgiving dinner on top of Katahdin. Funny guy, isn't he? The only good thing in stopping early on those rainy days was that I dried out. Or at the very least, I was not so soggy.

In the afternoon at Muskrat Shelter, a few hikers stopped for breaks. One of them was furious at Miss Potato Wedge, the hiker at Top of Georgia Hostel. He showed us where her dog, Potato Wedge, had bitten him. She had again left her pooch alone, but this time he was tied on the porch near other hikers' gear. When this hiker went to grab his pack, the dog lunged, biting him on the abdomen. Dogs can be scary on the trail. In hindsight, I am just glad Potato Wedge didn't bite me.

Later, I hiked upon a father/daughter duo resting. Their black lab perched on a shoulder-height boulder in the trail. The daughter, about 10, sat next to Fido. Dad stood behind them. My uphill approach placed them at a higher level than myself—in a dog's world, a stature of domination. As I closed the gap, the dog stood up on the rock, with hair raised.

The young girl hugged her dog. I stopped a safe distance away, then asked the man to hold the anxious animal. He became irritated and insisted there was nothing to worry about. All the while, the dog was showing his teeth and growling. I would not proceed until the dad, not the girl, had control of the dog. He continued to inform me I was being ridiculous. Again, I thought of brother John and the gift I refused.

We had been on the trail less than two weeks, yet I already felt so accomplished. I had done more personally challenging stuff in that time than I had in all my years up to that point. That's not to take away from previous accomplishments, but this was different. Reflecting on my lists, I realized those little lessons that seemed so insignificant were steppingstones toward helping me enjoy my hike even more. Each new task meant learning, which required me to make adjustments so I could grow and tackle the next obstacle.

6

100 Miles

Sunshine led the way the next couple days. The terrain was easy, my feet enjoyed the low mileage days, and our hiking bubble seemed more like family than strangers we had just met.

I hiked alone most of the time. Gilligan and Mozzie hiked ahead. Throughout the days, I leapfrogged with other hikers as well. The first two I met were collecting water from a stream that emptied itself over the trail from the right.

They highly recommended I camel up. "Camel up" is a hiker term meaning "hydrate as much as you can when water is available." It's easier to carry it inside you than on you. I never refused a good water source. When they were done, I took my turn.

Just as I was leaving, a trio of young college guys hiked up. One was from Texas, and the other two were from the University of Maine, my alma mater.

One fellow Black Bear was studying photography at UMaine on a self-guided course while on the AT. The other fellow UMainer had a friend who was taking a class from Dr. Butterfield, one of my professors when I studied there and who still remains my dear friend to this day. What a small world.

Here I was, out on this grand adventure for God knows what reason. Part of it was to just do it. But once out there, I realized there was going to be more than following the Nike slogan. I liked the escape. But the deeper I got into the trail, the more I was reminded of home.

I didn't mind. For some, it caused homesickness. But for me, it did the opposite. The connections I encountered were like God's way of saying I wasn't alone, like meeting Karl and Walking Man, who were from Maine and meeting the UMaine students. I may have been away, but home was still in my heart. The best reminders were all the flashbacks of Bruce. At home I would be busy with this and that, with no time to ponder and reflect. But the freedom of the trail provided hours for such things.

At one point, I passed Midnight. He'd had a rough night and wasn't feeling so well physically. His body and feet ached more than usual. Midnight suffered from a multitude of war injuries. He was disheartened, knowing he had to leave the trail.

That first night we met at Plum Orchard Shelter, he had shared with us that he was AWOL from a VA clinic. He had been in the hospital for over 18 months. They told him he would never walk again. Drugged up to control the pain, he had few faculties for decision-making.

One night with the change of staff, his medication had been forgotten. He regained his wits just enough to realize he wanted out of there. He called his daughter, who came and took him out without authorization.

Going cold turkey from the prescribed narcotics, Midnight freed himself from the addiction. Medical marijuana became his go-to drug for pain control. I am not an advocate of the substance, but even I noticed a difference in his ability to function without pain after a hit or two of his prescription.

But that day as I passed him, not much was helping his pain. I stopped and sat with him for a while. When I gave him a hug, he cried. He wanted so much to be healthy and to be able to function like he did before the war. I had all I could do not to cry with him, but he needed someone to be strong.

I have a huge soft spot in my heart for our military personnel—maybe that's why, without thinking, I reached over and hugged Andrew that cold night. I thought I was helping. Our service men and women sacrifice so much so that we can have the freedoms we often take for granted. More needs to be done for our men and women in uniform.

That day, all I could do was offer Midnight a hug. As I left, I gave him a mini rosary my goddaughter had made for me. It was priceless to me, but I felt he needed it more than I did.

March 22 was a great day. I saw a baby black bear. We passed the 100-mile marker. I climbed a fire tower. We stayed inside a real house. We cooked a real meal and I learned not to grocery shop directly after coming off the trail.

My bear sighting was so adorable. A memory is all I have, no photos. So it's like the fish that got away. I was walking along the trail alone, completely engrossed in my own thoughts and in my own world, a common state of being for me on the trail.

There were two other hikers about 30 yards or so ahead of me. I trekked forward, head down, enjoying the morning, when something caught my left eye. I immediately came to an abrupt halt. There it was, the tiniest baby bear. He could have fit into my hiking boot. I couldn't believe how close to the trail he was.

He was just sitting there, like a little puppy wanting to be held. His eyes spoke to me and said, "Please pick me up. I am so lonely. My mommy left me. I want to cuddle, and I am hungry." I fought back the urge to do such a thing, in fear that Mama Bear would hear him screech if I so much as touched a hair on his hide.

I did decide to yell ahead to the other hikers to beware of Mama Bear. Not sure how they missed Baby. They were curious, though, and came back to take a peek. But that's all they did, and the three of us scurried out of the vicinity as quickly as we could.

A little farther down the trail, we joined a few hikers who had stealth camped. We told them about the bear. They shared their story of how they heard a baby bear calling out, then the mother bear called from the distance in bear language, "Shut-up!" Baby bear would be silent for a while, then call out for mommy and again would be told to hush. They said it went on all night. My immediate thought was that it sounded so much like raising human babies. Another connection to life back home.

It was so amazing to be in the midst of such wild happenings. I was grateful to my family for supporting me on this trip and mostly grateful to God. It was hard not to feel close to His presence out there. Even in the misery. During those times I called upon Him even more. Just like Baby Bear calling out to his mother in the darkness of the night. But in the day when he could see, he was calm.

I too called upon God to help me through my darkness, the pain of my knees and feet, and to help me through the cold and rain. When all was well, I didn't seem to talk to Him as much. But that day, a day of lightness and joy, I made sure to give thanks for the good times.

Early in life, I wanted to be a nun. That was every devout Catholic mother's dream. I was born and raised in the faith, making me a cradle Catholic. Going to church every Sunday as a family was what we did. There was no choice. Well, there was, but the alternative was not a selection one would freely make. Attending Confraternity of Catholic Doctrine, also known as CCD, was a must.

Confraternity of Catholic Doctrine is a fancy term for Sunday school. In my youth, there were times I rebelled at CCD. I wasn't a terrible youngster, just a little too talkative, and I gave my teachers a hard time. That's what everyone else did, and I wanted to fit in. It's not that we were horrible. We just pushed the boundaries.

Looking back, I enjoyed my time learning about faith. When I was in junior high, I asked my mom to take me to a convent so I could experience religious life. Request granted, and off to the beautiful coast of southern Maine where Sister Marita, a friend of ours, lived in a convent on the beach.

Sr. Marita, who was from our community, would always take the time to talk with me when she visited our parish. I admired her, and it was so much fun visiting her at the convent, learning how I could devote my life to Jesus. After that visit, I was convinced that was what I wanted to do. I loved God and helping people. I thought I felt a calling.

Nope, wrong number! Somewhere between that visit and 8th grade, I discovered boys. They were pretty interesting to me. Not sure exactly when I went from beating them up on the playground (not really your typical nun behavior) and outplaying them in gym to wanting them to like me. No more convent visits were in my future. So went my mother's dream, washed out to sea.

Dances, first kisses, and boyfriends were capturing my attention. Unfortunately, I was not capturing the eye of the other sex. Guys were not too thrilled with the memory of years before when I would chase them and beat them up. Besides, living in a small town, most classmates and neighbors were more like brothers.

One guy did catch my eye, though. He was tall, cute, and tough. Just what I thought I wanted. It took me three long years to wise up and realize he was NOT Mr. Right. Sometimes I think I wasted those years and I wish I could undo the pain I caused my parents. But those were learning years.

Even though religious life ended up not being my vocation, my Catholic roots run deep, and I am so thankful that going to church was not an option. By making us attend mass and CCD, Mom and Dad were planting the seed; and even though it lay dormant for a few years, it was still alive, waiting for its time to grow and bear fruit.

If there was one thing I learned from all those years in faith formation, it was that there is a God who loves us dearly. Heaven is real, and those we love who have passed on are there helping and guiding us. I take comfort in knowing that Mom knows I am sorry and I do love her.

My failures are part of my past and part of the person I am today. We cannot change the things we have done. We can only learn and grow from them, using the knowledge and experiences as a trampoline to propel us to a bigger and brighter future.

Everything that had happened the first couple weeks on the AT were steppingstones toward success. All of it—the good, the bad, and the ugly.

The first milestone was one hundred miles. Wow! It seemed like we had accomplished so much. Albert Mountain was the second peak over 5,000 feet elevation so far. At the top stands Albert Mountain Fire Tower #1. It was built in the 1950s to replace an old wooden fire tower on Standing Indian Mountain close by.

The tower was used as a short-term live-in for wardens. I am not a fan of high places, especially high places on top of higher places. But I did climb that structure. I always enjoy the view once I make it to the top; it's getting there that is the difficult part.

After Gilligan's and my excursion up the tower, we enjoyed a snack at the bottom with fellow hikers. We then continued the almost 6 miles down to Rock Gap Shelter, where we thought we were going to spend the night. In the morning, we would hitch a ride into Franklin, North Carolina.

Andrew arrived ahead of me, as usual. While he waited, a man named Colin was there, drumming up business for the home he was renovating to be a hostel. Our original plans were to stay at the Budget Inn, where we had our drop boxes. But timing was good with this guy. When the opportunity struck, we took it. The idea of a real house and a home-cooked meal versus a hotel room and restaurant, made for an easy decision.

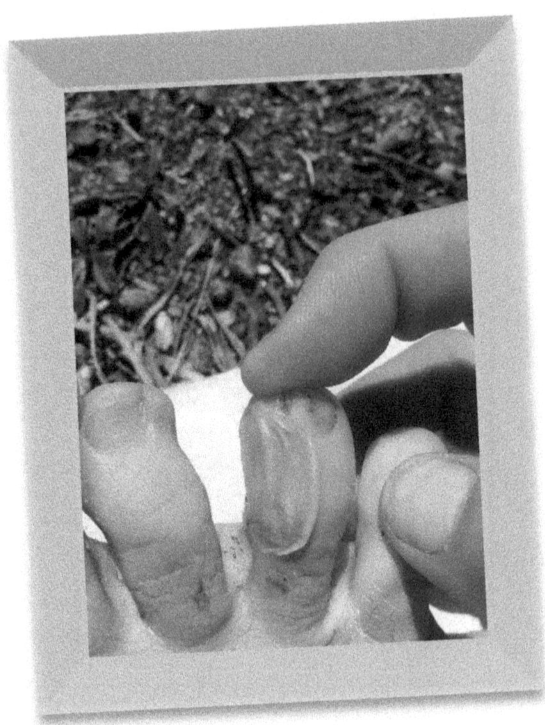

7

The Rescue

Colin had parked at the road, a tenth of a mile away from the shelter. He said he needed to shuttle his first patrons to the house but promised it would be a quick return. Andrew, Mozzie, and I waited in the parking area.

While waiting, I realized that I had blue-blazed from the trail to the shelter, then blue-blazed out to the parking lot, missing about 300 yards of white blazes. It wasn't a huge deal, but I wanted to stay to my purist ways, so I hiked back to where the junction for the shelter had taken me off the AT. I then hiked back down, thus missing no white blazes.

Andrew, Mozzie, and I nestled under a fir tree to gain shelter from the oncoming rain, while we learned the real meaning of "quick," We had enjoyed a couple days of dry weather and cowered from the cold, damp feeling that was returning so quickly. The evergreen provided just enough cover to keep us from getting soaked. The twenty minutes we were quoted turned into thirty, then into forty. Then just shy of an hour later, our ride returned.

Colin arrived none too soon, and we were off to town. First stop was the grocery store so we wouldn't have to backtrack. I offered to cook for us if Andrew would split the tab with me and help with the dishes.

An experienced grocery shopper knows the importance of going to the store with a list and a full stomach. I had neither. My stomach was below empty, as a matter of fact. I bought enough to feed a small army, which turned out to be good. There were two other hikers who accepted my offer to feed them for a $10/person donation. Feeding four hungry hikers is about the same as feeding an army.

The home-cooked menu was a bargain. It consisted of my family's famous chicken tenderloins baked in a secret sauce, caterpillar baked potatoes, and salad with homemade blueberry wine dressing.

The sauce I had made up at home one day when I was tired of plain chicken. I decided to be creative, using whatever was in the fridge. I didn't want a barbecue sauce. Mayonnaise, mustard, and ketchup found their way to the counter, along with what I call the quatro spices: pepper, onion powder, garlic powder, and salt. I mixed them up, coated the chicken, then baked.

The caterpillar potatoes are a large Idaho baker, sliced thin but not cut all the way through, placed in a shallow sheet pan. I prefer stoneware. The spuds are coated with lots of melted butter and freshly minced garlic, salt, and pepper, then baked. I baste the potatoes with the buttery mixture every 15 minutes until they are done. As they cook, they fan out slightly, resembling a caterpillar.

For the salad dressing, I used some of Colin's Maine wild blueberry jam and wine. When you bought this book, I bet you didn't think it was a recipe collection as well. My gift to you. You are welcome.

I went on this journey as a vacation from my domestic engineering duties and what was the first thing I did when given the chance? Cooked and cleaned. Yup, go figure. The next day wasn't any better.

Andrew and I decided we didn't want to go back out into the woods just yet, but we also didn't want to spend more money on lodging. So we made a deal with Colin. He needed some serious cleaning done, and we wanted to stay one more night.

We did a work for stay. More like, I did a work for stay. Colin charged us $30/person/night. If I helped to clean, he would only charge $30 for the both of us for the second night. I said that was perfect. Back home, I charged $15 an hour to clean, and I estimated it would take me two hours to spiffy up the areas he requested. Deal. Andrew needed to tend to some phone calls, so I told him I would take care of the dirty work.

Colin's home was a small ranch built in the late sixties (my guess) and not much looked like it had been changed since that time. Everything worked, it was just outdated, old, and not so clean—not filthy, just in need of some TLC. Colin was a nice man, a laid back, natural kind of guy. He expressed this through an overwhelming decor of Asian textiles, knickknacks, candles, and lack of lighting.

I set out to do my chores while our host ran errands. Four hours later, I was done, a little over budget on our deal. No problem. I have never minded doing above and beyond what was expected of me.

Just when I thought I could call it quits and actually rest on my zero day, Colin returned home. He asked me if I would go with him on a quick trip to pick up a van, then drive his car back. I figured I could squeeze in one more helpful deed. I failed to remember his definition of "quick."

The trip was not speedy. He needed a few things for the place and wanted my help. How could I say no? I spent my whole day off helping a stranger, and I still had to partially pay for the second night. I really don't think he had a clue what he was asking. I just so wanted to rest but felt bad for him. I did want him to have success with his new business.

Time to head back to the trail, but not before we filled our tummies at the hiker-famous First Baptist Church of Franklin. Every year in the spring, they offer a free pancake and bacon breakfast to hungry hikers. They will pick you up at the local hotels and deliver you back after breakfast.

Colin gave us a ride to the church, where we found some of our hiking buddies, Midnight, Lunch Lady, and Mighty Mouse. The friendly hosts encouraged us to eat until we burst. I could not eat the pancakes, but I did have an endless helping of bacon, orange juice, and hot cocoa.

Along with serving us food, they took our photo, printed it, and gave it to us with a note card. I sent my photo home to the boys so they could see I was doing fine. Midnight sent his to the VA clinic he had escaped to show he could not only walk but was out doing it on the Appalachian Trail!

The church had a two-hour window for serving. When it was time to finish up, a member of the group gave a reading from Scripture. It was a nice touch. They provide food, love, and fellowship. So many people will give you advice that is hypocritical, a "do as I say, not as I do" kind of advice. They were not just talking about how to live; they were living those words.

It was also a great reminder of the importance of service to others, the reason we are here on this earth. It helped to ease my frustration of the day before when my precious zero day was used to take care of someone else instead of my own needs. Good goes around.

March 25 brought us two days past Franklin to a stone's throw away from the Nantahala Outdoor Center, known as the NOC, in North Carolina. It is an adventure complex complete with lodging, food, gear, and home to the Olympic whitewater rafting trials.

We had been back on the trail for only a short 25 miles and were already in sight of our next hotel room. We were meeting my sister Becky and her husband, Pat.

The section was wonderful. My feet were happy, and the sun was shining. It was a great day to be in the woods. It was also prayer card day.

One of the schools that was following my adventure was All Saints Catholic School in Bangor, Maine. The fourth and fifth graders made prayer cards for me. Before I left home, I had uploaded each one of them to my blog for future posts on Wednesdays and Sundays. I had enough to last the whole trip.

That day's prayer requested I have a great trip. And I was having a great trip, even though things were not going quite as planned. I had way more foot pain than expected. I knew there would be rain, but one can never prepare for it in full. Our mileage was way behind my planned schedule, and I could tell Andrew was not enjoying himself, so I felt some of that stress also.

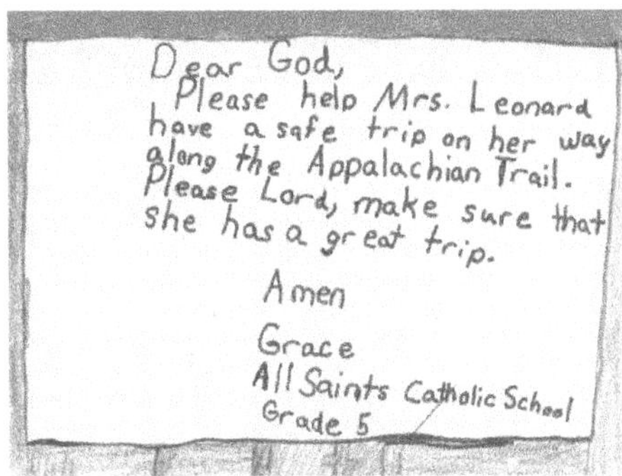
Dear God,
Please help Mrs. Leonard have a safe trip on her way along the Appalachian Trail. Please Lord, make sure that she has a great trip.
Amen
Grace
All Saints Catholic School
Grade 5

Despite all those circumstances, it was a great trip. I stayed focused on the positive the best I could. I allowed myself to have tiny pity parties and sometimes mini tantrums, but they were short lived. Then I would put my positive attitude back on and chose to have a great day.

Some days were more challenging than others. I would remember all my friends, family, students, and blog followers. With God's grace and their support, I had the strength I needed to persist.

I was ahead of Andrew, and I ended up hiking awhile with Papion. He was from Arizona and a very pleasant person to be around. We met up at Cold Spring Shelter, a quaint structure that was beginning to show its age. A spring crossed the trail right in front of the building and there was also a two-person picnic table next to a fire pit. It was the perfect location for lunch. We enjoyed each other's conversation and joked about the mice that were not bothered by our presence. In fact, they seemed happy we were there.

Papion did not like mice; no one did. He was all too aware of the nuisance they caused on the trail. He told me about the night he left a half-eaten Snickers bar on the mesh ceiling shelf built into his tent.

The next morning while packing up, he had forgotten about the candy bar until he saw the empty wrapper and a hole in the top of his tent.

Later in the day, another fire tower presented itself to me. I was alone this time and attempted the creaky old structure. Halfway up, the stairs took a hard left, changing from sturdy with a railing on each side, to a skinny, shaky rise with only one railing. I retreated to the safety of the ground and hiked on. I hadn’t gone far when I heard another hiker approach the tower. I watched as he climbed right up, as most of the young hikers do.

He encouraged me to do the same, promising to stay with me as long as I needed. It was another beautiful, 360-degree, unhindered panorama of the landscape. Just as I thought it couldn't get any prettier, it did! Thanks to Blaze for helping me with my fear of heights, I was able to take in just one more fantastic view on the Appalachian Trail.

The NOC was in sight. We had a six-mile drop between us and hot food. We arrived just in time to catch lunch at the River's End Restaurant, and yes, it was on the edge of the river. We sat outside while we feasted on burgers and fries, waiting for Becky and Pat to arrive. They were going to whisk us away to nearby Cherokee.

My sister and her husband lived in Georgia at the time and loved casinos. They were our trail angels that day, splurging for adjoining rooms at Harrah's Hotel and Casino. We kept the dividing door open, creating one large suite.

After I enjoyed a long hot soak in the jacuzzi while they tried their luck at the slots, we went to the Diamond Club, a lounge reserved for VIP guests. That would be Becky and Pat. Andrew and I just tagged along on their coat tails.

Aromas from hot and cold hors d’oeuvres filled the room, making our senses dance for joy and our tummies grumble. It was more than enough to make a meal. We ate until we were content.

Our plan was to spend just the one night, then get back on the trail. The room was so inviting, and it was nice to be with family. We found it hard to leave. So we didn't. Becky and Pat were gracious. They were planning on two nights anyway, so we stayed.

This made our third zero day on the trail and our seventh night with a real roof over our heads—in only 18 days! No wonder Bruce thought we would be celebrating Thanksgiving on the top of Katahdin.

Dinner the second night was the biggest AYCE buffet I had ever seen. Andrew skipped this and had alone time in the room and a walk around the complex with Mozzie. I was not skipping any chance to fill up. There was so much food that I didn't even get to all the stations. It wasn't the best I had ever eaten, but it did the trick. I ate until I couldn't move. Then I ate some more.

As much as we enjoyed the company of family and very much appreciated their generosity, the next morning it would be time to pack up and head back to the Nantahala Outdoor Center.

We woke up on March 28 in our cozy hotel to a fresh layer of powdery snow. A white carpet dusted the rooftops and the mountains. Stealing a line from the movie *Apollo 13,* I sent an urgent text to Bruce, who was in Florida now. It read, "Houston, we have a problem!" Back home, a nice little dusting of snow is welcomed; but today, this thrilled neither of us.

I was not a fan of the cold. I hated being cold. Cold was the worst. Nothing works right when the mercury drops. Your body, your gear, the ground, everything is off. I was glad we had taken the extra day, so I did not have to wake up to a snow-covered tent.

I was not prepared to spend a night in the mountains with forecasted temps dipping into the teens. In the spirit of minimalism, I had given Bruce all my extra winter gear I didn't think I would need until the Smokies. Becky and Pat offered to pay for a third night, but Andrew and I did not want to overextend our stay. We figured we could hike 13 miles that day, then Bruce could pick us up at the other end. If only we could reach him.

As we drove back to the NOC, there was more snow on the ground. Pat dropped us off exactly where he had picked us up. We had to walk through the NOC complex, which was officially AT-blazed. Becky joined us for this 1/4-mile section, then we said our good-byes.

There was no reply to the distress text I had sent hubby. Why wasn't he answering me when it was obvious I needed help? Why else would

I have used such a quote? Anyone who has seen the movie *Apollo 13* knows the crew was in grave danger when the actor Tom Hanks spoke those words to NASA. I, too, was in perceived danger.

We headed into the woods. We'd had a six-mile drop into the NOC, and the climb out was just as extreme. Still no reply from Bruce. I called again. No answer! For real? What was he doing? It was early morning, but we are morning people. I could not understand why he wasn't answering. Had he gone to the Sunshine State and forgotten about me?

I called his parents' phone numbers. He was there to visit and work. They said he was still sleeping. *Not anymore!* Was my thought. I didn't ask, I demanded, "Wake him up!"

Andrew and I hiked from the NOC to Stecoah Gap. It was a beautiful hike. The sky was crystal blue and the air cool and crisp. As we climbed in elevation, there was more snow accumulation. We were warm as long as we kept moving. Breaks were short and few. In places where the snow was deeper, the trail became packed and slippery from all the hiker traffic. For the first time since leaving Amicalola Falls, I slipped and fell.

A fallen tree blocked the trail. When I stepped over it, the slick surface caused my other foot to slide right out from under me. I slid a full body length down a slope, and catching the heel of each boot on something prevented me from sliding down the snow-covered, forested mountainside. It was a close one.

I lay on my pack, looking up at the sky and thanking God I didn't go any farther. It was by His saving grace I stopped when I did. Continuing down the slope would have been a rough ride, bouncing from tree trunk to tree trunk. When I realized I would be okay, I noticed my jellybeans were safely clutched in the bag I was holding in my right hand.

At Stecoah Gap, we hitched a $25 shuttle ride, arranged by my now-awake Bruce, back to the NOC where we had started that morning. We wanted to stay at a hotel closer to the trail, but they would not accept dogs. Refusing us was illegal since Mozzie was a service dog, but we were too tired to complain. Instead, we rented a bunk room at the NOC, also arranged by Bruce. It would be a far cry from Harrah's; but once we were asleep, we wouldn't know the difference.

Our shuttle driver dropped us off at the River's End Restaurant. We needed cash to pay him—a fact we were unaware of until we arrived at our destination. We just assumed he could take a check or a form of electronic payment, like all the others up to this point had done. Neither one of us had enough dineros and there was no ATM.

A lady at the bar overheard us discussing our dilemma and offered to front me the cash to pay the driver. Wow, I didn't expect that! I told her I would not be able to repay her until the morning when my husband arrived. She said no worries, she worked there and would be around. Trail magic comes when you need it the most and least expect it. Good continues to go around.

Before locating our bunk room on the NOC complex, we had barely enough time to eat. The restaurant was getting ready to close, but if we could order fast, they would let us in. Hamburgers and fries were a quick and easy choice. The burgers were so good there, best on the trail. Their beef was grass feed and locally grown. With full tummies and no worries of having to sleep in the cold, we hiked up to our cabin.

There we found Lunch Lady in the bunk room next door. She had received a care package with wine sent to the NOC, and she invited me over. She and I dug out our hiking cups and enjoyed a half bottle each of the relaxing juice. It was nice to have some girl time—something I did not realize I would miss out on the trail. It was a splendid end to a long day. It wasn't nearly as traumatic as I had perceived it could have been. As a matter of fact, it was an uneventful and a beautiful day on the trail.

Bruce wished he could have said the same about his day. Here's his version of the rescue.

> The rescue story really began when I left Emily, aka Black Bear, Andrew, and his dog, Mozzie, on top of Springer Mountain that cold, rainy morning. I thought they were never going to leave, so I left first and hiked south, back to my car at Amicalola. I flew down the mountain, covering the eight-plus

miles in about 2.5 hours. I had to catch a flight in Atlanta for a business trip.

Rain and cold filled Emily and Andrew's days while mine were packed with traveling for work and long hours taking care of business to fund this journey of hers. After leaving them at Springer Mountain, the plan was that I would meet them again at Neel Gap, after their fifth day of hiking. I would fly back to Atlanta. Travel delays prevented me from reaching them in time at Neel Gap, so Jimmy and I Believe stepped in. They collected Emily and her hiking partners and drove them south to the Holiday Inn in Gainesville, Georgia, where I had made reservations. I drove north from the Atlanta airport. We pulled into the Holiday Inn at the same time.

Jimmy and I Believe returned to Neel Gap where they had a cabin and where I would drop Emily, Andrew, and Mozzie back off less than twenty-four hours later.

But first, Emily was all business with her A-game on. While Andrew kept to himself and relaxed, Emily was full of orders. She gets like that sometimes. At home, when she wants everyone to know she has stuff to accomplish, she puts on her sarge hat from her NROTC days. Emily never did go into the service, but she acts like she did. She doesn't mean to be demanding; she just gets focused on the tasks at hand. And on this day, that task was getting ready to get back to the trail. So, I spent the evening following orders. Laundry, resupplying food, and the night's meal were part of my chores. Not really sure what she did.

The night was over before we knew it, and it was time for me to chauffeur them back to Neel Gap. Since I then had a seven-hour drive to Florida where I would be staying at my parents' and working remotely, I didn't stay to visit with Jimmy, I Believe, Andrew, and Emily. I have the luxury of working at home but also travel often, visiting customers.

It was March 14, our son Patch's birthday, when I left Emily, Andrew, and Mozzie for their zero day in the care of Jimmy and I Believe. I knew this was a difficult day for her since she would be away for the first time for one of our sons' birthday. The next day was my birthday, so she had two days to be homesick.

The plan was to reunite with Emily and her hiking buddies at Fontana Dam. She was off having fun in the woods and I was heading back to work, setting up office at my parents' place in Florida. I spent the next two weeks working extremely long hours with little sleep. I was looking forward to the leisurely drive to Fontana Dam to reunite with Emily.

That plan was foiled when my dad woke me and handed me the phone. It was Emily on the other end in a panic! I had a difficult time waking up. I had worked well past midnight on an urgent project for work, and now Emily was insisting I get up because she didn't want to spend the night in the cold, wet snow. What was I supposed to do? I was at least eight hours away!

I got up, that's what I did, and went into logistics mode. First, I needed to pick up a rental car. That required Mom and Dad to drive me one and a half hours in the opposite direction, from The Villages, Florida, to Orlando International Airport. After securing my rental car, I headed back to The Villages to pack.

From The Villages to the NOC is about 536 miles and about eight hours and forty minutes of driving time. When I was finally ready to head north, the interstate was a parking lot.

While I sat in traffic and crawled north, I arranged a shuttle to pick up the hikers at Stecoah Gap where Emily, Andrew, and Mozzie would end the day. The driver would take them back to the NOC, where they had started that morning. I also booked them a bunkroom at the NOC. In Emily's defense, they didn't have any cell service in that area to make the calls themselves. But she could have toughed it out and slept in her tent.

Over fourteen hours later, at about 2:30am, I finally arrived at the NOC. But I couldn't go to bed just yet. For the last 15 years or so, I committed to reading every day. So, before I went to the bunkroom, I remained in the car and did my daily fifteen minutes of reading. The three of them were snug in their bunks, and I was exhausted from the drive from hell. Once inside, I still couldn't close my eyes yet, because Emily was so excited to see me and insisted on telling me trail stories.

Finally, I was able to put my head on my pillow and fall into a deep sleep. But that didn't last long.

It seemed like I hadn't even gone to sleep when at 5:30am I was told we needed to get breakfast and get them back to the trail. That wasn't such a bad thing; the food at the River's Edge Restaurant was every bit as good as Emily boasted about. I may have been tired, but at least I was well fed.

I wish that was the end of the story, but my job was not done yet. Emily and Andrew had food drop boxes I needed to deliver to a trail angel, Connie. Connie had reached out to Emily during Emily's pre-hike planning and offered Emily, Andrew, and Mozzie a free shuttle and a night at Connie's house halfway through the Great Smoky Mountain National Park.

Once again, Emily and her hiking buddies hiked north, and I went my own way. This time I was headed to Knoxville, Tennessee, to meet up with Connie.

It was a two-hour drive. I've never minded driving. In fact, I enjoy new sights and visiting new places, but on less than 3 hours of sleep that day, it was not the day to travel the route I took. According to a Google search, in the May 26, 2014 edition of the *Conde Nast Traveler*, there was an article titled, *Extreme Drives: the 10 Scariest Highways for White-Knuckle Road Trips* written by Marisa Lascala. Listed in that article was Tail of the Dragon. She writes, "The 11-mile stretch of US 129 at Deals Gap, starting at the North Carolina/Tennessee border, is said to have 318 curves."

I didn't count the curves, with names like Pearly Gates, Brake or Bust Bend, and Gravity Cavity. I focused on not driving off them instead. While I heeded the 30 mph speed limit, others did not. The Tail of the Dragon is popular with motorcyclists and car lovers who seek the need for speed and the thrill of death-defying curves. In fact, spectators and professional photographers line this stretch of road, capturing the wannabe racers in their hair-raising feats of bravery or stupidity, depending on how one looks at it. I'm sure, though, me and my rented Ford Taurus were of no interest to any of them. I definitely need to visit this stretch of road again, but after a full night's sleep.

Safely making it through the Tail of the Dragon, I continued to Connie's house in Knoxville to deliver the food boxes. From Knoxville, I drove another 65 miles taking me an hour and forty minutes to Fontana Dam to meet Emily and Andrew. Side note: Emily never did go to Connie's house. That food drop required almost 4 hours of driving. If I had gone directly from Stecoah Gap where I dropped Emily off that morning, then drove straight to Fontana Dam where I would meet them at day's end, it would have only taken 20 minutes.

I pulled out all the stops to help Emily during those first weeks on the trail. It was a far cry from her initial plan of me only seeing her once a month. But I really didn't mind. She spent the first 25 years of our marriage taking care of our home and giving up her career to raise our boys. It was a joy for me to help her on this journey in the best way that I could. And if it meant I lost a few hours of sleep, so be it. She's worth it.

It was truly amazing after that stint that Bruce did not insist I pack up and go home. He has always been so forgiving. I didn't think anything could top the mercy he had extended to me back in 1988 when I showed up at the Ring Dance on crutches—but this rescue mission did.

I'd like to say our dating was smooth sailing on the courtship seas but that wasn't the case either. After two and half months of dating fun and excitement, out of the blue, he broke up with me. It was horrible and kind of mean.

It was another hockey-game date night. I had secured tickets for us and a couple of his friends. They were right on time to pick me up. I can't really remember exactly how our relationship shredded. What I do remember was I was ready to go to the game, and then I was suddenly dateless, boyfriendless, and crying. And he went away with all the tickets!

Apparently, an old girlfriend had decided she wanted him back, so I was thrown overboard, and she returned to the helm.

That night, I went to the library and wrote a few short poems for my writing class. Up to that point, my instructor and classmates hated my work. But the pieces that flowed from my pen that evening received great praise.

The work was dark, sad, and depressing. To this day I still don't understand why people relish in others' pain. We see it every day in the media, where the headlines are filled with horrific stories while the article about a good Samaritan often goes unnoticed. If only we as a society would be more excited about finding the good and exploiting the good, even if it is miniscule, how much happier we all would be. Just maybe, there would be less of the bad.

That's what I was reaching for on my hike. I really tried to focus on the positive, even when I was in the midst of not-so-happy events.

I focused my sadness that night of the breakup into my writings, and my C grade for Writing Pros turned into a B. Looking back, I don't think I would have been able to bring up my grade without the pain. Pain causes us to learn and grow, but we must not focus on it.

After a brief separation, Bruce decided that we should be together. Miss Ex wasn't so desirable after all. I mean really, once you have been exposed to all of my goodness, how could anyone else compare?

Our spring semester flew by, completing his junior year of college and my junior/senior year. I wasn't really sure what year I was. I was on the extended plan. Goodness continued. For a while, anyways.

8

Alone

After a late night and relatively short shut-eye time, we were up and packed early to continue on our epic journey. Bruce drove us back to Stecoah Gap. We headed north once again into the forest. We would reunite with him at the end of the day, once we reached Fontana Dam, fourteen miles away.

The day was comfortable, cool but not cold, sunny and bright. It was a long, painful day for me. Andrew hiked on. I never caught up to him. I was left alone to limp my way along with a bum knee.

My worries were getting the best of me by now. I was really beginning to second guess the integrity of my knee. After my surgery years back to reconstruct my anterior cruciate ligament (ACL), I did not have any serious ailments that kept me from participating in activities. I did give up soccer, but other than that, I was still very active with no issues.

But now I was having daily pain. Not the tired, lame aches from a hard day of hiking that went away with rest. This was sharp, intense, stabbing pain with each step, and downhill only made it worse.

Early in the day, I was afraid that hiking to Fontana Dam would be impossible. I prepared mentally, in the event I had to break the miles into two short days—as long as I could contact Bruce. I hobbled forward. The sun glistened through the trees, low in the sky and from the southeast. Its rays shimmered off icicles that had formed on the left side of the trail.

The night's frigid temps had suspended the mountain spring's flow into popsicle-sized ice forms. I plucked one as I went by, just like I had done as a kid back in Maine during the winter, when I'd snag one from the edge of the porch roof and eat it.

Painfully, I hobbled about 50 yards; in my condition, 50 yards might as well have been 50 miles. But then it dawned on me that I was holding and eating—ice! And ice was good for other things besides a refreshing drink.

I made my way back to the frozen spring and plucked a second icicle. This time, I did not eat it. I sat on the ground, rolled up my pants, and iced my aching knee. If I've said it once, I've said it a thousand times, "The trail provides!"

I was able to ice my knee three times that day using some form of nature's cure. I found frost coming from the ground and then an area where the snow had not yet melted. This allowed me to complete the distance and make it to Fontana Dam.

Yes, we say the trail provides, but I believe it is God that is actually doing the providing. He provides what we need when we need it. We just have to look around and be perceptive. It reminded me of a story about a storm that caused great flooding in a small town.

A man was in his house, and neighbors came by in a small canoe to offer him a ride. He declined, saying, "I am okay. God will save me." Time passed, and the water level increased. After some time, the man was chest deep in water on his front porch. Rescuers came by in a rubber dingy and encouraged him to get in. He declined again, saying, "I am okay. God will save me." The waters rose higher, causing him to seek refuge on the second story of the house. A larger boat motored to the window, and he still declined. He was forced to the roof. A helicopter came, and he said, "I am okay. God will save me." Eventually the waters overtook him, and upon entering the pearly gates, he said to St. Peter, "What happened? I trusted God would save me!" St. Peter said to him, "God sent you a canoe, a rubber dingy, a boat, and a helicopter, what else did you want him to do?" God will be there for us, but sometimes we have to help ourselves also. It is a two-way street.

Bruce rescued me yet again, and off to Fontana Village Resort Lodge we went. At first glance, I felt out of place as we entered the lobby. We were, for lack of better words, hiker trash. The rustic foyer with its cathedral ceiling, sunken seating area, and towering fieldstone fireplace outclassed us filthy hikers. But the friendly, courteous staff quickly snuffed out any feelings I had of not belonging.

First order of business after dumping our gear in the room was food. By now we were like bloodhounds. We had no problem sniffing out the location of the restaurant. No burgers or fries were safe. Our olfactory senses would rival any canine's. I never got tired of my go-to meal. Andrew chose a meaty steak to satisfy his appetite.

Bedtime happened later than we had hoped, well past 11:00pm. Morning came way too soon and with it, so did Andrew's decision to take a zero day. Bruce, in all his wisdom, persuaded me to at least hike the two miles from where he picked us up the day before, through a small stretch of woods along the lake to the dam. That at least would give me some mileage for the day in case Andrew decided to take a permanent zero. I slackpacked this section.

A few steps into the woods, I began to bawl. Big ole crocodile tears and sobs this time! I mentioned earlier that I wasn't much of a crybaby, but the trail was turning me into one.

I knew in my heart that Andrew was not going to return, so I decided to keep going after the two miles—which meant I would be entering the Great Smoky Mountains alone! When my friend Sharon had decided not to go on this journey, I didn't mind going by myself. I was only hesitant about going through the Smokies and the White Mountains alone. I figured I was sure to meet someone along the way to partner up with through those areas. But since I was hiking with Andrew, I had not yet made any other connections.

I sent Bruce a text asking him to bring all my gear so I could continue on. It was a tough choice but the right choice for me, just as Andrew had made the choice that was best for him. I was not mad or angry at him. I was scared for myself. I was less than three miles from entering the Great Smoky Mountains, and I was going in alone.

I gathered all my gear from Bruce. I double and triple checked everything. I was ready to go. I waited for him to finish a phone call. He was in the car taking care of business and I was standing on the curb, anxiously waiting to get started. I was really scared and nervous, fighting back more tears. I knew they would not help me. I needed to be strong.

All of a sudden, I heard the soothing sound of a familiar voice calling my name, "Hey, Black Bear, is that you?" I turned around, and it was Karl and Walking Man.

I burst out crying again! These new feelings were making a fool out of me. We had seen the father-son duo at supper, but I had not thought twice about them after that.

I quickly dried my watery eyes and explained my dilemma. I asked to use them as backup security. Not as a babysitter, just an extra pair of eyes to make sure I was safe as we passed through the Smokies. They were more than accommodating to my petition.

By the time hubby finished his call, the three of us had worked it out. We agreed each day to stop at a predesignated shelter. There was no promise to hike together, just a nightly check-in. We swapped phone numbers, and I also gave them Bruce's number. Bruce was relieved to know there would be someone else to watch over me. God is great, isn't He?

Fontana Dam is located less than a mile south of the Great Smoky Mountains National Park (GSNP) in North Carolina and is the tallest concrete dam east of the Rockies. The dam was built to support the war efforts of WWII. The secluded area of the Tennessee Valley made it a secure location.

Because of the remoteness of this place, the road needed improvement for heavy equipment. Housing was built for the employees; it was impossible for workers to commute. Construction on the dam began January 1, 1942, and the gates closed in November 1944, flooding the area of the Little Tennessee River above the dam and creating a diverse wilderness recreation area.

After construction of Fontana Dam was completed, the housing area was sold and is now a private wilderness resort for people from all over who come to enjoy the pleasures of boating, fishing, hiking, and more. The lodge where we stayed the night before was just one of those many structures.

The walk across Fontana Dam was impressive. We had the road all to ourselves that morning, since it was closed to traffic for construction and workers had not yet begun their day. It was too early for laborers, but perfect timing for hiking enthusiasts who were seeking adventure.

The visitor center would not open until May, so before heading across the mammoth structure, we glanced at as much of the historical information displayed in the windows as we could. This was one of the many benefits of hiking the Appalachian Trail.

Most of the trail is in the heart of the wilderness connecting rural towns. Following the trail takes hikers to parts of this great country one would not normally have a chance to see. Fontana is not a drive-by to some other well-known destination. If you want to visit this place, it must be intentional.

We traversed its 2,365-foot-long road atop the dam's high wall, enjoying the spectacular views both up and down the Little Tennessee River. The reservoir to our right provided over 200 miles of shoreline and over 10,000 acres of water for recreation.

The view to the left was framed by the mountains we had hiked the day before. A glance over the guardrail at the Little Tennessee River at the bottom of the dam's 480-foot wall, sent my stomach into acrobatic mode. I forced myself to take many looks and lean over the rail slightly. Even though I proved to myself I would be fine, I decided I liked the center of the road for the remainder of the crossing.

Less than a mile after leaving the dam, we entered the woods again. Our short jaunt on a park road brought us to The Great Smoky Mountains entrance trailhead. There, we deposited our park permits into the black metal box. Thru-hiker permits are required for passage through the Smokies. We had been able to purchase and print them out at the NOC.

Before us lay the most hyped-up section of the trail besides the White Mountains in New Hampshire. Horrible stories of severe weather, bear attacks, desolation, and difficult terrain were the focus of most conversations regarding the Smokies. If you listened carefully, you would hear hints of more positive elements. I tried to focus on those, even though I did have my reservations about going through this vast wilderness. Those reservations had been somewhat calmed with the presence of Karl and Walking Man.

It had been a very emotional day, which made the hike one of the hardest so far. Seeing two deer helped brighten my mood. They were my first wildlife sighting since the baby bear. Deer sightings were always most enjoyable. I never get tired of seeing them.

I went from the lowest of lows to the highest of highs, all within a few miles. The exhaustion from the roller-coaster ride of feelings weighed me down. It was as if someone had filled my pack with stones. I never thought I was a dramatic kind of person, but the trail was bringing out parts of me I had never experienced before. I was used to being in control of my feelings, the captain of my own vessel, very guarded and secure. All of a sudden, the floodgates were open, and emotions were flowing like the mighty Mississippi. If I had stayed on the bridge, my tears could have filled the spillways of the dam.

Part of me felt embarrassed about the outpouring of sensitivity, yet on the other hand, it felt freeing. I had nothing to hide anymore. I could just relax and not worry about maintaining the wall I had obviously built around myself.

9

The Smokies

The day's end brought us to Mollies Ridge Shelter. Tenting is permitted in the Smokies only if the shelter is full. The GSNP had lots of rules. I suppose it was to save the integrity of the outdoor experience. But their shelter rules were awful.

All thru-hikers have to pay for a permit to traverse the Smokies. The rules say you must stay in a shelter. Shelter spots can be reserved by section hikers who get first priority, and the last thru-hiker to arrive must surrender his or her spot to the hiker with a reservation.

So, as a thru-hiker, if I am the last thru-hiker to arrive and the shelter fills up, I must surrender my spot to a hiker with a reservation. Which means I must pack up my belongings and set up outside, no matter what time it is.

I understand not wanting to spoil the wilderness with overuse, but this isn't fair for thru-hikers. Many thru-hikers opted to set up their tents upon arrival, hoping the shelter would in fact fill up. But rangers regularly patrolled the Smokies, so setting up outside while the shelter still had space available was risky business for anyone who wanted to avoid a fine.

The worst day on the trail so far was followed by the best day on the trail so far. I started bright and early, not having to wait for anyone. I was on my own agenda. I left the shelter by 7:50am, which made for my earliest start after a night spent in the woods.

It felt so great. The day didn't claim any noteworthy events; it was just a serene walk in the woods with beautiful weather and beautiful views. The terrain was very interesting. It wasn't the same old winter-killed, dull forest I had been hiking through. It was changing from dormant, sparsely-leafed trees to more dense evergreens.

Partridge, or ruffed grouse, were abundant. I began hunting early in life, since my dad carried me in a pack basket. For just as long, I have heard the sound partridge make when they fly off. I will never become immune to that sound.

They make two distinctive noises. The first is the drumming created when the male strikes his wings against his chest or a log. Drumming is used by the male as a means of courtship. He relies solely on this non-verbal display to alert females in the area that *I AM HERE.* It starts slowly, a low sound you can feel as well as hear. *Thump----thump---thump---thump--thump-thump-thump....* It can be heard a long way off.

The second sound is so startling it will send you into fight or flight mode, no matter how many times you have heard it before. When the partridge feels a predator has come just a little too close, he takes to flight as fast and rapidly as he can, beating his wings hard and loud. This flushing sounds almost like a machine gun and is sure to pierce the nerves of the most placid person, sending them over the edge. The day's wilderness offerings were gorgeous sunshine and an endless supply of those sounds. I only wished I could have seen a partridge.

I also took a nap. Napping is my favorite activity, and I was not getting the chance to do it as much as I had hoped. Now I was solo and was getting ready to take a break. I rounded a corner, and straight up ahead two other hikers were lying on the ground with their feet propped on a log, soaking up the sun.

How perfect! I thought, and I asked if they minded company. "More the merrier" was their reply, so I stuck my poles in the ground next to theirs, undressed my feet, added them to the log, and reclined for a little nap

Derrick Knob Shelter was home for the night. I arrived just ahead of Karl and Walking Man, and it was already a full house. While we cooked our dinners on the shelf on the side of the building, we were pelted with driving hail. The minuscule overhang did little to protect us from the assault. It was short lived, and we carried on with our evening duties.

As more hikers arrived, one particular person took it upon herself to move other people's gear in order to make room for several weekenders who held reservations. She felt she needed to stand up for the newcomers, who were younger and inexperienced.

Well, that was the wrong thing to do with me around. My name was Black Bear for a reason. I tend to be very protective of my stuff. The list of hiking not-to-dos includes: *Don't mess with others' things*. I stopped her before she continued her actions. I mean, come on! She was dragging hikers' air mattresses across a dirty, splintery wooden floor. It was a great way to puncture them. Also, hikers have their own routine and order of business; mess that up, and they are apt to forget or lose something. I explained that I understood she wanted to help the young kids, but she needed to find the owners of the gear and let them move it themselves.

April Fool's Day was nothing foolish at all. It was more like a Halloween treat with no trick. It was even more magnificent than the day before. I was not sure if it had to do with the better weather and terrain, which always helped, or a mix of things.

For one thing, I was beginning to change and adjust on the trail, becoming one with it. Andrew had been gone for three days now, and other than leapfrogging and meeting up with Walking Man and Karl at night, I was a solo hiker. As much as I had enjoyed Andrew and Mozzie, I must have let his unhappiness spill over onto me. It wasn't his fault; he had never once complained. I can sometimes feel energy from others. Sometimes it's a blessing, and sometimes it's a curse. Now that I was alone, I was feeling free.

My hike began about 7:45am. I hadn't taken too many steps when I heard another partridge drumming in the distance. *I'd love to actually see one,* I said to myself. It wasn't more than a few minutes, and I flushed a bird who was sitting on the side of the trail.

It was so much fun to ask and then to receive—a thing that was happening more and more. I would have a random thought; and then later, that thought would come to fruition.

At the beginning of my hike, I had been on the trail a few days and was getting irritated with my electronics and my charging cables. I had four, one each for my inReach, iPhone, GoPro, and charging cell. I said to self, "Remember to get a couple twist ties from a bread bag next time you are in town." But when I was in town, I didn't think anything of it, forgot actually.

That night, I was checking for debris in the area where I wanted to set my tent, and I found a large green twist tie. It was long enough to cut, giving me the two twisties I had mentally requested.

On Purpose, a fellow hiker who starred in the Appalachian Trail documentary *Walking Home,* had a similar find. He was in need of a pair of tweezers. In town, he got out of the vehicle and on the ground between his feet was a brand-new pair of tweezers. Hmmm? The trail provides.

The terrain changed drastically, starting out at 4,900 feet just south of Sam's Gap in North Carolina and ending at Mt. Collins Shelter at 5,970 feet. The first ten miles were pretty much uphill until we reached Clingman's Dome, the highest point on the Appalachian Trail at 6,655 feet.

The trail is never "just" uphill or "just" downhill, though. When we covered such distances in a day's hike there were always pointless ups and downs (PUDS) that got in the way. The forest changed even more from the wintery, dead forest with bare hardwood trees to a magical, dense evergreen forest complete with the smell of fresh spruce, pine, and hemlock. It was like having my own aroma therapy treatment without the high cost.

Fruit Smoothie and Pumpkin Butt, a brother-sister pair from Massachusetts, appeared from a side trail when I was taking a rest at Clingman's Dome. I was still at the bottom of the tower waiting to take on the mass of tourists—not my favorite thing to do.

I had met the duo days earlier and they were becoming consistent faces in my ever-growing hiker family. I asked them where they were coming from since they showed up using a different trail from what I had used. They informed me it was the AT. I asked if they had used a blue-blazed trail. Nope, it was the AT.

I soon realized I had misread the signs somewhere and had taken a wrong turn. The guidebook even warns of possible confusion, and I still got it wrong. I had taken a side trail to the tourist parking lot, then walked up the very steep and crowded pedestrian road to the top.

It was like a zoo. And I was the animal. Hundreds of people were there to access the observation tower. Everyone was in their designer street clothes, all happy and fresh, smelling like cologne and dryer sheets. Not one person had a bag larger than a small fanny pack. I received many strange looks as I made my way through the crowd with my dirty clothes and pack. I should have held out a cup.

I felt bad for one young boy who was with his parents and sister. I'm not sure why they were out hiking in designer clothes, but they were. At least the trail was easy—it's always easy close to tourist traps. They were on the trail I thought was the AT; and since it was so easy, I should have known better. The young boy was about five, and he just wanted to be a boy. He wanted to run, jump, and make noise. The mom made him hold her hand, and she actually said, "Hush, we are outside, so you have to be quiet!" Really? In what world did she grow up?

I did not let the news of missing a small section of trail bother me, since I had done it in error and the alternate route I took was actually longer. The worse part was the people. It was the most uncomfortable feeling to be unexpectedly thrown into a huge crowd. I did all I could to not have a panic attack. I just wanted to get back into the woods.

But first, we needed to climb the tower. This wasn't the usual tower we were accustomed to seeing. This one had a ramp the width of a one-lane road that spiraled up to the top of the observation area. There was nothing to fear here except the masses of people on this opening day of Clingman's Dome. No wonder it was so busy.

The view was stunning, with sunshine, bright blue skies, and white fluffy clouds. We were very blessed; it is rare to have such a view from the top.

The view might have been grand, but the cell service was almost impossible. I was supposed to meet a trail angel, Connie. She had reached out to me before I even began my hike and offered to put me up for a night midway through the Smokies at Newfound Gap. She finds hikers on *Trail Journals* and offers help. Bruce had even dropped off a food box for me at her house. Jimmy and I Believe were also going to be in the area. But without cell service for the past three days to keep everyone updated, I didn't know if anyone would be there when I arrived the next day.

While Fruit Smoothie, Pumpkin Butt, and I sat in the sun enjoying a rest, Karl arrived. The four of us sat on the concrete ledge of the lower ramp and shared our snacks. It was nice to share. Eating the same thing day in and day out gets boring. I had made it a point not to eat other people's food because I didn't know them or their habits; but the more time I spent with certain hikers, the more I relaxed and was more comfortable with them, trusting their hygiene. Sickness is a big deal on the trail, and I did all I could to avoid it.

After our R&R and calorie intake, we headed for the trail. This time I went the right way. Karl waited for Walking Man. He was so good to his dad. Karl could have hiked on and met up with his dad at the end of the day, but he wouldn't do that. Each would hike their own pace, but they'd meet up for snack, water, and lunch breaks. They looked like they had a really great relationship. It wasn't until later that I learned they were just getting to know each other.

Still no service at Mt. Collins Shelter. I was able to send Bruce a satellite message through the inReach, asking him to contact Connie,

Jimmy, and I Believe. I decided I would stay with Jimmy and I Believe instead of Connie, whose home was almost two hours away. It was so nice of Connie to invite me, but my friends were staying closer to the trail. I didn't want to spend too much time driving.

I only had five miles to cover in the morning to Newfound Gap, and I hoped someone would be there for me. I was a little worried about the lack of communication, but not nearly as concerned as I had been when I couldn't reach Bruce back at the NOC. I felt it would all work out. Was that a sign of becoming patient? Couldn't be. Patience and my name have never been used in the same sentence.

Did I mention that day was the best day on the trail, even better than the previous?

Easter was in three days, making the current day Holy Thursday, also known as the Last Supper. Holy Week is a very important celebration in the Christian faith. Christmas marks the coming of our Savior into the world, but the Easter season seals the deal for our redemption, with Jesus' dying on the cross. I hadn't attended mass since I had left home. Until this Holy Week, I didn't realize how much I would miss it. Our very small parish at St. Leo's Catholic Church in Howland, Maine, is like family. I grew up in that church, made my confirmation there, got married there, and our boys and Bruce also made their sacraments there. The congregation is mostly older; it's like having an unlimited supply of parents and grandparents to share advice and comfort you when you need it. Everyone knows everyone.

Today I would miss Holy Thursday mass, the beginning of a mass marathon with the other services on Good Friday, Easter Vigil, and Easter Morning. I didn't always attend all four services growing up, but after having a family of my own and growing deeper in my faith with Bruce, attending all of Holy Week's services has become very enriching.

I would be okay, though. I knew missing church while I was out on the trail was not going to be the end of my salvation. God knows what is in my heart. I have heard many people use that very excuse for never attending church. A similar excuse might be, "I don't have to go to church to love God or be a Christian." I never understood that—it's like trying to take a bath without getting wet. But I did know that my short absence was not going to hurt my relationship with God. As a matter of fact, I spent more time in prayer while hiking the AT than when I was home. After all, Jesus himself also retreated to the desert and mountains for alone time to draw closer to God.

No church services were in the near future, but I was still blessed with trail magic twice, all by 10:30am. The first was compliments of Elizabeth. She had her SUV backed into the parking lot, with the hatch open. The trail exited the woods onto a grassy area abutting the parking lot. It then skirted the lawn a few yards, before disappearing back into the woods. I helped myself to some vanilla bean-flavored almonds and water. It was a chilly morning, and one look at Elizabeth had me thinking of home. She was dressed head to toe in L.L.Bean clothing to keep her warm as she tended to hikers.

The second trail magic was at Newfound Gap. When I arrived, there was no Connie or Jimmy and I Believe. But there was a pickup truck with its cap opened and a full spread of yummy food for hikers to enjoy. Several other hikers were filling up on the morning magic. Our trail angels were Bernie and Beth, a married couple. Beth saves up her tip money for the year and buys hiker supplies and food with it. They spend their anniversary week at Newfound Gap each year, feeding hikers and catering to them until the money runs out.

My friends showed up and so did Connie. She brought my food box. That was so nice of her. I was just expecting to forfeit it and then resupply in Gatlinburg. Connie was leaving for a trip, her itinerary had changed, and it ended up that it was better for her not to host me that night. Things always seem to work out for the best.

Before I had left the shelter that morning, I had said good-bye to Karl, Walking Man, Fruit Smoothie, and Pumpkin Butt. I was going to spend the night with my friends in Pigeon Forge, Tennessee, and the others were going to hike on. We would meet again if it was meant to be. I no longer felt threatened by the Smokies. I was over halfway through them and I felt quite confident in my abilities. Besides, there were so many nice people on the trail, and we all looked out for each other in one way or another.

First, off to Gatlinburg, Tennessee, for a quick tour. Jimmy and I Believe wanted to show me the sights. There was an outfitter in town and every other tourist-trap venue you could think of. It was wall to wall people and cars. My favorite things, NOT!!! But I do love to go to outfitters. I didn't need more stuff to carry, but it was fun to shop and make sure I wasn't missing out on anything.

Inside the store, we found Pumpkin Butt and Fruit Smoothie. She was in desperate need of a new pair of shoes. From there, the two were going to hitch a ride to the grocery store at the other end of town. Since I also needed to go to the grocery store, we waited for them so they didn't have to thumb it.

After lunch, we stopped at a little winery that offered samples. I Believe wanted to pick up a gift for her mom, and I was up for a little taste testing. While the sibling duo sorted their food on the curb, I Believe and I went inside. I had never done a wine sampling before, and I was excited to do something new. Who knew there was so much more to a thru-hike besides hiking?

I Believe chose a couple samples that looked good, and when they asked for our ID's, they refused mine. It had expired. I knew that. I was carrying my old one, so that I wouldn't lose my new one. I never thought I would need it for drinking purposes, since that wasn't a high priority on my list of things to do. I didn't think I even looked close to 30 years young, but the state of Tennessee apparently has a 100-percent photo ID check for the purchase of alcohol. So much for trying something new!

The kids were going to hitch a ride back to Newfound Gap to continue hiking, but they were not quite done repacking their food. Since we were going in the opposite direction, we could not give them a ride. I Believe and I did help them make a sign to hold. Traffic was heavy, and their luck at catching a ride would be good, providing there were locals out driving. Most tourists do not stop.

The sign was made, and I Believe and I held it up for the kids while they continued their chores. Car after car went by without so much as a look. We were close to a traffic signal, which made it hard for drivers not to notice us—but they still ignored us. One car even pulled over into the other lane to keep from having to make eye contact. I Believe and I were unsuccessful at snagging a ride for the kids; at least, we had made the sign.

We left them to try their own luck, and we headed to our hotel in Pigeon Forge. I was due for a hot shower, my own repacking before supper, and bed.

I really loved what the trail had to offer. The hiking was my favorite part, and that day had seemed so easy. I was getting stronger each day, my knee was doing so much better with the addition of a knee brace, and my feet had even been agreeable. The views were also spectacular. At one point, I was getting visual stimulus overload. The only thing better than the hike and sights was the people with whom I was enjoying it all. If for some reason my journey had to end there, I would have felt successful. But no such thing was happening.

In the next two days, I covered 34 miles. The first day out of Newfound Gap, I did just under 16 miles and ended at Tri-Corner Knob Shelter. The guidebook noted the shelter held twelve. This was always a conservative number. Over time, I noticed the max occupancy of any given shelter was always relative to the weather. Hikers have a way of making a sardine can roomy enough for whoever wants in.

That night, Tri-Corner Knob Shelter slept well over the suggested occupancy. The two wooden levels were full, as well as the dirt area in front of the regular sleeping area. In the Smokies, a tarp is secured to the open side of the building, making it more weatherproof. We greatly appreciated it that night.

About 9:00pm, a raging thunderstorm broke out, thrashing and howling all night. It was the worst storm I had ever been in. It was also my first storm at over 5,900 feet elevation. I am sure the elevation had something to do with it. The thunder sounded alive as it boomed, sending shockwaves through the air that you could hear and feel. We felt safe inside the shelter, but one is never really safe in a structure unless it is grounded. I was truly scared for those who had decided to set up camp outside.

The second day after Newfound Gap, I whipped out my longest day yet, 18.4 miles. It was a high-paced trekking event, and I loved every step of the way. Each step I took brought me closer to seeing Bruce. I woke up at 6:00am and was on the trail before dawn, this 6:45am start being my earliest yet. Breakfast was fast food—a Pop-Tart, gluten-free, of course.

I finally had the courage to head out while the sun was still sleeping. My headlamp barely guided my way. It was rather difficult to see the markings on the trees. The 90 lumens on my headlamp were not quite bright enough to give me the confidence to trek at full speed.

It was probably a good thing I was visually impaired by the darkness. I think the trail went straight up. I wasn't sure because I couldn't see, but my huffing and puffing with frequent rests told me this was probably true. Usually I study the guidebook to have some inclination about the morning hike, but I had not done so that morning. If I would have, the map would have shared a secret: I would be climbing 400 feet over a very short distance.

Hiking solo was relaxing. I could go at my own pace, take pictures when I wanted to, rest when I wanted to, and pray. I had developed a nice routine each morning.

The first twenty minutes or so I spent adjusting to the day's weather. I was always dressed too warm when I started out. Like clockwork, within a short time, I needed to de-layer. I tried a few times to start without my coat, but I couldn't. It was just too cold, and when I am cold, I tense up, which causes a headache, which usually turns into a migraine. After my morning fashion show of changing clothes on the wilderness runway, I pared down to my normal attire.

Once I was stretched and warm, I would say my prayers. I would have a conversation with God, then end with a meditation on the rosary. I no longer had my beads because I had given them to Midnight, but I had fingers to help keep count and an app on my phone.

I may have been hiking solo, but I was far from being alone. I leapfrogged with several hikers throughout the day. At one point, I came upon Fruit Smoothie and Pumpkin Butt. They were resting in the sun, next to a wide, swollen stream we needed to cross. The water was crystal clear and flowing fast. Once on the other side, I dropped my pack and undressed my feet.

I, too, enjoyed a rest and a soak in the cold water to smooth my aching knee and feet. Then a little nap in the sun was just the right ingredient to help me reach hubby by day's end.

I was excited to see Bruce. It felt like I was getting ready for a date. No fancying up, though. Just a wash in the stream would have to do. But there were several miles to go, so another layer of sweat and grime would accumulate.

I arrived at my extraction point where the AT crossed Green Corner Road, also the location of Standing Bear Farm hostel. I was not going to the hostel. Instead, Bruce was going to whisk me away to a hotel. It was 3:45 in the afternoon. I had done the 18.4 miles in record time—for me. I was ready for the day to end and our "date" to start.

It didn't matter to me that our date was just a rescue from the woods. Our dates were always simple, anyway. Seldom were they grand and over the top. But that's probably what made them so special, the simplicity of them.

I remember one date early on; we had planned a dinner in. I was cooking. He even brought flowers. How sweet!

Back then, a popular TV show was *Dallas*, a primetime soap opera about a slick-dealing oil tycoon family led by J.R., who, in a cliff-hanging episode, was shot by an unknown person. The headlines back then were "Who shot J.R.?"

This particular date was to consist of dinner and watching the video recordings of *Dallas* episodes Bruce had missed while at school. His family loved this show and would watch it together. I didn't really care for television, and I could only handle about one episode.

After enduring all I could, I requested the entertainment be changed to something more interesting. He was agreeable to pleasing me and said something on the lines of, "Sure, what do you have in mind?"

My response: "I have some videos of me playing soccer!"

He was game, so there we sat on the couch and watched me, my favorite subject. I am sure he would have preferred catching up on his *Dallas* drama, but he was already showing signs of a loving, caring, and appeasing character that was so darn attractive to me. He is still just as wonderful now as he was back then. To this day I still do not know who shot J.R.

Bruce had not arrived yet, so I spread out my sit-upon, the piece of Tyvek I Believe had given me for a ground cloth. I hung out on the side of the road, enjoying the warmth of the sun and the success of a wonderful day of hiking. While I was doing so, I looked up the road and saw Karl and Walking Man making their way back to the trail.

They had stopped for lunch at the hostel. Lunch wasn't the only item served; they said they were able to taste some of Tennessee's finest home brew of white lightning. I bet this backwoods brewery didn't card them.

It was a treat to see my hiking buddies unexpectedly. I didn't think I'd catch up to them. But now I was headed off trail and would see them down the road after my date.

April 4 marked the end of my journey through the Smokies. I was blessed with great weather, except for the one storm. But even so, I had found the Smokies to be beautiful and much easier than I originally perceived. In fact, I finished them one day faster than planned.

I had been so worried and scared about that section. But it ended up being so grand. Sometimes our fears can be crippling when we try to tackle them on our own. But with the help of prayers, a good attitude, and action, my fears did not stand a chance of ruining my journey through those mountains. I was living my mantra poem and didn't even realize it.

You gain strength, courage and
confidence by every experience
in which you really stop
to look fear in thc face.
You must do the thing
which you think you cannot do.
-Eleanor Roosevelt

10

We Are Family

I slept in on Easter Sunday. I slept so well that Bruce was up way before my eyelids considered flickering. I don't usually sleep soundly, but that night, I did. It amazed me how difficult it was for me to fall asleep and stay asleep on the trail. I have never been a good sleeper, but I had hoped that it would be different out on the trail. I thought I would be exhausted from hiking. That wasn't the case; I still wasn't getting the rest I needed. So, I was grateful for the shuteye I received that night.

This was the first Easter we did not celebrate with our sons. They were home while Bruce and I were away. I had already missed Bruce's and Patch's birthdays, and I would later miss Stephen's twenty-first birthday celebration. Now I wasn't home for Easter. We had left them alone to fend for themselves. Stephen was 20 and Patch was 19—not exactly kids, but they were not out on their own, either. We would have no sunrise breakfast at church and no traditional Easter egg basket for them, or our family meal with everyone at the house. It was just me and Bruce in our hotel.

Our day was filled with the ordinary hiker chores of resupplying, repacking, laundry, and bathing. I was very spoiled in this department. Bruce tended to my every need. He was the best support a hiker could have. He did my laundry, drove me around as needed, got my food, figured the next section's logistics, and even gave me foot rubs. Most of the time, I didn't even need to ask; he would be one step ahead of me and would have what I needed before I even requested it.

Bruce was my hero on this trip. I had spent the last 25 years tending to his needs while he was the breadwinner for our family. But now he was spoiling me, and the roles were reversed, kind of. He was still the money-making machine; but he was also the domestic god.

Zero days were always too short, and before I knew it, it was time to hit the trail again. Later in the hike, I found the best zero day was preceded by a nero day so all chores could be done upon arrival that first day, then I'd have a full day to rest and/or enjoy whatever the town had to offer. But this time had been just a regular zero day, filled with chores.

I was back on the trail about 8:30am the next morning, and it was a very slow start. It took me a long time to get back the hiking momentum after such a nice zero day. My pack was loaded with extras—three pounds of tangerines and two pounds of jellybeans—to share with other hikers at the shelter that night. I often carried extra treats to give away. It was more weight, but the enjoyment it brought to other hikers was worth the burden. But this was not a good day to be carrying an extra five pounds.

Fifteen miles were between Roaring Fork Shelter and myself when I started out that morning on April 6. I started at 1,775 feet, then climbed to 4,263 feet, dropped back down to 2,929 feet, up to 3,855 feet, down to 3,500 feet. Then I pushed up and over Max Patch at 4,629 feet and finished at the shelter at 4,036 feet.

I was on top of Max Patch when the temperature started dropping and clouds rolled over the top of the bald mountain. I saw the ominous formations way off in the distance and prayed they just looked bad and would not be anything more than that.

Being the cautious soul that I am, I scurried off the open bald as quickly as I could, just in case Mother Nature had other ideas. And she did. The clouds thickened and darkened as the breeze picked up. I did not want to be in the open if lightning accompanied the approaching storm. I hastily descended Max Patch to the safety of the woods.

I continued my brisk pace to try and beat the rain to the shelter. I wanted to stay dry. During that hurrying, I failed to keep an eye out for white blazes and just let the trail lead me on. Unfortunately, it led me to a dead end. When I realized my error, I turned around—only to be closed in by the forest. I realized I wasn't even following a trail.

My fear of being wet was immediately replaced by fear of being lost. Turning around and seeing no sign of a trail made my throat close. I felt a panic attack rising quicker than yeast in a hot oven. And that ball of dough in my throat was choking my air supply. Not only was I going to be caught in a storm on my own, I was now lost.

My first reaction was to run as fast as I could in the direction I thought I had come. But from somewhere deep within, a soft voice said, "Breathe."

So, I did. And the dough lost some of its puffiness. I went to run again. I heard, "Breathe." I breathed again, and the dough decompressed a little more. One more time I heard, "Breathe." Again, I listened, and the dough collapsed.

Had I just stopped a panic attack? I was puzzled. I was lost. A possibly dangerous storm was almost on me. And I was okay with all that. Wow! Let's add—I was proud of myself, too.

So, what now? I slowly examined the woods and noticed I was in a small clearing that may have once been a campsite. Taking my time and making sure I took notice of landmarks, I slowly worked my way back in the direction I felt I had come.

After what seemed like eternity, I did find a trail, but it was not the AT. I followed it back, using the clouds. The sun wasn't out, but I remembered the direction the clouds were moving in relation to the trail as I was descending the mountain.

There it was! In my frenzy to get off the open bald of Max Patch, I had missed the double white blaze that noted a turn, and I'd gone half a mile into the woods on another trail that slowly dead-ended into nothing.

It was a long day of PUDS and a wrong turn, all while carrying an extra five pounds. When I arrived at the shelter and emptied my load of fruit and sweets, it was met with gratitude by the other hikers. The heavy burden soon was forgotten.

After sharing my goods and having my own dinner, I claimed a spot in the shelter, changed into my warm wool PJs, then climbed into my sleeping bag. I wanted to retain what warmth I had before the weather got any colder. It was still too early to sleep, so I just sat up and socialized with the other hikers. No bag dancing this time.

Way back in the beginning of the hike, I had met another Andrew and Armeaus, a hiker and his dog. They showed up now. Andrew was about to tie Armeaus to a tree so he could cook his dinner. I offered to hold Armeaus so the dog would not feel abandoned, and Armeaus showed his gratitude by crawling headfirst into my zipped-up sleeping bag. He was by no means a small creature, a Doberman, easily weighing ninety pounds. It was quite cozy for me as well; he was like a little furnace.

When Andrew was finished cooking his supper, he called his companion. Armeaus ignored him. I had to unzip my bag and push him out. I felt as reluctant as the dog. I would have been quite content to have the furry companion to cuddle with during that damp, chilly night.

The clouds were kind and did not dump their payload until nighttime, when everyone was safe and dry in the shelter or their tents. Then the weather was still amiable, and the rain stopped just before sunup. I was glad I was in the shelter. I had been on the trail for just two days short of a month, and I was already tired of packing up a wet tent. It wasn't necessarily the wetness that was so bad, it was the cold morning air that made it so difficult. My fingers and hands would stiffen up and ache, making the simple chore of packing miserable.

Seven and a half miles into the morning, right after Bluff Mountain, it began to rain and did not stop until just before Hot Springs. It was another wet soggy day on the Appalachian Trail. By now I had forgotten how many days and nights it had rained. I quit counting.

I recalled Paul Stutzman stating in his book *Hiking Through* that the year he hiked the AT had been the wettest year ever. I was beginning to wonder if this year might outdo his. Not only did it rain, those dark clouds I saw on top of Max Patch caught up to me and produced more than just precipitation. The storm was accompanied by thunder roaring and lightning flashing in the distance, not too close, but close enough to have me singing Hail Marys and hiking a little faster than I safely should have.

Hot Springs was one of my favorite little towns. The trail dumps you out of the woods onto Bridge Street, which should be called Main Street because everything is on that street. The 2010 census reported the population to be a whopping 560. Hot Springs isn't what you would call a booming town, but it was full of friendly faces and great hospitality.

Before arriving in this little hiker sanctuary, I received a text from Karl asking of my whereabouts and ETA into Hot Springs. He and Walking Man secured a slot for a mineral bath at the famous Hot Springs hot tubs and wanted to know if I wanted to join them with their other friends.

Hot Springs is known for just that—hot springs of natural mineral water heated deep within the earth. Legend has it that the crystal-clear, carbonated waters and mineral content have healing powers. It has been a resort destination since the 1800s. Native Americans were the first to discover the rich waters; then as word spread, the sick and lame from the early colonies came. In Hot Springs, President Andrew Johnson's son, Frank, met his bride, the daughter of the hotel owner, Bessie Rumbough. Today, the resort pipes the waters into jacuzzi tubs set in private outdoor settings overlooking a stream.

When I received Karl's text, I had no time to spare. I was fifteen minutes out, and they were already in the tub. Originally, I was going to stop at the hostel to dump my gear and wash off the day's rain and mud before exploring the one-road town, but there was no time for such tasks; the clock was ticking, and I wanted to see my friends and enjoy a mineral bath before their scheduled time had expired.

I arrived at the check-in desk and asked where the showers were. They told me a shower was not necessary.

"Really?" was my reply. I thought to myself, *How disgusting is that?* They assured me a shower wasn't needed, and my friends had not showered, either.

One of the friendly staff escorted me to the secluded bathing area. I had no swimsuit, but neither did my friends. My Smartwool undergarments would have to do.

It was reassuring how these fellow hikers who I had known less than a month were like family. I felt no reservations about undressing to my base layer in front of these guys. Out on the trail, friendships and bonds build quickly and easily. I found people for the most part were not judgmental and were very accepting of others.

We all came from different walks of life, different socioeconomic statuses, and various religious beliefs, but out there, we all had a common goal, to seek the woods and whatever it had to offer. Modesty was set aside in a very respectful manner. There were no his or her bathrooms or locker rooms. The wilderness was one big gender-neutral space. The only privacy one had was their own tent or the diverted eyes of fellow hikers as you did what you needed to do. Modesty was just something hikers didn't worry about.

The soak in the healing waters did as much for the mind as it did for the body. And it was well timed for an event that was spur of the moment. If I had done my chores first, I may not have ventured back out to explore the spa.

After the hot tub, I headed to Elmer's hostel to check in. It was an old house, complete with antiques, dust, and the smell of my grandmother's attic. The place was clean other than dust; I don't like to dust either, so I felt right at home.

When I arrived, Elmer and his helper were in the kitchen preparing supper. It smelled delightful. I would not be staying for it, though. I had plans to meet with the guys at the local pub.

Bruce had left a food box for me. I extracted it from the disarrayed pile of other packages waiting to be claimed. Opening it was so mundane. I wish I would have slipped in a few treats as a surprise. Food was fuel, and the treats would have to come when Bruce was around or from unexpected trail magic.

I was reorganizing my pack when I noticed a couple of silver insects on the nightstand. I picked them up, squished them, and put them in the trash. I found another one and did the same. No big deal, it was early spring, and bugs were beginning to find their way inside. The room had poor lighting, so I pulled the curtain back to allow in some sunshine. When I did, several more of these insects fell to the nightstand. I examined the back of the curtain closer, and it was covered with them. This was more than I could handle. I went down to Elmer and asked if someone could remove the curtain and dispose of the critters. The dust may not have bothered me, but the creepy crawling things clinging to the curtain next to my bed had me reconsidering my stay in this historic bed and breakfast.

Laundry was next. I took a shower after packing my food bag, then walked to the laundromat. It was five o'clock when I put my load of hiker filth into the machine and noticed a Mexican grill next door. I like tacos even more than burgers and fries. Should I go or should I stay? Dinner plans were at six o'clock with Walking Man and Karl, but that was an hour away and I was starving.

My two tacos were a great way to pass the time as my clothes were being washed. While they dried, I called a reporter from a Maine newspaper back home who was writing an outdoor piece on Mainers hiking the Appalachian Trail. I entertained her with my experiences so far and let her know about Karl and Walking Man, since they were also from Maine.

It took me a while for my appetite to develop. At first, I did not experience the ferocious hiker hunger everyone talked about. I gave lots of my food to Andrew in the beginning, especially the oatmeal. I didn't like to cook in the morning. My goal was to get on the trail as fast as possible. If I did cook at supper time, I hardly finished my meal. I would eat half, then share with Andrew. When Andrew went home, Karl gladly became the recipient of my leftovers. But by Hot Springs, the hunger was in full force. I had no problem eating a taco appetizer then finishing my three-course meal at the pub, complete with a couple adult beverages.

The bar was full of other hikers seeking a night off the trail. I ran into Benji, a nice guy I had met way back in the Smokies and hiked with a few times. He was having some ankle issues and was going home. It was dark when we left the pub, so he offered to walk me back to Elmer's, making sure I was safe. Most hikers were like that. I didn't need protecting, especially in the friendly town of Hot Springs, but it was nice to know chivalry was not dead.

The healing waters worked their magic on me that night. I laid my head on the pillow, and I zonked out. When I woke up the next morning, I was in the exact position as when I fell asleep. Another great night's sleep, compliments of a real bed and pillow. I liked the routine of hiking a few days in the woods, and then sleeping inside. The wonderful night of rest made for an easy day of hiking, and my original plan of eleven miles for the next day was stretched to fifteen. I made it all the way to Allen Gap at mile 289.2.

Karl and Walking Man also stopped here, as well as several other hikers. A dozen or so of us managed to find suitable spots for our tents. Maybe not so suitable. We were pitched just inside the woods, off the road. The guidebook highly suggests not to camp close to road access. It could be dangerous in some areas where the locals are not too friendly toward the hiking community. We all felt safe with our numbers that night. It was a good place to stop after a double-digit day of hiking, and best of all, there was a small convenience store.

I took full advantage of this little hole-in-the-wall establishment. It literally had holes in the walls. I was learning to become a risk taker, but that day I played it conservatively. I stayed away from the "fresh" food items. I was afraid anything exposed to the inside of the store might harbor pathogens requiring shots.

I preferred the safety of the packaged choices full of preservatives. I grabbed a soda, a bag of chips, and a Snickers bar. That was the treat I craved, the first of such delicacies since being on the trail. I had given them up for Lent before I started my journey. Lent had ended three days earlier with Easter.

It may not have been a nutritious dinner for the night, but it was high in calories and taste. Later, I even yogied another Snickers from a fellow hiker named Bloomer. Yogiing is when a hiker manages to gain food from others without directly asking for it.

After consuming Bloomer's handout, I wished I had not done so. The first bite was hard and dry. I thought it was just a little worn from being stuffed in a food bag. I finished it, but soon after, my stomach was not happy I had done so. I later learned it was a candy bar Bloomer had from a previous hike several years ago. I vowed not to break my rule again—the rule of not taking food from another hiker who was not in my close-knit group.

The sun was starting to think about disappearing, not quite dusk but the time you know darkness will follow soon. A few of us were sitting on the ground, sharing stories. We were nestled less than 100 yards into the woods. We looked up through the trees and saw a lone hiker walking on the road. We couldn't see the road, but we knew he was on it.

He looked just like Jesus. The fact that this hiker's trail name was Jesus was even more fitting. We all had a chuckle, but I couldn't help but wonder what Jesus would look like today if He were walking down the street. Would I just watch from afar and make jokes, or would I approach Him? Would I even recognize Him? I went to bed that night with a heavy heart, wondering if I was doing all I could to be the best person I was meant to be.

Four long days of hiking took me from Hot Springs, North Carolina, to Erwin, Tennessee. The second day out, I hiked eighteen miles alone. It was hot, buggy, and hilly. I was alone but not alone. There were other hikers at Flint Mountain Shelter who I had come to know by trail name only, just familiar faces in the woods.

Walking Man and Karl were not going to make it that far. My feet hurt. I was tired and beat. The plan for the next day was to take it slower and do fewer miles.

So much for taking it easy and letting my feet determine my miles. The next day I hiked alone again, and this time did just under 19 miles. It brought me up and over Bald Mountain, at an elevation of 5,516 feet. It was a long, cloudy climb up to the bald. As I approached the summit, the clouds vanished, revealing an unhindered 360-degree view. I had never seen anything so spectacular.

I took a selfie video of myself with the view, and as I did, I broke down and sobbed. Again! At this rate, I wouldn't have a tear left in my body by the time I reached Virginia.

I was so grateful to Bruce and the boys for supporting me on my adventure and to God for giving me the strength to thrive. It wasn't just the view that made it so grand but a combination of that and all I had gone through to get to that point.

Clingman's Dome back in North Carolina had an incredible view but did not cause an emotional breakdown. Visitors can drive to the top of that attraction. There I was surrounded by tourists, making it less appealing. But to witness the grandeur of Bald Mountain, I had to earn it; and I was there alone to enjoy it by myself.

The last two days, I had been lonely because I was solo; but God had a bigger plan for me, and hiking by myself was part of the plan. He had a treat waiting for me at the top of that summit. My solitude on top of the bald gave me the privacy to breakdown emotionally and give thanks to Him, Bruce, and everyone else who made my trip possible.

From the summit, it was a short hop to the shelter, and I seemed to float in on wings. I don't even remember the 1.2-mile hike to my resting spot for the night. What I do recall is arriving at the shelter elated with what I had seen and felt, and I couldn't wait to share it with the others. I wanted to see what they thought of the bald. I was full of joy and openly shared with them as I proclaimed, "Wasn't that marvelous and so spectacular!" There were four or five other hikers there and they all looked at me like I had three heads and two were cut off.

"What?" one of them replied.

"The bald, the view! It was so awesome!" I said. They only became more perturbed with my happiness and ignored me after that.

Apparently, the summit was socked in for them, making their moods as damp as the day had been. As far as I know, I was the only hiker in those few days who was blessed with the sight.

The next day I would be arriving at Uncle Johnny's Cabins two days earlier than planned. But first, I had to work off the night's party effects. My shelter mates insisted on indulging in some weed for most of the night. I did not partake in the mind-altering pleasure, but it was so stuffy in the shelter that I could not escape it. I did all I could to keep from breathing it in. I despise smoking of any kind. My mother died young because of lung cancer from smoking cigarettes. I also had many friends growing up who wasted their lives with marijuana.

It was too dark and too late for me to set up my tent outside, and I didn't dare speak up. I was the only one not participating, and I didn't want to cause any trouble, so I suffered through it. I had my excitement on top of the bald; the others were creating their own visuals in a different way.

The next morning, I was sick to my stomach and my throat hurt. It took three hours of hiking and breathing in fresh air before I felt better. Most hikers on the trail were considerate and would ask if it bothered anyone. This group did not care about anyone except themselves. They were there to have a good time, no matter who they bothered.

I also had to deal with very cold temps in the morning. It was 38 degrees, but with the wind chill, it felt much colder. The only way to warm up was to hike. Just as the morning sickness passed, so did the morning chill, and it turned out to be a very pleasant and enjoyable hike.

At No Business Knob Shelter, I had a great lunch. There were five high school guys out for the night. They were great kids. One gave me a tangerine, one shared his chocolate covered raisins, and another went on a water run. The water boy took one of my hydration bags also. I had great trail magic right there.

The water boy was taking forever to return. One of the others went to look for him, with no luck. I still needed to do a little over 6 miles and it was early afternoon, so I packed up and left. The lunch break had already lasted an hour and a half. The remaining kids filled my spare pouch from their supply, and I was off.

Just outside of Erwin, I caught up with two men. This was very unusual; I never caught up to anyone unless they were injured or aged. Brothers Chris and Todd were neither. They had been section hiking the Appalachian Trail for a few years. Twice a year, they backpacked as far as they could for one week.

I caught up to them just as they were scouting for their 4:00pm break. They explained to me that their earlier hikes were all about the miles and getting it done. Then they realized they were missing the whole point of escaping their lives of work and stress. So, they stopped rushing and were now taking it slow and easy.

They carried heavy packs with luxury items like camp chairs and comfy mattress pads. They also had a 4:00pm ritual of stopping and having a cocktail with appetizers. I joined them for a break with my snacks and sport drink as they mixed up their beverage of vodka, schnapps, and Gatorade, with a snack of salami and cheese. My yogiing skills failed me that day.

The descent into Erwin went on and on and on. I stopped counting after the seventeenth switchback. I remember thinking, *Enough already! Just get me down. I don't need a ramp!* I made it to the cabins about 5:00pm. I splurged and rented the private cabin for $30; it was overpriced by about $29.99. It came complete with dirt, a cold shower, no curtains, and a hole in the threshold that was home to the largest black spider I had ever seen. He did not survive long. I should have let him live to eat the mice that visited me the two nights I stayed.

Uncle Johnny's was known as a party place, and it was loud, with all the other hikers staying there. But it was warm, dry, and had a bed. I was not sure it was a clean bed, but it was a bed.

The guidebook stated that there was a shuttle to town for dinner. It did not state the time of that shuttle. I arrived too late. I begged and pleaded with the cabin keeper, but he would not bend. I was so hungry. I was now in full hiker-hunger mode every day.

I had my resupply box and Andrew's. We had dropped them off on our way down to Georgia. I pawed through them but did not want more trail food. I went to the cabin store and bought a Klondike Bar, a Snickers, and a bag of chips. That did little to fill the caloric cravings of my nutrient-deprived body. I went back to my room sulking.

Later, I went back to the front of the store where there was a picnic table. I hung around, hoping someone might stop by so I could hitch a ride. No such luck.

I noticed a tub of onion dip and a half-eaten bag of chips unattended on the table. I vaguely remembered seeing those items there earlier that afternoon. They were still there. They had been sitting in the sun all afternoon. I looked at the food and wondered how sick I would get if I ate them. I was that hungry.

Forgetting the vow I made to myself after eating Bloomer's Snickers bar, I consumed all the sun-melted dip and stale chips. They tasted great, and I was fine. That night, my paradigm of food safety changed.

Despite the cold and sickly start to my day and the lack of cleanliness and hospitality at the cabins ending the day, the middle of the day was fabulous. The weather was nice, and meeting the two groups of section hikers taught me a lesson about remembering to enjoy it out there. I almost envied them. They had no real schedule. They were not controlled by hammering out the miles and getting to the next destination. For them it was all about the moment. I was beginning to despise long-distance backpacking.

I was in no hurry to go back out the next day. Karl and his dad would arrive, and I was up for a zero. I still needed to resupply. I had my food box, but I was in need of fresh food. It also gave me a chance to do another pack shakedown.

I shipped a few items home. I no longer needed my hat, a pair of gloves I had found, my liner, an extra bandanna, my GoPro and batteries, camp fork, and headlamp. Karl had found a better headlamp and gave it to me since mine of 90 lumens was not bright enough. I also retired my Jetboil. I had quit cooking awhile back.

On the zero day, I was able to catch the shuttle to town for breakfast with a few other hikers. We were dropped off at a local diner and given our pickup time. I was tickled pink when I read the menu's heading, "Any meal any time of day." My breakfast crew was astonished when I ordered a cheeseburger, fries, and strawberry milkshake.

"What?" was my reaction to them. "I'm hungry!"

I resupplied later in the day when the cabin keeper dropped me off at the store on his lunch shuttle run. He said he would be back in about an hour or so when he retrieved the lunch crew. My resupply was quick, so I decided I would try my luck at hitchhiking. I had never,

ever hitchhiked before. That was way out of my comfort zone, even though I grew up in a small town where all the local kids did so.

Erwin was supposed to be a hiker-friendly town, so I decided to give it a try. It was Sunday, and the route back to the cabin was lined with churches. I was feeling lucky. I passed several houses of worship as godly people were leaving. Not one person so much as gave me a wave! I was clean, smiling, and carrying a few grocery bags. I was sure someone would see my desperation and offer me a ride.

I was less than half a mile from the cabin when a car finally pulled over. I opened the back door and there was a hiker friend already in the back seat. The only reason the driver pulled over was because of my friend. Glad I did not place any bets. Even though I had felt lucky, there was no luck in the cards for me that day, unless it was the fact that I had not been run over.

Karl and Walking Man made it to Uncle Johnny's, along with several other hiker friends. We all spent the day hanging out, repacking, and socializing in the backyard. If you saw the documentary Walking Home by Ryan Leighton, you will recognize this scene. It was a nice time of hiker comradery and storytelling. Most of us had been on the trail for a month or so, and we all shared the same highs and lows in one way or another.

After a great day in the backyard, we took the supper shuttle to a Mexican grill. Eight of us shared a table, and the trail bonding continued over beers and very large margaritas. When the oversized platters of tacos, burritos, fajitas, and more came, mine was mixed up with Wookie's. He had already started eating it before we noticed. The waiter was apologetic, offering to make me a new one. I reassured him it was no big deal. I figured if I didn't get sick from the chips and dip, I would be fine from Wookie's double dipping his fork into my dinner. After all, we were all becoming one big happy hiker family.

A trip across the parking lot to Walmart was next. Some of the hikers took the shuttle over. Karl, Walking Man, and I walked. We more like, stumbled over. Their gigantic beers and my one margarita bowl had us a little tipsy. Walking Man and I stumbled on the sidewalk. We had hiked roughly 350 miles over hills and through the woods without any major mishaps, only to almost be done in by a curb. Or maybe it was the hops and tequila.

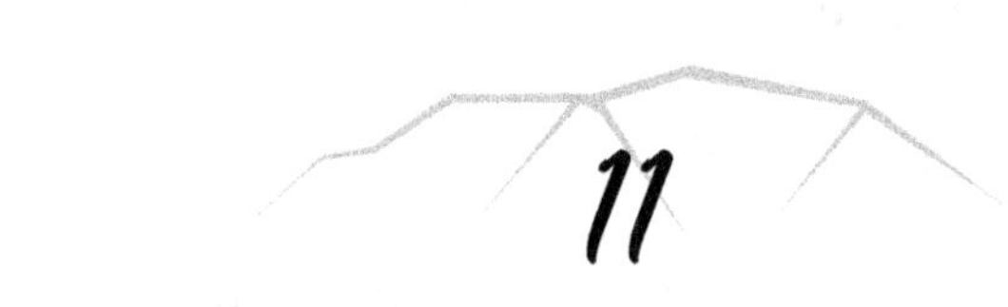

11

Hypothermia

A nice hiking rhythm was taking shape for me. I would hike a few days, come to a town, resupply, clean up, do my hiker chores, rest, and do it all over again. It was a simple life, filled with so much adventure and friendship. Some days were great, and some days were miserable. I never knew what the day would have in store, but I was always excited to find out.

Good weather didn't always mean good days, and bad weather didn't always mean bad days; everything was relative to how I was feeling on any particular day. My mental state was the main factor contributing to how the day would go, so I would try my best to put forth a good attitude—even on some days when I had to fake it until I made it. But leaving Erwin on April 13, I didn't have to do any artificial positive attitude adjustments.

My hiker rhythm was on autopilot, and the two days' rest had me ready to go. The 17-mile hike to Cherry Gap Shelter seemed effortless. I was ready to push on past the shelter, but three hikers from my current bubble already had a nice fire going. They encouraged me to stay.

August, Cray-nip, and Nomad had already claimed space in the shelter. I set up my tent. I liked to be in the shelter when it was raining, but my preference was my own tent. Shelters usually had mice and almost always had snoring. After I erected my tent, I joined the crew around the fire for some chitchat while I ate my supper.

Nomad and Cray-nip were already conversing about dating. Nomad was boasting that he only dated older women. I believe he was in his twenties. Feeling a little feisty, I decided to join in on this conversation. Growing up with four brothers and mostly guys in my neighborhood, I was used to locker-room talk. It went like this:

Me: "So Nomad, where would I fall in the spectrum of your dating possibilities?"

Nomad: "How old are you?"

Me: "49."

Nomad: "No offense, but that's just outside my upper age limit."

Me: "Why do you limit yourself? You don't know what you are missing! Us older women know how to treat a guy. We know what to do to make you happy and you don't even have to ask."

By this time, August, who had been silent up to this point sitting in the back of the shelter, burst out laughing and shouted, "AND THAT'S EXACTLY WHY I ONLY DATE OLDER WOMEN!" We all started laughing. I am not usually so fresh, but it sure was funny.

Bad days are usually followed by good days and vice-versa. The next day was wet and miserable. My journal entry for that day was one sentence long: "Wet, rainy, windy, and muddy, enough said!" I can remember that day and the next like it was yesterday. Not only did we battle the rain and wind, we had to climb up over Roan Mountain the first day, then Hump Mountain the next.

Elevation was just over 1,700 feet at Erwin. We ended at just over 6,100 feet at the top of Roan Mountain. The shelter was located at the summit, making it the highest shelter on the Appalachian Trail. The day was soggy and miserable, and as we climbed, it only got colder.

Rain started early in the day and kept us soaked. Several of us on the trail leapfrogged from time to time. Familiar faces included brother-sister duo, Pumpkin Butt and Fruit Smoothie, and Karl and Walking Man. These four were my hiking family. We didn't always hike together, but the five of us kept close tabs on each other.

Late in the afternoon, the clouds dried up and the sun peaked out with a soft, teasing breeze. It looked like I would be dry before reaching the shelter. That thought barely finished in my brain when the heavens opened without any warning and re-soaked me. I didn't even have time to pull out my rain jacket. So much for being dry. It rained so hard that the trail, now a trench worn out by years of hiking, turned into a stream bed. I was hiking up and the water was gushing down. Wherever the trail may have been flat, there was over five inches of standing water to tread through. My feet were soaked and cold, but I noticed they didn't hurt.

The hike to Roan Mountain Shelter seemed to never end. I caught up to August at one point, who usually hiked very fast. He was tall, lean, and fit, but he didn't like the rain.

This wasn't his first rodeo. This was his sixth thru-hike. One time I had asked him why he hiked it so many times. I enjoyed the friendships, views, and peacefulness of the trail. I was even liking the routine. But I was dreading the long distance and suffering. I couldn't even fathom doing it a second time, let alone six times. He never gave me a definitive answer. Instead, he replied, "Ask yourself that question after you have been home for a month, and you will have your answer."

August was familiar with the trail, but even he was fooled by the many false summits we experienced on the way up Roan Mountain. Just when we thought we were there, the trail would turn and continue upward. It was like being in line at Disney World; it just kept going and going.

I finally arrived at the blue-blazed trail leading to the shelter. A couple dozen hikers were already at the cabin. I secured a spot in the loft, then decided to claim the last one on the main level instead so I could slip out early in the morning without being too bothersome. The spot I claimed was extra wide. I was holding a place for Walking Man. Pumpkin, Smoothie, and Karl set up outside; they did not like shelter life. I didn't either, but I liked cold rain even less.

Saving spots is frowned upon, so I just set my stuff up wide, and then when Walking Man showed up, I made room for him to squeeze in. The guidebook quoted fifteen for the occupancy of the shelter, but hiker magic almost doubled that number. It was a full house.

Whenever several hikers are in such close quarters, there is bound to be a disagreement of some sort. Some want the door open. Some want it closed. Some want music, others do not. It was almost guaranteed that when the last headlamp turned out and the last sleeping-bag zipper zipped, inevitably the pungent smell of weed would fill the shelter space. Did they really think no one would notice because it was dark? I was not going to go through that again. I loudly requested that the activity be stopped—or go outside. I didn't make any friends that night, but I did sleep better.

Clothes drying overnight was wishful thinking. They were too soaked to dry under my raincoat as they had on earlier days. I hung them on pegs and nails, hoping for the best. By morning they were just as I had left them, only colder. There is nothing like the feel of putting on cold, squishy, dirty clothes to start the day. I had a clean pair of socks, but why bother; my shoes were so wet it would not have done any good. I decided to keep them for later as a treat for my feet.

The rain may have stopped temporarily but the trail-bed streams were flowing just as strong as the day before as the precipitation found its way to lower elevations. In some places, the runoff was uncontrolled. It cascaded across the trail in mini flash-flood zones. Trail design attempted to control the flow with channels directing the anticipated rains away, but even these gullies were no match for Mother Nature.

The flat areas were like small lakes, collecting all the water. There was no going around; straight ahead was all I could do. A few times, I stopped to capture video of my walk through the deepest parts. Up to this point, I had only taken pictures of beautiful scenery. I also needed to show everyone back home my misery. It wasn't too bad; it was kind of fun—until it got cold.

The fun didn't last too long. The cloud cover never went away, and it rained on us again that second day. The tree cover was surprisingly thick on Roan Mountain, sheltering us from the wind. As the trail descended, the trees became less dense and opened up to a large, windy bald. At one point, I looked up. Ahead, I could barely make out a large figure through the mist and fog.

It was Walking Man fighting his way up the muddy bald. He was fashionably wearing his ground cover cloth as a skirt to help thwart the rain pellets that were beating down on us. He was listing to the right in an attempt to brace himself against the wind blowing him off the trail. I myself walked with the same posture. The wind was so loud, nothing else was audible. I caught up to within in a few feet of him before he knew I was there, videoing his laborious journey. Walking Man and I hiked together for a while. It was nice to have company on such a dreadful day.

It was a five and half mile drop at the end of a very long day. We all were tired from the past two and half days of mountains combined with torrential elements, so we sought the refuge of town. The guys were headed to a hotel where they would meet up with Ryan, a friend of theirs from home. I was headed to Mountain Harbour Hostel. From afar, Bruce had also contacted a hotel to make a reservation for me; but the poor cell service prevented his message reaching me.

Dreary weather brought everyone in from the woods, and space at the hostel was limited. When I arrived, only tent sites were available, so I reserved one. The last place I wanted to be was out in the rain. Pumpkin and Smoothie were tenting also, but they were far more adaptable to the cold than I was. The tent site rental at least gave me access to the hiker pad and laundry. It wasn't much, but it was dry and warm.

The converted upstairs of the barn made a college frat house look like a five-star hotel. It had a small loft with a few beds, a semi-private room, a main area for sitting, a dining table, and a kitchen area. In the back hall leading down to the animals was a single private room and second bathroom.

A few of us late arrivals missed the free shuttle to town but were able to call the local restaurant that advertised shuttles to their establishment. We had a few minutes to spare, so I went to rinse the ick from my shoes and socks with the hose.

I didn't realize how cold I was until I attempted the simple task of cleaning my footwear. While I was hiking and moving, my body was warm; but as soon as I stopped, I was no longer producing the heat and circulation to my extremities. Now nothing was working.

Broadway, a young kid in his early 20s, offered to assist me. I am not one to accept help, unless it's from Bruce. I like to be independent and, in most cases, I like to be the one doing the helping. I politely declined Broadway's offer and thanked him.

I did not realize how pathetic I was, but he did. Without saying a word, he took the hose, my dirty socks, and my shoes; and then in a very assertive yet caring way, he said, "I got this! Go inside." He explained that I did not look well.

His sternness snapped me out of my zombie state and alerted me to the danger I was in. I was trembling all over, and did not even feel cold anymore. I was hypothermic. Thank God for all my hiking friends.

The trip to the restaurant was almost a disaster. After we finished our meal, we let the manager know we were ready for the shuttle back to the hostel. He informed us that the shuttle was no longer running for the evening. That would have been nice to know when they dropped us off. I was thinking clearly now that I was dry and had a tummy full of hot food, so I didn't panic. I secured us a ride with some of the patrons who were getting ready to leave. It was amazing that I would freely get into a vehicle with strangers while out on the trail. If only the whole world was this way, strangers helping strangers, what a wonderful place it would be. Thanks to these nameless trail angels, August and myself climbed into the back of the Explorer and did not have to walk back to the hostel.

It was getting late, and I had not yet set up my tent. I went into the hiker lounge to retrieve my items. Nomad and Broadway asked where I was headed, so I told them. They insisted I stay inside and said I could sleep on the floor. I did not feel comfortable with this, since I had not paid to sleep inside.

They were really concerned for me since I was so cold earlier and still had not completely warmed up. They did not relent, so I asked the others who were staying there if they minded if I crashed on the floor. Who was going to say no? I decided to accept the offer. I reasoned that at least I did pay for the tent site and I would pay the owner the difference in the morning, even if it was just floor space.

I was out early, but not too early. I waited for the hiker store to open. Twenty minutes after the opening time listed, the door was still locked. I decided to leave and forgo paying the difference for the inside space I had occupied. I would plan to catch them in the future.

It was a pleasant morning as I hiked back to the trail with another hiker. There was no rain, and it looked as if the sun would come out. Moreland Gap Shelter was my destination for April 16, day 38 on the trail. I would pass the 400-mile mark.

It was 18 miles of easy hiking, winding through small backyards, by a cemetery, through fields and clearings. The trail may have been easy, but my feet were tired, and I was exhausted from the past two and half days of rain, cold, and tough terrain. I took my time to cover the miles. It didn't matter if I was tired, I had to cover the distance. I was just thankful the trail was so gentle; it gave me a chance to rest on the move.

My exhaustion caused me to be relaxed. I was too tired to even think. My mind was clear, and I was able to truly enjoy the hike without any distractions. I had never experienced that kind of euphoria before—exhaustion combined with joy. I just let the trail lead me on.

Every day brought something new. It could have been easy to get bored with the humdrum of doing the same tasks day in and day out, but I would have missed so much. It was the little things out on the trail that made the experience so grand. I never in my wildest dreams would have thought so much joy could come from being so tired. I earned the tiredness by hiking peaks over 5,000 and 6,000 feet. I pushed my body through wind, rain, and mud. I saw views one can only access by foot. And through that tiredness, I found peace.

A stream next to the trail that day provided some cool relief for my feet. They had been waterlogged for too long, but the coolness of the stream that day was a nice relief. As I dried them, I noticed the pads of my feet were pruned and pitted, looking like someone had pricked them with hundreds of nails. It was quite gross, and I feared I had some sort of fungus or jungle rot. I powdered and dried them extra dry, then continued for the day. That night at Moreland Gap Shelter, while we were all sitting around having dinner and airing out our feet, I noticed I was not the only one with pitted soles. It seemed to be a common ailment.

When I arrived for the night, I hadn't expected to be reunited with my hiking family. But one by one, they all showed up. Pumpkin and Smoothie arrived first, followed by Karl and Walking Man with their friend Ryan. By now, Karl's charm and good looks had caught the eye of many female hikers earning him the trail name GQ. Their friend Ryan was producing an AT documentary of the father-son hike. I went from thinking I was going to be alone—not counting the antisocial crew in the shelter—to having my tramily (trail family) to keep me company. I even had a tent mate.

Nomad also made it to the site. He slept in the shelters. But by the time he got there, the shelter was full. He hiked light, too light. He carried no tent or tarp. So, he rolled his sleeping bag on the cold ground and was going to cowboy camp.

Being the kind soul that I am (more like too naïve), I offered Nomad a space in my tent if he behaved himself. I felt bad for him. I had a soft spot in my heart for Nomad. He seemed to have a tough life—I am sure no doubt due to poor choices and unhealthy behaviors—but deep down I felt he had a kind heart. After all, he had come to my rescue the night before when I crashed on the hostel floor.

It is amazing how the body heals after a night of rest. The next morning, the holes in my feet were gone. Gold Bond and air do a body good. The weather was clear, the temps were nice, and we were six happy hikers ready to take on the day. It wasn't discussed formally, but we all somehow agreed we would hike together and Pond Flats campsite would be our destination for the day, only eleven and a half miles.

The trail took us by Laurel Falls, a scenic stream with a waterfall. The guidebook cautioned against swimming due to a dangerous whirlpool, so we heeded its warning and enjoyed the view from a distance. Besides, it was still early spring in the mountains and no one felt like swimming

Nine miles into the hike, the guidebook also showed a side trail to town. Everyone wanted to take the blue-blazed trail for a quick jaunt into a grocery store and fast food for lunch. It was an extra two miles round trip. My feet may have been hole free that day, but they were not pain free. There was no way I was doing any extra miles.

I offered to stay on the trail and wait for them. They all felt bad, until I reasoned I could rest my feet, nap, and watch their gear so they could do the trip without the weight of their packs. Then it was unanimous. They were quite pleased to slack it into town, and I enjoyed a long nap by the babbling stream. It was heaven.

I was so glad I stayed behind. The climb from the junction of the AT and the blue-blazed trail to town was a series of switchbacks that climbed from just under 2,000 feet to 3,700 feet in two and half miles. It was easy terrain, it just went up, up, and up.

When we arrived at the campsite later that day, there were several other hikers already there. I looked at my guidebook, my iPhone app, and the terrain, but something was off. It was a clearing, and there was a spring, but the distance didn't feel right. I usually just go with the flow, but this night I persuaded the gang to continue a little farther. We went about another quarter mile and came to a much better and less crowded site. One solo hiker had set up there. We all decided this would be home for the night.

There was plenty of space to pitch our tents. I set up farther away from the group so I could start earlier than normal the next morning without disturbing any of the others. After all our tents were set up, we built a fire together where we sat enjoying the delightfully dry yet cool evening. By the fire, I savored my chips, Snickers Extreme, and soda they had bought me as a thank you for waiting with the gear earlier.

Once everyone had their end-of-the-day chores done and meals eaten, we joined for together-time around the fire. Ryan and GQ set up a GoPro in a tree to record the evening events for the documentary. It felt like our own version of tribal council on *Survivor*, but no one was being voted off.

Ryan brought a protein bar to share with us. We could only have a piece of it if we allowed him to record us as we ate it. It was not your ordinary sports bar. This one was made of powdered crickets. I was looking around to see if Anthony Bourdain was lurking behind a tree for some reality tv show. I promised Ryan I would try it.

I have never been too daring in trying uncommon foods. But why not? This whole adventure was about experiencing the unusual. To all of our surprise, it was quite tasty. If I had not known it contained insect parts, I probably would have never known; but since I did know, I was a little reserved in the chewing and swallowing. I did finish what I took, but I did not ask for seconds.

As the sun went down and the blueness of the sky faded to pinks and oranges and then to black, tiny lights flickered in the distance through the trees. During the day as we walked over the mountains, there was no sign of a town anywhere, and we felt so far from civilization. But as darkness overtook the woods, we could see shiny specks of life. We all wondered if any of the people below knew such a trail existed in their own backyards.

The woods seemed void of life other than the occasional hiker passing through, but where I chose to set my tent was a colony of some sort. I was sitting up in my tent, writing in my journal, when I felt something move under my bottom. I didn't think anything of it, but shortly after that, I felt it again, an even stronger push. This time I moved my hand to where I felt the movement and began pressing hard. There was a release and a pop as an insect's exoskeleton gave way.

I felt confident I had taken care of the bug. I had no idea what it was, and I didn't want to. My imagination took over as I envisioned a giant, nuclear-grown caterpillar escaping from the depths of the earth to swallow us whole as we slept. It had to be one strong insect for me to notice it moving as my not-so-small buttocks sat on it.

It was 9:20pm, well past hiker midnight. My 5:00am start was going to come fast, so I finished my journal and lay down—only to be woken by the sound of a large redneck-sounding pickup speeding away in the distance. I'd grown up in Maine with that kind of truck. I pictured one of my brothers sitting behind the wheel with me on shotgun, having fun on a hot summer night.

I drifted off to sleep again with those fond memories—only to be woken again, this time by more of the same movement from under my tent. It wasn't just one; it felt like the bottom of the tent was coming alive. I squished and popped more of the mystery squirmies as though I was popping bubble wrap. I adjusted my sleeping pad and added whatever else I could find to layer between me and the tent floor so I would not feel it anymore. I love nature, but sometimes she gives me the willies!

I didn't quite make a 5:00am start. I was on the trail by 5:50am instead. Breakfast was on the go as I left in the pre-dawn darkness, guided by my headlamp. I had a short 3.4-mile hike to Hampton, Tennessee, where I would meet Bruce for my resupply. I was full of excitement. It had been almost two weeks since I had last seen Hubby Bear.

The meeting point was a beautiful lake. The sun was barely up when I arrived, and the morning fog still covered most of the water. The air was crisp at 52 degrees, but that did not stop me from taking a plunge. I have a rule about swimming in strange water, and I never break it. If the water is murky and I cannot see my body parts, I don't swim, ever! I examined the water's clarity and then proceeded to change into my bathing suit. Bruce had it with the rest of my gear in the vehicle. It was a quick, refreshing dip. I was dried and dressed in no time.

The main advantage of having a support vehicle was that I always had what I needed. I had tons of extra gear in the vehicle. Bruce helped me unload my luggage, boxes, and bags so I could resupply and tweak my backpack. I was always tweaking. It was advantageous to have my supplies follow me, but it was also a burden. The trail was teaching me to be streamlined, and the more stuff I had, the more work it was to go through it.

12

Homeless

While I was going through my gear, a hiker exited the trail and asked Bruce for a ride to town. I had stuff to do and we were waiting for the rest of the gang, so Bruce helped him. They took off, leaving me to go through my belongings in the parking area.

A county sheriff pulled up slowly to investigate. He asked if I needed any help. I told him I was fine. He left to patrol the rest of the park, then returned, asking me again if I was okay. I reassured him I was. He asked again. I then told him I was a thru-hiker and my hubby had just gone to help another hiker and would be right back.

Apparently, the sheriff was concerned that I had been abandoned and wanted to know if I needed a ride to a shelter for women. I chuckled and thanked him for his kindness while reassuring him I was fine. After he left, I chuckled to myself again, wondering just how destitute I must have looked. Then my heart went to feeling sad.

We never really know how good we have it until we open our eyes and look around. The sheriff's concern for me made me realize not all women are as fortunate as I am. I gave thanks to God for giving me a wonderful husband who delighted in my goals and dreams as much as I did. A small tingling stirred in my soul as my love for Bruce grew even more.

It wasn't long until the gang reunited at the beach. No one else swam, but we did take a snack break with Bruce before continuing on for the day. Walking Man, GQ, Ryan, Pumpkin, and Smoothie hiked ahead. I would eventually catch up. First, I needed to repack all my extra gear to load back into the car. It was still strewn all over the ground in the parking lot.

Possessing an abundance of stuff is comforting and comes in handy when you need it, but with owning more possessions comes more responsibility. Instead of being content with what I carried on my back and enjoying the beautiful spot with awesome friends, I was knee deep in trunks, totes, and bags. Eventually I finished repacking and was also reconsidering having so much stuff. Bruce drove ahead, then hiked south to meet me at Iron Mountain Shelter.

Less than a mile after leaving the recreation area, I caught up to Smoothie and Pumpkin.

"If you don't tell her, I will!" Pumpkin said to Smoothie.

She looked at me with pain in her eyes and said, "I have a really bad rash, and I don't know what to do!"

The wet conditions over the past week, especially the drenching before and after Roan Mountain, had everyone dealing with skin issues. But Fruit Smoothie had the worse chafing I had ever seen.

I flinched when I saw it and tried so hard to hide my concern, but I failed. The tops of her inner thighs were so raw they looked like fresh hamburger. I had known she was uncomfortable, but I had not known how bad it was. The baggy shorts she switched to did little to relieve the pain.

We had fifteen more miles to go for the day, and there was no way she was going to be able to do that. Continuing on would have risked deepening the wounds and/or infection.

I was able to reach Bruce by text. He was still close and returned to the swimming area where we had left him earlier. The kids backtracked, and Bruce drove them to town, where Fruit Smoothie could buy what she needed to heal and hike more comfortably.

The remainder of the day was a pleasant hike with GQ, Walking Man, and Ryan. Sometimes I would hike alone. Sometimes I would be blessed with the company of one of the guys. Usually GQ blazed the way out in front, and the three of us trailed behind.

Ryan often kept pace with GQ, but by the end of the day, he was dragging. GQ, Walking Man, and I had over 400 miles under our boots, but this was only Ryan's third day on the trail. To make matters more challenging for him, he had no hiking poles and was carrying a pack loaded with gear and all his camera equipment.

Before this hike, I had never used hiking poles, not even when I went snowshoeing. One summer when Bruce and I were climbing Katahdin, we saw some hikers using hiking poles on their descent and they seemed to effortlessly glide over the rock scrambles. Bruce and I said if we ever climbed the mountain again, we would use a pair. I did some research, asked around, and decided on a pair of women's Black Diamond Trail Pro Shock Trekking poles. They were my best friends out on the trail.

We still had a few miles to go before we reached the shelter, but Ryan was tired, hungry, and low on water. He and I stopped for a rest. I shared my snack, energy cubes, energy-enhancing supplements, and water. I couldn't do much, but it was all he needed for the final push to the end of the day. As we left our little break area, I handed him my best friends to use for the last few miles.

When I arrived at Iron Mountain Shelter, Bruce was already there with the rest of my hiking family. He had hiked southbound from the parking area at TN 91 with Smoothie and Pumpkin. GQ, Walking Man, and Ryan arrived before I did. They all welcomed me like I was an Olympic champion finishing my leg of the relay. I was home, and not homeless, at least for the night.

The seven of us set up our tents, randomly dispersed among the trees surrounding the shelter. It was a fabulous spot. The shelter was basic, but the area around it was level, dry, and soft, a real treat. After I set up our tent and took care of my miscellaneous tasks, I delivered trail magic.

Bruce had packed in Honey Buns and orange juice for everyone. He had already passed around a six pack of PBR—Pabst Blue Ribbon. Everyone knew who the real trail angel was. Bruce always made me look good. Rumor had it that hikers tolerated me because wherever Black Bear was, Bruce and all his kindness were close at hand.

Ryan remained in his tent; he had climbed in shortly after setting it up. It is quite normal for a hiker to disappear once reaching camp. We all like to withdraw to our own space for various reasons. But quite a bit of time had passed, and he hadn't reemerged as he had the previous two nights.

I "knocked" on his tent to see if he was interested in a Honey Bun and orange juice. He unzipped his tent just wide enough so I could pass him the items, graciously accepting the offering without saying a word, he zipped the tent back up, and we never heard from him until morning. I secretly giggled at him. I knew he'd be okay. He was at the spot in his discomfort where all of us had been—400 miles ago.

Once I had delivered the treats, it was time for me to indulge in mine. Bruce had packed in a Subway sandwich for me. I placed my footlong on the picnic table situated under the shelter's overhang. Several other hikers sat in the shelter, and all eyes were on me.

I was taking my life into my own hands as I proudly and teasingly unwrapped the sandwich. I slowly ate all the contents held within the roll and left the soggy carcass bun on the wrapper, since I don't eat anything made with wheat. I turned to the hikers with their puppy-dog eyes and asked, "Do any of you..."

I could not even finish the sentence before they all replied, "Yes!"

After an evening filled with trail magic and extra beverages, nature called late in the night. Both Bruce and I took a little stroll to take care of business. Thankfully, this midnight potty break was uneventful, not like our first nighttime escapade back at Springer Mountain.

Upon returning to the tent, I could hear Smoothie rustling in hers. Then she called to me in a hilarious kind of panic. A mouse had run across her face, waking her up. She heard me and called out. She wanted help making sure the little critter was no longer inside. We laughed and squealed like little girls as we emptied the contents of her tent, looking for the rodent. Once we were positive it was gone, we returned to finish the night's sleep. Oh, the joys of wilderness camping.

Morning came early. Bruce and I were packed up and on the trail by 5:55am. We all wanted to make Damascus, Virginia, by the end of the day.

Damascus is a small town with a population of 1,000 plus. It is home to Trail Days, the largest event on the AT, with presentations, hiker reunions, music, gear reps, and retailers on hand to assist hikers. We would be arriving a month before this event, so there would be no partying for us unless we returned later. Many hikers do take a leave from their thru-hikes to attend Trail Days. I had no desire to do so.

It was a pleasant morning, even with the drizzle. The easy terrain was an added bonus, and since I had continued loaning Ryan my hiking poles, Bruce shared one of his poles with me.

We reached the vehicle quickly. From my resupply in the car, I grabbed minimal food for the day. Bruce would be meeting me somewhere the AT crossed a dirt road to hand off a mid-day, calorie-boosting Big Mac and fries and a few extras, in case I couldn't do the hoped-for miles. Damascus would make a 26-mile day, my longest if completed.

I gave Bruce a hug and kiss, he gave me both poles, and I was on my way.

At some point during the day, I called Bruce to confirm I wanted to push all the way. The rain was coming down harder and I didn't want to stay in the woods that night. We also confirmed the rendezvous point for my power lunch. I hadn't eaten fast food in years but felt the need for it that day. I did not have enough calories for a 26-mile day. I was looking forward to my "two all-beef patties, special sauce, lettuce, cheese, pickles on a sesame-seed bun."

The rain had intensified along with the wind, and the temperature was dropping. The mild start to the day was long gone and misery was settling in.

Our rendezvous was at McQueens Gap. I arrived ahead of Bruce and found a tree to stand behind to protect me from the elements. The skinny timber did little to divert the driving rain from buffeting me. I was cold, wet, trembling—and Bruce was late. I called to check on his ETA, and he was 20 minutes out.

I dreaded the wait in the cold but needed the food. I did not have enough to continue the hike to Damascus, nor did I have enough to spend the night on the trail. I could have done it, but it would have been pure misery. The shelter was only one mile away. I put failure in my brain, conceded I would not make Damascus, and waited behind my toothpick tree for Bruce.

Through the wind and rain, I faintly heard a voice. "Mama Bear!" I looked up to see Fruit Smoothie and Pumpkin Butt exiting the woods.

I told them that I was waiting for Bruce and a Big Mac and that I had decided to stay at the shelter. They were heading on to Damascus, 11 miles away, and encouraged me to join them. I lacked confidence in my ability, but they built me up and said they would share their food. I called Bruce and canceled the drop.

The three of us rallied together and headed up the hill, singing and laughing at the rain. I no longer felt so incompetent.

The kids rescued me that day. I don't do well in the cold; I get grumpy really fast and let misery take over. So much for happy hiking. With their good attitudes rubbing off onto me, I was able to delight in our rainy journey. It reminded me of the saying, "When we share our joys, they are multiplied; and when we share our sorrows, they are divided."

That thought made me think of people who say they don't need to go to church to love God or to be a Christian. Which in one sense is true, but not what God has intended. God doesn't want us to attend Sunday service for Him; He wants us to participate in a faithful community so we can share life with others and, in sharing, joys and sorrows can be multiplied and divided. That day my sorrows were not only divided but turned into joy with the help of my "cubs."

We quickly arrived at the shelter. We filled our water bottles and shared some oatmeal. In the shelter sat a grumpy man from Germany. I thought I had been having a pity-party, but he made my earlier demeanor seem delightful. He was not sharing any joy with us and his misery was only multiplying. He went on and on about how boring the Appalachian Trail was and how he had hiked all over the world and this was the worst trail ever!

We attempted to help him find good in the trail, but he wasn't accepting. So we finished our snacks and moved on. It was late in the day, and we still had 10 miles to cover in the rain.

Three and a half miles out from Damascus, we reached the Tennessee-Virginia border. A solo hiker was just hanging out in the rain. We asked if he was okay, and he reassured us he was. He was waiting at the sign for some friends to have a celebratory toke. While he was still sober, we asked him to capture our moment of victory entering our fourth state.

The trail had crisscrossed the borders of Tennessee and North Carolina for approximately the last 200 miles. It was nice to have that flip-flopping from one state to the other behind us. We finally felt like we were making progress.

The kids and I made awesome time. We were crushing it, at just under three miles an hour. Every 45 minutes, I would send a text to hubby letting him know how many miles we had left. We were making tracks fast. Our time was incredible. Our photographer at the border sign and his hiking buddies made us look like snails, though. They were flying high as they cruised past us, singing and laughing. Whatever they had used to celebrate was floating them into Damascus.

For 9 miles, the three of us were full of energy and strength. Not bad, considering my quitting state of mind earlier. We had no problem keeping pace and pounding out the miles. We laughed, sang, and hiked along. Then, with 2 miles left, we hit a wall. It was as though our off switch had been flipped, and we had all we could do to make it to Damascus. The cold, wind, and rain got the best of us, and we were zapped of our energy. With wet, soggy feet, sore muscles, blisters, and various degrees of more chafing, we managed to make it to the trail town in one piece. It was our highest-mileage day, 26 miles, and 23 of those were in the rain.

Bruce was not late this time; he was there with the SUV, a cold Big Mac, and fries. We were beyond soaked, muddy, cold, and hungry. Bruce layered the seats with towels to protect the new rental from our dirt. We looked like pigs that had just wallowed in mud, but we weren't as happy. The attempt to keep the vehicle clean was futile. We soaked the towels through, and the mud from our boots left a nice layer on the floor mats. Another chore for Bruce. Once we were in the truck, Bruce handed me my burger, but I no longer wanted it. As famished as I was, the thought of a cold burger seemed very unappealing. Pumpkin was happy to accept it, while Smoothie and I ate the fries.

We were not sure where we were going to stay. None of us had reservations. The kids liked to go conservative, and I liked whatever luxury Bruce would allow. After several calls and not much luck with either cheap or five-star places, Bruce finally made a connection with the owner of some cabins. He gave us an incredible rate, which the four of us gladly shared. It was the best of both worlds. The cabins were fully furnished and clean, at a more-than-reasonable price. Our cabin was cute, cozy, and set next to the river that was overflowing from the rains.

A quick stop at the grocery store to purchase items for supper was all that was needed for the evening. We had a combined effort preparing a feast consisting of curry chicken, special sauce chicken tenders, jasmine rice, and salad. I am so glad I passed on the Big Mac.

The next morning, Smoothie and I awoke to extra-sore feet, so we all decided to take a zero day to recover. We enjoyed another combined effort at breakfast with eggs, pancakes, and fresh fruit. It was so nice to be inside, warm and dry.

Ryan, GQ, and Walking Man caught up to us while we zeroed. With a late start on their previous day, they could only make it to the shelter, where they took refuge from the rain with the grumpy German. GQ kept me updated on their ETA in Damascus, and Bruce and I met them at the trailhead about noon. The trail runs through the town, as it does in Hot Springs. I continued walking with them back to the cabin so I wouldn't miss any of the white blazes.

Before they arrived, Bruce had arranged with the cabin owner for us to switch to a larger cabin the seven of us could share. The proprietor was accommodating and gracious with his rate. He let us have the larger space for the same price even though three more hikers were joining us. Back at the cabin, my hiking family was reunited once again.

Our zero day was spent like most days off the trail, completing chores of laundry, resupply, catching up with family back home, and relaxing. Ryan had his own chores to do. He conducted interviews with us for his documentary.

We had the added duty of drying all our gear. Everything was soaked and smelly. Bruce and I collected everyone's dirty clothes and went to the laundromat in the next town over. We volunteered so that everyone did not have to spend the time sitting around, waiting for laundry to be finished. We were a great group; it was a nice circle of give and take. Everyone had something to offer to help make the experience more enjoyable.

When we dumped the clothes into a bin at the laundromat, "smelly" was a kind way of describing the stench that escaped the bag. Imagine a high school locker room after a hot, wet football game that went into overtime and all the players had left their gear and clothing on the floor in soggy clumps. Put that smell into a non-breathable bag. Close it tightly and leave it in a hot, muggy corner for a day or two. Now open it and add a month of used cat litter. Seal it up really good for another week. Now bake on high for about another day or two. Open the bag, and take a great big deep breath. If you are still standing, congratulations! If not, you will know how we felt.

The rain stopped, allowing us to have a barbecue. The seven of us pitched in, creating another feast. Chicken, steak, hot dogs, potatoes, salad, and veggies filled our plates. The food was fantastic, but it was the company of my new family that I will always remember. We crowded around the table, sharing stories and planning for the next section of the hike.

It didn't take me long to realize a thru-hike is more than just a walk in the woods. It is so much deeper than that. It's also about relationships: the relationship with myself, with the environment, with my Creator, with my spouse, and with family. That night, the focus was on the friendship I was developing with my hiking family.

It was close quarters when it came to bedtime, so it was a good thing we were becoming friends. The two-bedroom cabin was meant for 3-6 people. It had a double bed in each room and a fold-out double bed in the small living area. Since our group included only one couple, that meant we had to be creative.

Bruce and I did not need to have our own space. It worked better for GQ and Walking Man to double up in one room. Ryan got his own private bed. Smoothie and I split the pull-out, and Pumpkin and Bruce drew the short straws and took up floor space. It looked like a teenage sleepover. The price was right, and it was so much better than being outside.

We had one more co-op dining experience, with GQ claiming the title of head chef in the morning. He prepared fabulous breakfast sandwiches. We finished off the pancakes from the day before as well. "Stuffed" was an understatement by the time we had consumed everything edible.

It was normal hiker refueling. It's feast or famine out on the trail. It did not matter how much we ate; we knew we would burn it off—and then some—as soon as we were back on the trail. Long-distance hiking was the best weight loss plan ever! I ate whatever I wanted and still lost weight.

A few days earlier, that police officer might have suspected I was homeless, but that was far from the truth. Yes, I was in the woods and far from home. For all practical purposes, homeless. But my temporary family surrounded me with love and kindness, and it was impossible to feel neglected.

13

Ponies, Bear? And Cows

We left Damascus at different times on April 21. The kids needed to check on stuff at the outfitter. Ryan was heading home to Maine after he finished up one last interview with Walking Man and GQ. All I had to do was go back to the trail. Bruce walked with me to the north end of town where the trail disappeared back into the woods. He wasn't going too far after we said good-bye. He would be meeting me where the trail crossed Route 58. Everyone else would continue to the campsite just past the road crossing, and I would catch up with them the next day.

The trail out of Damascus follows the Virginia Creeper Trail for half a mile. When I first heard the name of this section, I was a little "creeped" out. My wild imagination took over, wondering how this trail got its name! Little did I need to worry.

The name did not derive from some crazed lunatic. Rather, the 35-mile trail was a former railbed from Abingdon, Virginia, following the Whitetop Laurel River to Whitetop, Virginia. It was a pleasant stroll on level ground for a morning stretch before my 16.7-mile hike.

The hike that day continued to be easy. The terrain was rolling hills easily climbed and descended. The only issue of the day was a detour I chose not to take. I came to an intersection where a sign posted on a tree read, "Northbound AT hikers: Bridge washed out 1/2 mile ahead. Best route to continue on AT..." I took a picture of the sign because there was no way I was going to remember the series of directions for the detour.

Then I pondered the wording of the sign. It didn't say, "Trail closed" or "Detour." It merely read, "Best route to continue..." I interpreted this to be a free-will choice. I wanted to be a purist and not miss any section of the trail. I noted the time for reference, and I went left instead of right.

I hiked and hiked and did not come to a bridge. I hiked for twenty more minutes. The terrain was easy, so I was sure I had completed over a mile. After I no longer saw any blazes and the trail dead-ended, I decided to turn around. Retracing my tracks at the expense of another twenty minutes back to the sign, I chose to heed the advice of the notice nailed to the tree and went right.

Free will is a wonderful gift. It is what distinguishes us from all other life forms. It is the root of our salvation. God sent His only Son to die for us. We are saved by that very act; but in order for us to take advantage of that salvation, we must choose to accept Him. And in doing so, by design we will have eternal life with Him.

Every day we are confronted with choices that will affect us, and when we are not sure which option to take, we have a great guidebook we can refer to, the Bible. Sometimes we think we have to figure everything out on our own, but all the answers have been provided for us if we just look at what is right in front of us.

When we close our eyes to the truth, we may have difficulty in our lives we could not foresee. That day I chose not to heed what was right in front of me. I had the answer to the question, which way should I go? But in all my infinite wisdom, I thought I could do it my way. I was wrong and needed to retreat back to the sign for directions. God also works that way. When we insist on doing things our way and then fail, all we have to do is admit we were wrong and seek Him. He will then guide us the right way, His way.

I made it to Route 58 with plenty of daylight left. A car was parked next to the road on the north side. But it wasn't Bruce. I found a spot as far off the pavement as I could safely sit and still be seen by oncoming traffic. The road was winding and narrow. I attempted several times to call and text Bruce. Poor cell service prevented any hope of communication.

I sent a satellite text using the inReach but had no reply from him. He probably lacked reception also. I waited over an hour, and there was no sign of him. The campsite was only three tenths of a mile in from the road, but I could not continue on because Bruce had my tent and sleeping bag. I was slackpacking, and regretting that choice. Another day of not having what I needed.

The sun was setting, and the temps were dropping. Thank goodness it was dry. I started to go into panic mode again. Then realized I had been going into panic mode quite a bit on the trail—and it never helped. So, I took a deep breath and decided to stop the next car that went by. It was not a busy road, and during the time I'd sat there, only one vehicle passed. I flagged it down and confirmed with the driver that I was in fact on Route 58.

I sat and said a few prayers and started to devise a plan to sleep outside without my gear. Just as I had given up all hope that Bruce was going to rescue me, I heard a vehicle coming around the bend.

Saved! Bruce finally showed up. I relaxed and jumped into the SUV. He had been worried about me and explained that the coordinates in the guidebook were wrong and had sent him to some other place. Luckily for me, Bruce is one smart cookie. He was able to figure out where I was and find his way there.

We drove back to Damascus for the night. We did not rent a cabin or room but instead slept in the back of the Ford Expedition in a parking lot.

By April 26, I had made it to mile 566.5, one quarter of the distance to Katahdin. I was having so much fun. I enjoyed my new life of hiking, meeting new people, and being in nature. The scariest part about the journey was not knowing what each day would bring; but that was also the best part.

Looking back, I realized my panic times came from the lack of knowledge of what lay ahead; but this was also exhilarating. The panics were caused by poor planning, change of events, or both. It was in those times of despair I had to reach down inside and find that inner strength we all possess.

If we want to harness that asset, we just need to follow the protocol for a fire. Stop. Drop. And roll. When a situation gets heated or seems to be overbearing, we just need to stop. Stop talking. Stop overthinking. Stop feeding the fire with our negative thoughts and behaviors. Then we need to drop. Drop to our knees and pray for God's guidance. Pray for the direction and wisdom we need to put out the flames. And finally, we need to roll. Roll with confidence and conviction. Roll under the smoke and the flames. Don't stop rolling until we emerge on the other side and into the fresh air.

One unexpected joy of hiking the Appalachian Trail was all the time I was able to spend with Bruce. During our initial planning, he was only going to join me on the trail about once a month to check on me. His work was demanding, making it difficult to take vacation.

I had been gone almost two months, and we already had more "dates" than we had since our kids were born. His job allowed him to take his office on the road, providing he had internet and cellular service. So while I was hiking, he would find a place to work; then at the end of the day, he would meet me.

Bruce had joined me the last few days, delivering trail magic for my hiking family and me. Other hikers who just happened to be at the right place at the right time also reaped the benefits of his services. He would meet us at trail crossings with snacks and cold beverages. Sometimes he would hike southbound on the trail and meet me. It was an awesome sight to see him hiking toward me when I would least expect it. The tingling kept growing stronger each time I saw him. It was like our younger years all over again. I couldn't get enough of him, and not because he was delivering treats. It was because he was giving of himself to help me succeed.

The last several days had been exciting. I saw wild ponies in the Grayson Highlands of Virginia. I saw many deer. I slept in my tent through a raging thunderstorm. I survived hurricane wind gusts while on an open bald. I saw very little sunshine. I celebrated Walking Man's birthday with him, met a friend from 25 years ago and did not even know it was him until later, and I met a famous songwriter.

Grayson Highlands State Park is located next to Mount Rogers National Recreation Area in Virginia. The park is located within Jefferson National Forest and is spread over 4,822 acres. For 2.8 miles, the Appalachian Trail wanders through Grayson Highlands State Park. The park is popular for hiking, camping, biking, and horseback riding. It is home to The Grayson Highlands Fall Festival and weekly music jams. Hikers remember this splendid landscape mostly for the wild ponies that inhabit the hills.

I was hiking with Walking Man through this section. He was 20 yards or so ahead of me when he stopped and waved his hand for me to quickly yet quietly come forward.

It immediately reminded me of my youth while hunting with my dad. I would be following my father; and when he heard or spotted a deer, he would stop, raise his arm with a halt gesture, followed by the rapid flick of his wrist waving me to his position. Walking Man did the exact thing. For a split second, I reminisced about those hunting days.

I had always loved the outdoors. I grew up with four brothers and two sisters, and Mom and Dad scraped out a meager existence on an Army pension and a teaching salary. So grand vacations were not heard of. Hunting and fishing were our thing. These did not require much money or travel since we lived in the woods.

I just longed to go on overnights. Only the boys were allowed on such expeditions. I voiced my young opinion on this subject every time the annual winter snowmobiling and ice-fishing trip came around. But I was left behind once again. I'd get the same excuse: "It's no place for a young lady."

When Bruce and I married, we bought a piece of lake frontage on Cold Stream Pond in Lowell, Maine, with a view of Katahdin. We wanted home to be on the water and close to the woods so that we didn't have to leave home to go on vacation. Recreation was outside our front and back doors. Bruce travels a lot for work, so when he had time off, he did not want to go anywhere.

Many times, I would express a desire to pack up and go camping. This posed a couple major challenges. First, Bruce didn't want to go camping; and second, we owned no gear. So I never pushed the issue hard and never went camping. Occasionally we would set up the kids' small tent down by the shore and sleep in that on warm summer nights. Before I started my hike of the AT, I could count on one hand the number of times I actually slept in a tent on a site not at home. Now here I was, living the dream after years of thinking it was impossible.

When I reached Walking Man's spot, we could see several wild ponies on both sides of the trail. I pulled out my camera and videoed him calling one closer. We continued on. Up ahead were more ponies closer to the trail. We saw a young one, old ones, and a very pregnant one. The young one was more timid than the older ponies but curious at the same time. With some coaxing and gentle pets, I was able to capture a selfie with him.

Walking Man picked some fresh grass to feed the ponies. They very quickly grew bored with the offering. I had some oatmeal, and they nibbled it from my hand. I remembered a bag of whole grain rice crackers in my pocket, and as soon as I pulled it out and opened it, the rustling sound of the packaging caused a mature pony to come trotting down the hill. He bullied his way through the herd to us, then the others followed in hot pursuit.

We were surrounded by several of these creatures. I was rethinking my decision to feed them. They were just like our dog. Whenever you open anything in the kitchen, Barney is there waiting for his share. These ponies were not strangers to human interaction or processed foods. Once we passed the far side of this area, we saw signs instructing us to keep the "wild" in "wilderness" and not to feed the animals. Nice try, but I think it was a little too late for that.

We were at Partnership Shelter near Mt. Rogers Visitor Center in Virginia on April 24. This is the only shelter on the trail with a shower. With its location so close to the road, it also offered the luxury of pizza delivery.

Bruce gave us a ride to town for resupply and we secretly purchased a birthday cake for Walking Man. We celebrated that evening, with everyone around a fire and, of course, pizza.

A couple, Lefty and Righty, were section hikers also at the shelter. They were fun to converse with and tell stories. They were a nice addition to the party, especially since it was also her birthday.

It was a full house that night. Since we were parked near the road, I slept in the SUV again with Bruce. I wanted to get an early start, as usual; and with the full house, our sleeping in the vehicle left more room in the shelter for others.

Another long day was scheduled, 17.6 miles. Bruce would meet up with me for lunch in Atkins at The Barn. I left as planned, and Bruce hung around helping other hikers. He gave Lefty and Righty a ride.

Their section hike ended at Partnership. While Bruce was chauffeuring them, they chitchatted and the normal conversation of where are you from, what do you do, led to their realization that we all knew each other. Since everyone used trail names and it had been 25 years or so, plus and minus a few pounds and several gray hairs since we had last seen them, we didn't recognize each other.

His name was Rich McDuff, a musician entertainer we would see at a local bar in Bangor when we were dating. We were loyal fans and developed a friendship. Like all things, changes occur with time, and we went separate ways. It was such a nice surprise to meet them again and rekindle our friendship.

The 17.5-mile hike to Crawfish campsite offered easy terrain. I started the day at 3,220 feet elevation and hiked up Glade Mountain at 4,120 feet over five miles, making it an easy stroll, nothing too strenuous. Then it was mostly downhill to Crawfish campsite at 2,600 feet. The terrain was gentle, but the air was chilly and damp that day. I did not have my warm hat or mittens and was wishing for them.

Around mile 540, the trail passed Lindamood School. The old one-room schoolhouse is now part of the Settlers Museum of Southwest

Virginia. The door is left unlocked for hikers to take a respite. Upon entering the building, I felt like I was stepping back in time. I could see the children in their handmade clothes, the girls with their hair up in a kerchief and the boys with their suspenders, sitting attentively and listening to the teacher. I could hear the students asking questions and helping each other.

The wood stove was strategically placed in the center to give warmth on a cold, damp day like that day. The school was quiet now. There was no children's chatter or the sound of a teacher's lesson. With the silence, I was hearing volumes of a simpler life. I could have stayed there for hours.

Before leaving the historic building, I helped myself to the bountiful trail magic a local church had left in the back corner. I did not seek out the food or beverages. Instead, I found warmth for my head, neck, and fingers. A large plastic tote was filled with handmade hats, gloves, and scarves. I felt so blessed.

Not wanting to be greedy, I chose what I thought would be the least desirable items for my hat and gloves. But the scarf I chose was a fleece with a print of ponies. It reminded me of the Grayson Highlands.

Bruce was right on time for lunch. We met at The Barn. I was ahead of GQ, Walking Man, Pumpkin Butt, and Fruit Smoothie. I didn't mind. It gave me longer to sit inside and warm up. While Bruce and I were enjoying our meal, a gentleman stood up and introduced himself. He was eating solo when we arrived, and as I passed his table, I gave a friendly smile and hello. He seemed like the rest of us, just in for a bite to eat. But he was the famous John Ellison, singer and songwriter.

I did not recognize his name, but when he offered to sing a song for us I did recognize the lyrics, "Some Kind of Wonderful." Mr. Ellison wrote the song and was the first person to sing it. He said the song has been recorded by more artists than any other song.

Mr. Ellison was passing through on his way back to Canada. After he sang, people lined up to get his autograph. I had him sign my buff and my AWOL guide page. The trail never ceased to surprise me.

After lunch, I said good-bye to Bruce. We would see each other again at Chestnut Knob Shelter, two days out.

GQ, Walking Man, Pumpkin Butt, Fruit Smoothie, and I hiked out for Crawfish campsite. It was a leisurely hike back into the woods. My hiking family stayed together for most of the afternoon.

The little camping area offered access to a stream, flat ground, a fire ring, and plenty of places to pitch our tents. I choose a spot nestled under a thicket of rhododendron trees. I enjoyed these plants. The rhododendrons reminded me of a stand of staghorn sumac trees that grew adjacent to our yard when I was a kid.

Sumacs are not at all like the rhododendrons in flowering or leafing design. It was the small woodiness of their trunks and branches that were similar. It was the perfect hiding place for my brother Buddy and I to play. We felt like we were in our own little world. Several times on the trail, I was able to pitch my tent within a stand of rhododendrons, hiding me from everyone else. I felt like a kid, once again in my own little world.

After our personal evening chores were done, we all pitched in to build a fire. Another great benefit of those wonderful trees was the never-ending supply of dry, dead wood they produced. I am not sure if using the debris fit a purist trail etiquette, but we used it anyway. We never cut or broke anything green. We only used what was already dead. My reasoning was that we were cleaning up the area, making room for new growth, like pruning a garden.

It wasn't terribly cold that night, but the air was damp and had a chill. Besides providing a heat source for our suppers, the fire kept us warm. We sat around it, talking and telling stories as we consumed s'mores. The fire also dried out our clothes. In fact, it did too good a job. I managed to melt my neoprene knee brace. Lucky for me, I had a spare.

After we were all fed, dried, and ready for bed, we disappeared one by one to our tents.

It wasn't long before the calm evening changed with a vengeance. The rain poured down, and a storm thrashed all around us. I was so happy to be tucked in among the rhododendrons buffered from the storm. As the thunder played out its symphony, I surprisingly was able to sleep. Storms on the trail were no longer bothering me. I wasn't sure if that was a good thing or not.

The hike to Chestnut Knob was another seventeen-plus-mile day, complete with clouds, cold, intermittent rain, and wind. But I would always say, no matter the weather, it was a great day to be on the trail. Some days I believed it; and other days, not so much. But a rainy, cold day on the trail really does beat a warm and sunny day at work. Besides, for some reason when it was cold and rainy and my feet were drenched, they didn't hurt as much.

We traversed many fields on the way to the shelter. The last three and a half miles was a steady push up over a 2,100-foot incline. I think it was a huge bald or farmland. I couldn't quite tell. It was so cloudy and damp that at times we could only see a few yards ahead. The shelter was a sight for sore eyes, our safe haven from the day's elements. Bruce was already there.

Chestnut Knob Shelter was completely enclosed. It had a door and even windows. Two hikers were already there when I arrived. They occupied the bottom bunks next to the door, leaving a platform with room for four and two bunks above the lower platforms.

One bunk was a single and the other was for one or two, depending how cozy you wanted to be. Bruce and I first claimed space on the lower platform; my hiking crew was right behind me. It would be a full house. Before they all arrived, another hiker arrived. He claimed the smaller bunk. That now left three places for four people. Pumpkin was going to take the last bunk, but Bruce and I decided to cuddle up on the top bunk, since we were a couple and wouldn't mind the closeness. That gave the remaining platform to my hiking buddies. No one wanted to set up outside at 4,400 feet on an open field in the cold rain. We assumed it was open—we still could not see anything.

By morning, the drizzle and rain had stopped. We were lucky; we woke to only a light frost. The fog lifted also, and we could see down into the valley at the quaint village below. Bright and early, Bruce snuck out to visit the privy, and when he stepped outside, he interrupted two deer feeding a few yards away. They were not bothered by the shelter or the happenings going on inside.

Bruce and I were packed up and out before anyone else. He had a flight to catch in Charlotte for work. Someone had to keep the funds coming in for my adventure.

The day remained cold. With the frosty start and the temps low most of the day, we made only quick stops. I had to put on an extra layer whenever I took a break. It seemed as if we were hiking north faster than spring was arriving. Late April in Virginia was colder than March in the Smokies. The last several days of cold and rain were wearing on me again. I just wanted to be warm.

God delivered my request. The next day was beautiful. The terrain was easy, and it was warm and sunny. We all arrived at the shelter early. GQ and Walking Man set up inside. The brother-sister duo set up their tent, and so did I.

There was a nice stream down over the bank, just off to the right of the shelter. With the temperature surprisingly warm, I decided I would head downstream to bathe. I wasn't the only one with that idea. As I strolled along, I looked up at the wrong time—or maybe it was the right time.

I managed to catch GQ in almost all his glory. One slight turn to his right, and I would have seen more than my fair share. I turned away and yelled to him, "Sorry! You should have told us where you were going and what you were doing!"

His reply was so humble: "Black Bear, I thought we were beyond that." We may have been, but I was still a little flushed.

That night after supper, we relaxed around the fire and shared each other's company. The air was dry and comfortable. I retired to my tent to journal and write postcards, all the while chitchatting with Fruit Smoothie through our tent walls.

Just after nightfall, we heard a strange sound. My blog post was short: "As we all are settling into our tents and/or shelter on this beautiful evening, Fruit Smoothie and I are startled by a sound. And that sound just happens to be a bear calling in the distance. Oh yay!!!! My food bag is hung. All should be safe. If I don't post again, you'll know otherwise."

The next day began like all the others—get up, pack, eat, hike. A few yards up the trail, we could see farm country. We had no idea we were so close to civilization until morning, when we could see the fields scattered down below us. The beastly noise that had scared Fruit Smoothie and I was just a lonely cow! It sure was a weird-sounding heifer. We heard "bear" all day long.

It was another glorious day of hiking. Blue skies and sunshine led us the whole day. The five of us hiked throughout the day as usual. I left early, only to be caught and passed by everyone else. Then we would leapfrog as we took turns resting.

Right before arriving at VA 606, we crossed a hiker-only suspension bridge over Kimberling Creek. The long, narrow wooden bridge swayed and bounced as we traveled its length. It caused my stomach to perform flip-flops as my nervousness increased with each wave caused by Walking Man's steps.

Once across it, we had a mere tenth of a mile to the road, then only a half mile west off the trail between our stomachs and a lunch counter at Trent's Grocer. The day could not have been more perfect. We were all together, the weather was cooperative, and we did not have to eat out of our food bags.

Only one girl was working the lunch counter and the store. It was not a stop for anyone in a hurry. Thankfully, on this day we had time on our side. We relaxed as we sipped our milkshakes and smelled the deep fryer as it cooked.

Normally, the smell of frying food would upset my stomach, but not out on the trail. It was a delicacy, calories galore. I enjoyed a burger, no bun, and fries with my shake, my standard off-trail meal. Then I topped it off with a bag of corn chips and a soda.

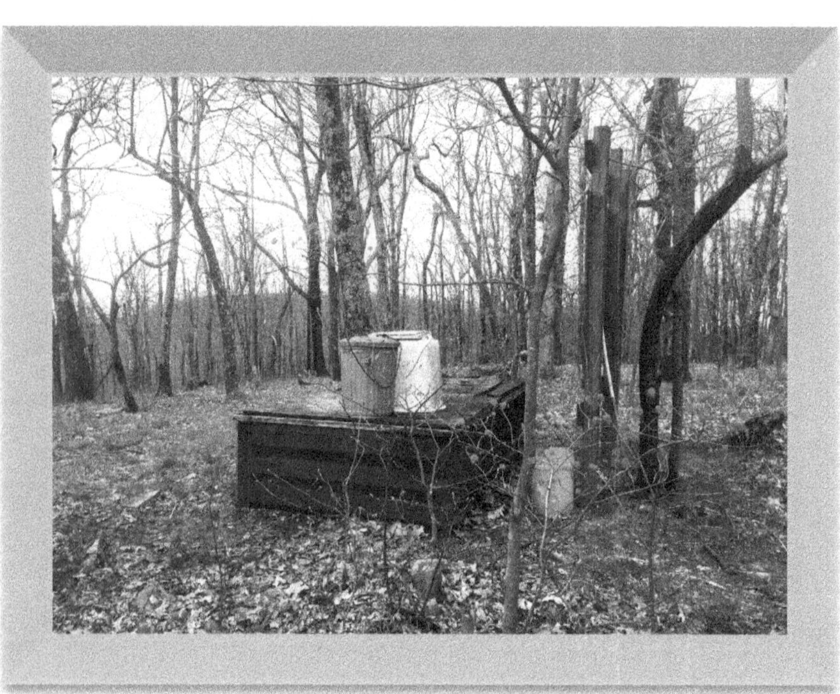

14

Sometimes Bad Things Happen

After our lunch break, we slowly sauntered back to the trail for a leisurely hike to our shelter for the night. We arrived by 3:00pm. Considering our day was sidetracked with a visit to Trent's Grocer, we still logged fourteen and a half miles and had the afternoon to enjoy.

We were doing just that at Wapiti Shelter. Camp chores filled our afternoon. We collected and filtered water, aired out gear in the sunshine, journaled, and tended to our feet.

During supper, another hiker stopped in. We asked if he was going to join us for the night, and he said, "No, way! I'm just stopping for a snack. Don't you know what happened at this shelter?"

I replied, "Thanks to you, I remember now."

We all knew what had taken place, but I had forgotten it was here at this shelter that it had happened—until that hiker so eagerly reminded us.

At Wapiti Shelter in May 1981, Robert Lee Smith befriended two hikers from Maine, Robert Mountford and Laura Ramsay. In the middle of the night, Smith shot one of them and fatally stabbed the other.

He was convicted of the murders and sentenced to 30 years in prison, only to be released on mandatory parole after serving only 15 years of his sentence. In May of 2008, he attempted to kill two fishermen in the same vicinity. Smith stole the truck of one of the victims, then crashed it while fleeing from the scene. He died in the hospital four days later.

There have been ten murders on the Appalachian Trail since 1974, more than on any other trail in the US. Crime happens everywhere. One murder is too many, but considering the trail opened its first section on October 7, 1923, the number is pretty low for a span of 92 years. My home state of Maine had 22 homicides in 2019 alone, not to mention thousands of other crimes committed in a year.

It was still a little unnerving to know what had gone on in that shelter. But we felt safety in our numbers. Besides, that was a long time ago. We were all set up, and the mileage for the day had us ending at Wapiti Shelter, so no, we were not leaving.

No murderous nightmares haunted me that night—which was good because the next day was an 18.3-mile hike into Pearisburg, Virginia. We started with a quick 1,300-foot climb out of Wapiti Shelter, then a 2,000-foot drop to our destination with PUDS sandwiched in the middle. I was up by 4:00am and on the trail by 4:45am. I headed out solo, in the dark.

The absence of the morning sun hid the incline from me. I was glad I could not see it. I was not really interested in thriving on the trail at that moment. I wanted the day's mileage over as fast and as soon as I could get it done. I was beginning to forget why I was out on the trail. The cold, the pain in my feet, and the high-mileage days were taking a toll on my attitude.

Over the last 28 days, we had been hiking 14-plus-mile days with only 2 zero days and only 3 days under 14 miles. Sixteen of those days were 17-plus-mile days. I was letting the negative get the best of me, and I was forgetting my own advice. I was far from a happy hiker. I was more like a grouchy black bear.

I looked forward to our nero, even though town days were not as relaxing as a hiker would like them to be. There were always the chores: laundry, resupply, repacking, and airing things out, not to mention time spent on real food and bathing with modern conveniences. Completing those tasks didn't leave much time for resting and elevating tired, sore feet. Since the group's plan was to nero, time was precious; I was not going to waste a single minute of it.

The descent into the little town of Pearisburg was steep at times with switchbacks offering some relief. In places, hikers were rewarded with stone steps. They came at a time when my knees were screaming, and the metatarsals were joining in the misery chorus. It was still painful, but the semi-consistent pattern of the stones was easier to navigate and required less thought process as well.

Thinking could be challenging at times on the trail. Most people don't realize the mental awareness needed to hike challenging terrain. It's not as technical as walking across metal ladders traversing 100-foot-deep crevices in the ice fields of Everest, where a one-inch error in foot placement will end in death. But on the Appalachian Trail, mental acuity is still needed for a successful and injury-free hike.

Whenever the trail had steps, it was one less thing I needed to concentrate on. I didn't need to calculate the height, depth, or angle of my foot placement for the least painful step. I could just walk and enjoy the hike the best I could.

I was very grateful for those stone steps. I was also in awe of them. Sometimes they would be close to town and other times they would be miles back in the heart of nowhere. I was amazed at their design and ingenuity. Steps on the trail were possible because of the many men and women who volunteered their time, skill, and brute strength to build them so we could hike more safely. I was tired just carrying my pack. AT volunteers have to carry their gear and then have the added burden of tools of the trade. I always took the time to thank trail volunteers for their efforts.

The trail snuck between two houses before emptying onto the street. Conveniently positioned under a shade tree was a picnic table, and I briefly stopped there to reference my AWOL guidebook. I decided to hike the half mile or so to the Plaza Motel, where my food-drop box was waiting for me. Once again, my superhero Bruce had delivered it on his way out of town.

Pearisburg offered everything hikers needed within walking distance. There were several restaurants to choose from, including pizza, fast food, AYCE Chinese, Mexican, and local diners. Also close at hand were a grocery store, a Dollar General, and a hardware store.

The lady at the front desk of the motel was super nice and checked me in speedily so I could begin my chores. The hotel was old and outdated, but it was clean. The shower ran out of hot water before I could finish, but I didn't mind. I was now fresh. I had the bonus of having my laundry done for me. That service came with the room. It was early afternoon, and I had completed 18.3 miles, showered, and was now resting, waiting for the rest of my hiking family to arrive so we could go eat.

Pumpkin Butt and Smoothie shared my room, and GQ and Walking Man checked in at the hotel next door. I wouldn't see the guys until the hike out the next day. After the kids settled in, we went across the street to the Food Lion grocery store to resupply. I only needed a few small items to complement my food-drop box.

Once we dropped our groceries in our room, we went back across the street to the Mexican restaurant. Yum! The portions were huge. We couldn't eat it all, even with our hiker hunger. We were more than happy to take the leftovers for our lunch on the trail.

Virginia had been a nice, easy walk. The path was pleasant and the terrain easy for the most part. Still, the everyday of roller-coaster walking was getting to me. What goes up must come down. When we went down, we knew there soon would be another up.

I did call the guidebook and the app I was using "the book and app of lies." I'd study them to get a feel for what was to come and I'd think I had it figured out; then reality would put a huge incline that I wasn't expecting at my feet—it kept it all interesting. Overall, the book and app were worth every penny.

I had completed 634.9 miles of the 2,189.2. By this time, I was suffering from only one sore toe that hadn't quite healed. I was healthy physically and, more importantly, mentally. My friends Fruit Smoothie, Pumpkin Butt, GQ, and Walking Man were awesome. They made hiking the AT all that much more enjoyable. The dynamics of our hiker family were hilarious and comforting.

Pumpkin Butt was a gentleman and clown; Smoothie was sweet and sensible. GQ was flirtatious and strong. Walking Man was levelheaded and full of wisdom. Then there was me, Black Bear, also known as Mama Bear. Add Bruce, our hero, to the mix, and we had one heck of a hiking family. We didn't always hike together during the day, but we would meet up at night. I called it hiking alone but together.

The woods were slowly coming alive with spring. I had been waiting so long for consistently warm weather. The cold was getting old. A few days before Pearisburg, I had a discussion with myself that ended with my inner self saying, "Stop complaining or go home!" Well, I wasn't going home, so I had to be patient as Mother Nature set her own pace.

May 1, leaving Pearisburg, the brother-sister duo left the hotel about 9:30am. They needed to do some big miles to meet up with their mom on Sunday, May 3. GQ and Walking Man met me at Dairy Queen for a quick lunch before heading back to the trail. I don't eat fast food, but that day I scarfed down two DQ value meals, which included two sundaes. I could have eaten more but decided I was already pushing my luck.

After our fast-food feast, we headed back to the trail. We were rested, restocked, and ready to go.

Our pace was leisurely as we road-walked back to the trail that continued to sneak between private homes. For almost two miles, the trail followed pavement. We crossed the Senator Sumate Bridge over the New River, then climbed down the steps to circle under the bridge. Walking on the even ground was a good warm-up as we slowly woke up our hiking muscles for the eight and half miles planned for our nero day.

We crossed a small stream that looked more like a ditch with running water. It was milky white. I commented on its color and stated that I was glad we did not need to collect and filter any of it. I would have had to pass. Shortly thereafter, we approached the area designated for crossing the three-foot-wide stream. Attached to a metal post was a sign in bold, all-caps lettering "NON-POTABLE WATER DO NOT DRINK." I did not need that sign, but it confirmed my initial instinct.

We crossed the water, crossed the dirt road right after it, and continued on the path. We were paralleling the dirt road as we began a slight incline. It soon became apparent why the water not only looked bad but was also not good for drinking. The stench in the air was horrible! It was worse than a meat packing plant I drove by once in Grand Island, Nebraska, with Bruce in the 90s. Worse still than the privy back on day one. I did all I could do to keep down my two burgers, fries, and sundaes. The trail was bordering a landfill. We quickened our pace to limit our suffering.

Once back in the wilderness where the air was fresh and clean, we hiked on together. The day had started out warm and sunny, but by late afternoon it was cloudy, windy, and cool. No rain, but the guys put rain covers on their packs, just to be sure. My pack was waterproof, so I didn't need to add the extra layer of protection. I was always ready in that department.

We reached Rice Field Shelter late. It was your typical three-sided structure with a picnic table out front, nothing to write home about. The privy was even less inviting. But it was something to note. It was missing its walls! Not only was it a stage for the world to see, it wasn't even strategically placed for privacy—the trail went right by it.

The view from the shelter was phenomenal. At an elevation of 3,372 feet, the shelter sat on the edge of a field, exposing the landscape below. Your eyes drifted down the treeless slope then floated across the valley to the never-ending horizon. It would have been a great place to wake up in the morning. But the shelter was almost full, and we still had energy to press forward to a campsite at mile 643.4.

Our chosen spot was spacious, providing room for all of us. A few young men were already set up and attempting to build a fire. After we erected our tents, we joined in the task of collecting dry wood and debris to burn. It was a hard chore since almost everything was wet from the recent rains. The ground was blanketed with last year's leaves, but they were too soggy to catch fire. With persistence and patience, GQ and one of the other young bucks managed to get the smoke to turn into a flame, and they soon had a fire burning.

I was not hungry enough to cook. I was still full of the DQ value meals. I did, however, snack on a couple leftover fajitas. I had a total of eight. I surprised GQ and Walking Man with three apiece. I loved being a hiker who also provided trail magic. It was so worth carrying the extra weight. I was too impatient, though. I ate mine cold; they warmed theirs over the fire.

When I was scavenging for sticks to burn, I uncovered a new-ish, 12-inch skillet left behind by someone. I was always finding stuff. Sometimes I would pack it out, other times I'd leave it. I put the skillet next to the fire for others to use if they wanted. If my pack had not been full of five days' worth of food, I would have packed it out. But I still had 3 or 4 days of hiking before meeting back up with Bruce, and I was not going to carry it over that many miles.

I was ready for bed by 6:00pm. It was a wonderful nero day. I was able to sleep in, eat lunch in town before hiking out, log over 8 miles, and finish with camp chores by early evening. It was great! The mountain air was turning crisp, so I decided to take full advantage of being done and went to bed early.

15

Virginia Blues, Never

May 2 was a peaceful night with the exception of one incident: a mouse attempted access to my tent. He was denied. The night was cool but not cold, perfect for sleeping, which I did until just after 7:00am. That was "sleeping in" for me. It had been a long time since I had such a great night's sleep. No pains, no worries, no snoring, or any other major disruptions of my slumber.

I woke ready to take on the day. First, I had to wipe down my tent. It hadn't rained, but the tent was soaked, not just on the outside but under the fly and on the screen. The moisture buildup was worse than on any other night when it had actually rained. I used my bandannas to sponge off the moisture before packing up the tent. It took a couple go-rounds of wiping and wringing before I could tell a difference.

We were headed for Bailey Gap Shelter, a hair shy of fifteen miles. So far, Virginia had been treating us well, with easy and enjoyable terrain that did not present much difficulty. The variety ranged from rolling terrain, moderate ups and downs, and a path that was neither obstacle filled nor smooth sailing. It was interesting and beckoned me on with each step.

The first seven miles of the day hovered around 3,300 to 3,400 feet. It was a stroll in the park. We rolled and tumbled over a ridgeline all day with spectacular views.

The day offered several interesting features. The first was a section of woods arrayed with rectangular, vehicle-sized boulders. The terrain was not rocky, so those boulders seemed out of place, but they were too large to have been placed by man. They were so random, I wondered how they came to be. Their unusual nature captured more than just my fleeting interest. I attempted to look up information on them but had no results. Poor service. Google would not be able to expand my knowledge that day. I just had to savor the unknown. That can be risky for me.

My brain decided to fill in the details that Google couldn't. I imagined those stone rocks to be alien cells lying dormant on planet Earth. Completely camouflaged as natural structures, they wait for the right time, and then through telepathic communication, the stones will crumble and supreme beings will rise and take over the world. Once I was satisfied with my explanation, I hiked on.

Whenever my imagination was on pause, Mother Nature would take over. Dazzling black, yellow, and orange millipedes were out and about. They were stunning little creatures. They seemed to float along the forest floor on their one thousand legs. Those little arthropods captured my attention and camera lens all the way to Maine. More flowers and the sweet notes of songbirds were bringing life to the woods.

Man-made structures were points of interest also. At mile 655.6 one can camp at the "The Captain's." If that is not your destination for the day, you can at least stop by for a free soda, every hiker's craving. But this beverage wasn't really free. In order to claim your drink, you first had to zip-line across the river. I wasn't feeling zippy that day. Filtered water from the trail would have to quench my thirst.

GQ, Walking Man, and I stopped at Pine Swamp Branch Shelter for lunch. It was only mid-day, and the shelter was already filled. Several other hikers were taking a break as well. I claimed my spot next to the shelter, dropped my pack, and headed for the privy.

Another hiker recognized my actions and politely suggested a tree might be better. I do prefer the concealment of a large tree instead of the dreadful outhouse, but since the area was packed with people, I thought I'd be a little more discreet. I apologize for the descriptive crudeness that follows, so if you have a weak stomach, you may want to skip ahead.

I decided I would check out the facilities and judge for myself. Upon first inspection, the outhouse looked clean and well-built, unlike several privies on the trail. It was better than our family's hunting camp outhouse.

So does a bear poop in the woods? This Black Bear should have.

As I sat on the clean seat, too tired to hover like I usually do, I placed an initial deposit. In horror, I felt the wetness of backsplash! Already in full deposit mode, the strongest of sphincter muscles could not hold back, and there was a *plop-plop* but no *fizz-fizz*, rather, a *splash-splash* back up to my heinie! OH, MY GROSSNESS! I used half a bag of wipes and a small bottle of hand sanitizer. My relationship with trail privies will never be the same.

It's funny now, but it wasn't then.

We started the day at northbound mile 643.4, and the hike was very generous and gentle. Near the end of the day, we passed a sign that read, "Bailey Gap Shelter 1.1 miles." *Great,* we thought. *We will be there in 30 minutes, max.* That was roughly based on our miles per hour that day plus calculations for collecting water before we ended.

After 45 minutes of a grueling uphill climb with the aid of only two small switchbacks, we still had .2 miles to go before reaching our destination. Walking Man and I struggled with every step. We felt slightly better when we reached GQ, who was waiting for us at the junction for the spring. He too was feeling the pain, just not quite as bad as us more mature folks. When he offered to take all the water bags down the trail to the source, I did not hesitate to accept the offer. I usually like to be self-sufficient but had no pride that day. Later that night, others who made it to the shelter also commented on how tough that last mile had been. We named it the "Hardest Mile in Virginia."

Bailey Gap Shelter had an electrical outlet. How cool was that! We wanted to experience the wilderness, but heaven forbid if our iPhones, iPods, or iPads died. I wasn't fooled for a minute. I knew the outlet was a joke, but just to be sure, I followed the wiring around to the back of the shelter, hoping it might be attached to solar panels. Nope, no such luck! The prank was on me. Maybe I was fooled a little bit. One could have only hoped for such an amenity out in the woods.

You never know what you will see in the woods. On May 3, someplace between Bailey Gap Shelter and Sarver Hollow Shelter in Virginia, I saw way more than I wanted to. It was a sparkling, sunshiny day. GQ was way out in front, not to be caught. Walking Man was ahead of me also. I was strolling along in my own little world.

I had just crossed a road when the trail became a plank boardwalk for several hundred feet. It meandered gracefully through a slightly wooded forest before ending back onto a gravely trail. I passed an established campsite with unattended gear strewn everywhere. I thought, *How odd?* But that was not as strange as what I saw next.

There were two young coeds on the bridge crossing a stream. A girl was sitting on the edge of the ramp and a guy stood beside her. Okay, they must be the owners of the messy campsite. As I approached them, I noticed a third person off to my right in the brush, a young man buck naked.

He was standing alone with his back to me, and as I closed the gap between him and myself, he greeted me with a very happy, "Hi there, how are you today?" As he spoke, he turned around and I got the full monty! I did not skip a beat and replied (after a full inspection, of course), "Great, at least I am not naked! How are you doing?"

I got lots of mileage out of that visual. It powered me through another long, hard day in the mountains. It's rumored that hikers get the Virginia Blues in this middle state. Virginia is the longest state on the Appalachian Trail, but it is far from boring, and after a 21-mile day, my second-hardest day in Virginia, I doubted the Blues would ever come.

The day was long and hard at times, but it did offer sweeping hills with rolling farmlands, blue skies with wispy white clouds that looked like angel wings, and the largest oak tree in the South. The oak is over 300 years old, with an 18-foot circumference. It is second in size only to the Dover Oak in New York. The three of us took time to photograph this behemoth and pondered the three centuries of stories it could tell if only it could speak.

May 4 was by far the most challenging, mentally and physically. The last few days had been crazy hard. I was tired beyond the point of exhaustion. Even though the terrain had been more gentle, the long days, little rest, and poor nutrition were catching up to me faster than a cheetah overtakes a gazelle. The only difference was that for the gazelle, misery ends quickly.

I was trudging along, dragging my feet. As I climbed the steep slope carved through the forest, I felt I was attached to a rubber band anchored at the bottom of the mountain. My head hung low with the weight of my pack. My hiking buddies had long ago hiked on ahead, and I was doubting my ability to meet up with them. I was not in a good spot mentally, but I kept going, one slow stomp at a time, forcing myself forward and upward.

I was thinking I could not go another step and thought about calling it quits for the day. I rounded a switchback, and a few yards up the trail was Walking Man, sitting on the embankment along the trail. The terrain was so steep to the left and right of the path that it was difficult to find a spot to sit without sliding downward. But there was one area that looked perfect for two weary bodies in need of repose.

"You are a sight for sore eyes!" I shouted to him. A cliché, I know, but that's all I could think of at the moment. He shuffled to his right, patted the ground next to him, and said, "Take a seat." No sweeter words were ever spoken. I joined him in his misery, and all of a sudden for both of us things didn't seem so impossible.

Walking Man and I hiked together the rest of the day, enjoying a break from the deleterious course we had been schlepping all day. The trail eased up soon after we reconnected, helping us to forget our earlier anguish.

At the top of Brush Mountain, we paid tribute to Audie Murphy, the most decorated American soldier of WWII. A blue-blazed trail welcomes hikers to a monument in his honor. He died May 28, 1971, in a plane crash on the slopes of Brush Mountain, near New Castle, Virginia.

Hiking the Appalachian Trail is so much more than just walking in the woods. It's not a random path sliced through the forest, either. The trail visionaries and engineers put great thought and concern into where the path takes its travelers. They were artists etching a masterpiece, one that when you first look at it seems like any other painting hanging on the wall. Closer inspection reveals its details and secrets.

A thru-hike of the AT is much like staring at a piece of art. Your first look at the trail looks like any other route; there are trees, stumps, rocks, and views. But as you take the time to examine and look closer, you see beyond the obvious. You begin to feel the trail and experience its hidden treasures.

Each person finds unique riches. For me, the trail was showing my inner strength and also my weaknesses. It was giving me attagirl pats on the back with each new accomplishment, and also "humbling chats" on areas I needed work.

Besides the self-improvement crash course, the trail was providing other enriching gifts as well. Not material or monetary, but something much more valuable. Visiting Audie's memorial was just one of those gifts that day. It wasn't anything I could tuck in my pack and make a fortune on. It was something I could hold in my heart—gratitude.

It's men and women like Audie who served and who continue to serve in our military giving us the freedoms we have in our country. When I told friends and family I was going to hike the AT, they told me how brave I was. I felt uncomfortable with that. Hiking the Appalachian Trail is not brave. Serving in our military is brave. Facing cancer is brave. Overcoming addiction is brave, and so on.

I was too scared to serve in our military; my bout with cancer was scary but for all practical purposes, mild; and for the most part, I've had a pretty cushy life. On that fourth day of May 2015, as I sat with Walking Man on top of Brush Mountain, reading about Audie Murphy, I was grateful for all the real brave men and women who serve and had served for the Red, White and Blue.

Walking Man and I continued meandering along as we began our descent. It was an easy three and a half mile drop to Trout Creek and the footbridge that would carry us to the other side. GQ was long gone. We had not seen him all afternoon. We knew we would cross paths again at the end of the day.

As Walking Man and I approached the stream, we could see GQ sitting in the middle of it with his clothes hanging on a nearby tree, an all-too-familiar sight. We chuckled—then joined him. The water was cool and refreshing. With the added luxury of biodegradable soap, we washed the day's dirt, sweat, and anguish downstream.

We sat for a long time, enjoying nature's spa. It was just what we needed after the demoralizing day of hiking we had experienced earlier. The soak was over way too soon, but we still had one last big climb and a descent into the shelter. I was eager to rest and dream about seeing Bruce the next day.

After a restful sleep at Pickle Branch Shelter, our goal for the day was Campbell Shelter at mile 712.4. It was a lofty goal of 17 miles. The trail's PUDS had other plans for our destination. The AT had rocky inclines and descents between us and Campbell.

Despite Walking Man's and my own tiredness, it was a fun hike across the ridgeline of Cove Mountain. The views were plentiful. Another pleasant gift today was lady's slippers, a rare orchid flower with swollen, ball-shaped tubers varying in color from dark magenta to the even more rare white. I saw the more common color dark pink and several rare light pink. I was not lucky enough to see the endangered yellow lady slipper.

We hiked separately for most of the day. I started out early and stayed in front until just after the blue-blazed trail for Dragon's Tooth. The trail had offered so much that day that I declined to hike the short 0.1 mile to see the stone monolith called Dragon's Tooth. I was viewed out.

As I was descending that particular section, I met a young couple with their dog, headed up to Dragon's Tooth. I didn't usually offer advice to other hikers because, frankly, I don't really care about another person's perception of the trail and I assume other hikers feel the same way. But this particular section was quite challenging. It was not dangerous, but its spiny ledge formations and narrow footings made it difficult. I feared for the dog's safety, not theirs. My judgmental thought of them was *What idiots, venturing out with flip-flops and a puppy!* So I told them about what lay ahead and advised not taking the dog. The arrogant response from the owner was typical. "Thanks, he'll be fine." I smiled and continued on my way.

At the bottom, the trail flattened out completely, and in the middle of a clearing was a 4-way trail intersection with a small tenting area, fire ring, and a long log for resting. The perfect spot to pause and enjoy a snack. As I sat solo on the log, I heard Bruce's voice calling me. I strained to see through the thick trees, but I could not see him.

After several minutes had passed and he did not appear, I gave up and decided I had imagined it. During that time, GQ had conquered the Dragon and joined me on the log. We decided to wait for Walking Man before continuing on. As we rested in the sun, the haughty couple returned and with a humble voice admitted their poor choice. I did well not to say, "I told you so"—a saying that is overused in society and seldom does any good when it is utilized.

I was not going crazy just yet; it *was* Bruce I had heard. But just as he had called out to me, he had received a work phone call and stopped mid-stride to tend to business. He was on an outcropping just above the trail intersection where I sat. He had stopped descending to my location in fear of losing his signal. He was parked about a mile up the trail at VA 624.

We decided to hike out to the vehicle while GQ waited for Walking Man. My pit stop at the car was short, as the guys were right behind Bruce and myself. Bruce leapfrogged ahead with the car, detouring into town before meeting up with us again farther up the trail.

He stocked up on supplies and met us at a trailhead on VA 311. There we had our fill of snacks provided by Bruce, our personal trail angel, that included juice and pulled pork. Protein, especially in the form of meat, was such a treat. Our bodies craved it.

Our original day's destination was Campbell Shelter at mile 712.4 but due to the steep and rocky terrain, our mileage was cut short by almost two and half miles. The parking lot was at mile 708.0. It was already late in the afternoon and we were all tired, especially Walking Man and myself.

Catawba Shelter became our stopping point. It was only two miles ahead on flat terrain, easy peasy. We would be there in less than thirty minutes. GQ and Walking Man headed out first. I needed to resupply from the car, and Bruce needed to get geared up to spend the night with us.

Bruce and I filled our packs with our needs, then we headed off together across VA 311 and up the trail. We followed a dirt fire road for several minutes and realized neither one of us had seen any white blazes. We were too busy laughing and catching up.

Just as in our early days of courtship, we were oblivious to our surroundings, even if we should have been paying attention. I checked my GPS trail app, and it confirmed we were headed in the correct direction. Several more minutes went by and we still didn't see any blazes. I should have known better, and Bruce was just following my lead.

I decided we needed to backtrack until we saw a white blaze. We had been hiking for about 45 minutes and should have arrived at the shelter in that amount of time. So back we went, a little faster than we had been doing. We saw our costly mistake and corrected our course. Even though the trail is well marked for most of its 2,189.2 miles, it is still easy to get off course if you do not pay attention. I was beginning to lose count of my off-track jaunts. Lucky for us, we were together and safety was not a concern.

Once back on the white blazes, we saw why my GPS showed we were headed in the right direction. The trail paralleled a fire road. The gap between them was only about thirty yards. From the trail we could see the road, but we were not able to identify the trail from the road.

We made it to the shelter, and the guys had already claimed their spots. We took up residence next to them. It was a clean, well-built structure, and we had it all to ourselves. Several other hikers passed through, but no one stopped.

After doing our camp chores, Bruce unpacked his goodies to share. There was beer for the guys, chips, salsa, fixings for guacamole, hot dogs, rolls, and stuff for s'mores. It was quite the feast! With our later-than-expected arrival, darkness came soon but it made for a cozy gathering with just the four of us.

It's common for hikers to get the blues when they reach Virginia. Some have the misunderstanding that Virginia will be easier because the highlands are not as aggressive as in other places on the trail. Not true! Some speculate it is because it is the longest state to hike through, so it seems to take forever to cross a new state line. True! But there was so much diversity in Virginia—and I wasn't even through the state yet—how could anyone be blue? For me, as I rested with Bruce sleeping by my side at Catawba Shelter, all was great.

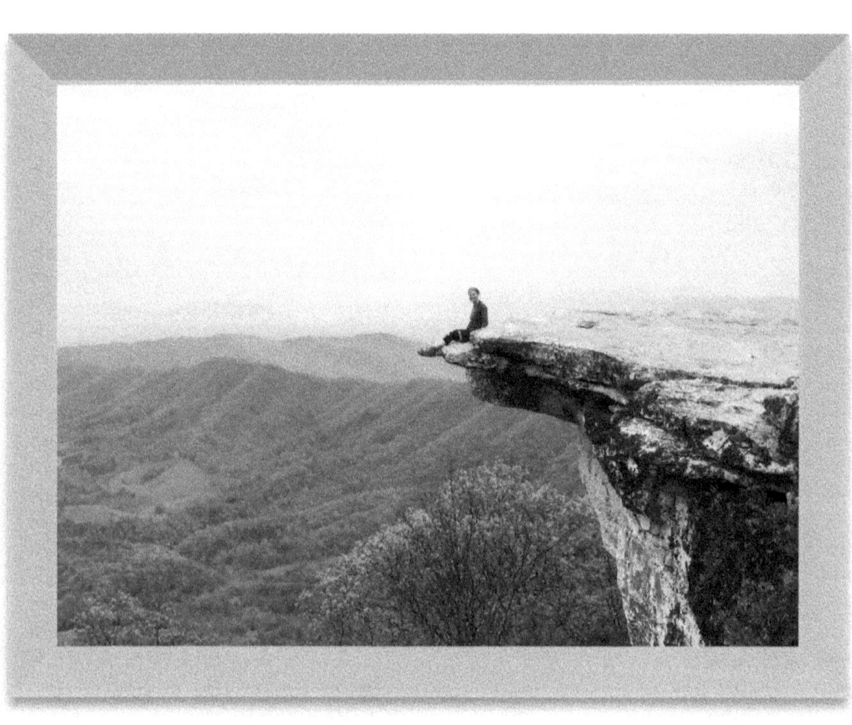

16

McAfee Knob

McAfee Knob here we come! The most photographed spot on the Appalachian Trail was a modest 1.7 miles away and just under a thousand-foot climb. After a wonderful night of rest, Bruce and I were up and ready to go early. Not surprising, but this day I was extra excited to hang my legs over the rocky outcropping and dangle them in space for the iconic photo. I didn't care how scared I was of heights; I was going to do it!

Bruce and I left the shelter, walked a few hundred yards, and came to a junction of the trail and a fire road. It was at that point we realized if we had stayed on the road and not backtracked the night before, we could have shaved over an hour off our hike. But who knew? We had done the best we could with the information we had.

Taking risks is important for growth, but when in doubt, it is always better to be safe than sorry. We only lost an hour or so, but time spent with Bruce is always time well spent. Besides, I would have missed all those white blazes.

Discovering what idiots we had been, we laughed at last night's wrong turn. I giggled and stood next to the junction sign while Bruce took crazy photos of me with a staged look of bewilderment. We naturally have a laid-back outlook, but sometimes life beats us down. On the trail, we were able to reconnect with that inner free spirit we loved so much about each other.

It was nice to escape the real world and be out there, having fun. So many couples give up on their marriage because life beats them into a place where they fall out of love. But love is a choice, not a feeling. It may start out as a feeling, but then it is a choice to stay in love.

When life cornered us against the ropes, we would use those ropes to tie ourselves closer together. We made a commitment for better or worse. Being out on the trail helped us to grow even deeper in love than we already were by allowing us to reconnect. Our motto has always been "The couple that plays together, stays together."

We arrived at the famous McAfee Knob in no time. I don't remember the climb being all that difficult, but I was impressed with a runner we saw who passed us on the way up. He was out for a morning jog. My idea of a morning jog was not a 1,000-foot ascent under 2 miles. But then again, most people's idea of a hike probably doesn't involve a 30-pound pack and 2.200 miles. It's all relative.

And there it was, McAfee Knob! It was just as impressive as the photos I had seen in books and Facebook posts. Green mountains stretched in all directions, like elongated spines of sleeping lizards. The valleys resembled indentations of their vertebrae.

The jogger who had passed us was at center stage on the Knob. Bruce and I stood in the wings to let him enjoy his time. It was early in the morning, and no other hikers were around, so we had time before it was our turn. After several minutes, the jogger rose and began his exit. I struck up a conversation with him before he escaped.

We learned he had just joined the National Guard. He was using his run as training before boot camp. We asked if he had time to snap our picture before he headed back down the mountain. Maybe Bruce and I met the next Audie Murphy.

Bruce and I enjoyed our brief time together on the natural landmark. It was a thrill to share it together. But 18 miles were on the POD (plan of the day), so we said our good-byes. He headed south and I headed north. It would be a short separation. Bruce would collect me again, once Walking Man, GQ, and I arrived in Daleville, Virginia.

One mountain with some cliff walking was our only challenge that day. It was followed by several miles of very little elevation gain or loss. Then a quick drop into town and we could eat, shower, and rest. Bruce and I knew in advance where we would rendezvous.

On a road trip home from Florida the previous summer, we detoured into Daleville. It was exciting to be on the trail and experience the unknown. But after a stretch of the unfamiliar, there was something very comforting about the familiar. When I stepped out of the woods, it was reassuring to know where I was. It wasn't just another town. For over a year, Bruce and I had this marked as one of our places to stop. The main reason was the Cracker Barrel restaurant where I wanted to feast.

Walking Man, GQ, Bruce, and I met at the local outfitter. More than 700 miles had taken a toll on our gear. We needed various items to replace worn out ones. While we were taking advantage of being inside, the clouds let go and dumped Niagara on the little town.

Timing is everything. Sometimes it's arriving at a trailhead just before trail angels are packing up. Sometimes it's meeting a day hiker who is going to the town you need a ride to. And sometimes it's getting to a shelter before Mother Nature shows you who is boss. That day, timing was on our side as well.

Bruce braved the elements to get the car, then he shuttled us across the parking lot to our eatery of choice—not Cracker Barrel, though. We chose a local place known for its barbecue, called the Three Little Pigs.

Timing was on our side once again. We were the last party to have its order cooked before the establishment lost power. Was it the timing fairy that was looking out for us? Was it coincidence? Maybe, maybe not? I believe good goes around, and we had done a lot of good for others on the trail so far, not because we were hoping for something in return but because it was the right thing to do. You reap what you sow, and it was our time to be on the receiving end of good.

While we waited out the storm, devouring our meals, we concurred we would not sleep in the soggy, storm-drowned park. GQ and Walking Man booked a room at the Howard Johnson's, while hubby and

I headed to a Sheraton Hotel in nearby in Roanoke, Virginia. It was heaven.

When asked if we wanted one king bed or two queens, I quickly interjected, "Two queens!" Not because I didn't want to be snuggly with hubby. My motives were selfish, but for a good reason. Two beds meant more pillows. The Sheraton equips each bed with four pillows. Even with my poor math skills, I knew 2 x 4 is 8. That's eight more clouds of comfort than when sleeping on the trail.

Bedtime rolled around, and I, being a pillow glutton, took 7 of the luxurious feather puffs, leaving my noncomplaining trail angel with one solitary piece of comfort.

The lucky 7 pillows lulled me swiftly to sleep that night but did not keep me coddled for long. At exactly 2:44am I woke up, famished. Most Americans never truly experience hunger, at least not in the third-world sense of it. We only think we know what it is to be empty in the gut when we have to fast for 24 hours for a colonoscopy.

That night I had feelings of hunger that were maddening. I tossed and turned and could not go back to sleep. I got up as quietly as I could in the hotel room and made myself a PBJ, opened a bag of chips—try doing that quietly—and a can of soda. Then I proceeded to have a full meal just before 3:00am. I was wired from the sugar rush, so I started repacking my gear for the next day. By 6:00am, Bruce joined me, and we went to breakfast, meal number 2, all before most people think about waking.

So many weird changes were happening to me on the trail. I was becoming a sentimental, blabbering fool, I was doing things I didn't know I had the strength to do, and my body was changing as well as my mind. It was like I was being peeled apart, layer by layer.

Midnight hunger attacks became common, but most of the time, I couldn't do anything about it because my food was hung in a tree, hopefully safe from critters. Fortunately, that night I could get up and eat. Or, unfortunately I could get up and eat, which then kept me awake.

Now it was going to be a long day on the trail. I was so hoping for a zero, but I was committed to doing whatever the guys wanted to do. The least it could be was a nero day. We all wanted to do laundry in the neighboring town. It would be an afternoon start at the earliest.

Daleville has a sister town, Troutville, that lies next door, separated by 1.5 miles of the easiest stretch of trail. Since we all needed to do laundry and we hadn't taken a zero in several days, we decided we deserved it. YAY! I was relieved. Well, it was almost a zero. I gave Bruce my gear, and so did the guys. It was the first and only time I had seen GQ and Walking Man slackpack.

We started where we had ended the day before, crossed the road, and disappeared into the woods. I was freed from the weight of my pack and ran the short distance to Troutville, arriving in under 15 minutes. I didn't even break a sweat. It was such a great feeling to be in that kind of shape. The guys were not far behind. The four of us were back together once again, and we drove the ½ mile to the town park and pitched our tents.

I fell in love with Troutville. I am not sure why; there wasn't much to it. It was a small, welcoming town, allowing hikers to camp in the park for free. There was also free laundry for hikers at the fire station across the street. While Bruce did my laundry, GQ, Walking Man, and I each went our separate ways, napping in the park. It wasn't long until our stomachs brought us back together, and off to supper we went—this time at Cracker Barrel. With another full tummy packed with carbs and protein, we made our way back to our home for the night.

A gentleman was waiting for me at the entrance to the park. He asked if I was the owner of the tent close to the playground. I confirmed ownership and explained why I put it there. It was close to the bathroom.

He informed me I needed to move it because the parents in the town get nervous when hikers have their tents too close to where the kids play. I laughed politely and said I understood. Despite suspecting me of being a threat to society, Troutville remained one of my favorite places so far. But if there is ever a next time, I will remember to stay on my side of the tracks.

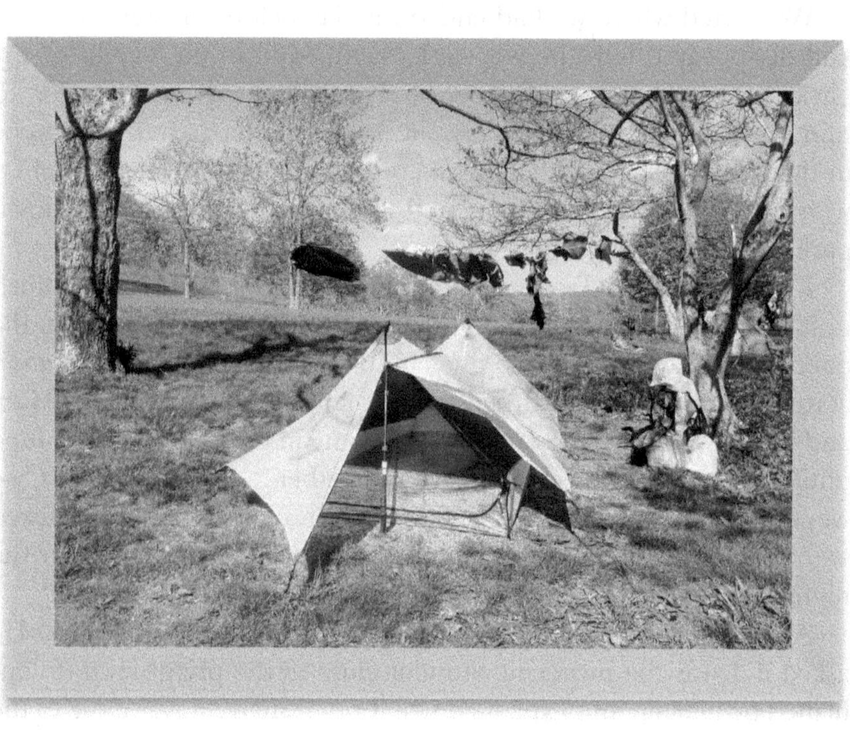

17

The Key to Success is Preparedness

A week of struggles and challenges began after we exited Troutville. We had another long day planned. Long days and big miles were the norm lately. It was a nice day of hiking. The forest was starting to spring into life with new growth and more animal sightings.

At Blackhorse Gap, mile 97.7 of the Blue Ridge Parkway, we met up with Bruce again, accompanied by his parents. Wendall and Josephine, aka Dad and Mom, were on their annual migration north to their summer home in Maine. They provided some snacks and beverages to my hiking buddies, officially making them trail angels.

Also in attendance on the trail were two large, shaggy dogs. They looked like giant, bushy black labs. We were in the middle of nowhere. They were obviously lost. Luckily for them, phone numbers were on their collars. I was secretly hoping Bruce would not be able to contact the owner. I wanted to keep them.

After I spent time cuddling and sharing my snacks with those lovable canines, I looked down at my leg and there it was! A black dot just below my knee on the outside of my leg. I couldn't freak out because I was surrounded by my in-laws and hiking family. I couldn't let them know just how crazy I was.

Ticks were my number one fear of hiking the Appalachian Trail, and this one had attached itself. I had spent a couple hours in Troutville treating my clothes and gear with permethrin to prevent a tick attack. But I was not wearing what I had treated. The weather was nice, and I had delayered, exposing bare skin. I did not apply repellent because the bugs were not out bothering me. My theory was that the tick came from the dogs.

I did not have any tweezers; I had sent them home in the spirit of ultra-lightness. Thanks to Cookie Monster, who did have a pair, I was able to safely remove the disease-carrying parasite. And then I frantically called my doctor's office back home, knowing he would wire me a prescription for an antibiotic, just to be safe.

But I was out of luck. Dr. Ritter was not in, and the receptionist told me to call the local authorities and they would advise me on the area's risk factor. That was not the answer I wanted! I knew in my heart it was not the answer Dr. Ritter would have given me either. I drew a circle around the bite site to watch for signs over the next few days. I was relieved no signs or symptoms appeared.

I limped my way across the James River bridge, ending my 20-mile day. I sat at the trailhead waiting for the guys. We would share a hitch into Glasgow for the night. I enjoyed the break, people-watching for 30 minutes until Pumpkin Butt arrived. I managed to snag us a ride to town. The driver graciously waited for GQ and Walking Man to join us.

Town was 6 miles away, and we were glad to have a hitch, even if our driver was packing a Glock on his waist. When he opened his trunk to throw in our packs, he had to rearrange his AK-47. Neither one of us was phased by his arsenal. Must have been our New England upbringing.

Our driver was all too aware of our need for transportation. He was a young hiking enthusiast who wouldn't let us pay him. He apologized for his weapons and explained that he was returning from the shooting range.

Glasgow, like Troutville, had a spot for hikers to camp sponsored by the town and Boy Scouts. There was even an eight-bunk shelter with power outlets, a fire ring, an outdoor shower cleaner than some hostels, and a porta potty. It was a small town, and all we needed was within a stone's throw of the camping area. Since we had done a 20-miler and I was still in pain from the day's hike, I was glad the restaurant was less than a hundred yards from my tent.

It was Mother's Day and I was solo. I was a little sad, but at the same time, I was there alone by choice. I try hard not to get caught up in the commercialization of such holidays. My family is always so good to me on a regular basis. I don't feel the need to receive such showering of praises.

Stephen and Patch contacted me earlier in the day to send love and greetings. Bruce had stayed the night before with us at the shelter, and he filled my empty cash pouch with money to splurge on a meal, since I carried minimal cash to prevent losing it. Even though I don't expect anything from my loved ones, I never refuse any gifts and greatly appreciate them.

Pumpkin, GQ, and Walking Man were not ready for supper when I was, so I celebrated alone. I had the usual: fries, a burger, salad, and a strawberry milkshake. The portions were huge. My leftovers provided GQ and Pumpkin with an appetizer. They were always very willing to consume what I could not eat; even though I was in full hiker-hunger mode, my bottomless pit did fill at times.

I slept soundly and woke up refreshed, which was a good thing since we had 15 miles planned for the day. With a late start, we headed back to the trail for another eventful hike in the woods. The sun was shining, and we were logging the miles.

The sunshine lasted only so long, and we ended the hike in a thunderstorm. It was really close, so close, that one burst of lightning caused the hair on my neck to stand, and I looked back to see if Walking Man was in fact still walking.

Our goal was a campsite noted in the guidebook. We searched and searched for the campsite, backtracking a short distance. All we encountered were private property signs. After no success and diminishing daylight, we stealth camped.

The rain stopped just as we were unpacking our tents. As soon as I was set up, I noticed fresh bear markings a few feet away. I let the guys know, and we all decided we'd risk it. We were wet and tired and not going anywhere. We didn't even hang our food bags. Not sure that was a smart idea.

It rained during the night. Everything was wet in the morning, but at least the rain had stopped by the time to get up. The guys wanted to do a big day. I was not so thrilled about it. I was lagging behind more than normal. About 10 miles into the day, I was going to stop at a shelter and send a text to the guys so they would not worry about me.

But when I reached the junction for the shelter, a sign informed me it was a half mile down a blue-blazed trail. No way was I doing any extra steps just to sleep, so I pushed on and soon came to a beautiful open meadow with a few scattered shade trees. I decided to stop there, instead. I tried to send a text to the guys, but there was no service. I figured they had pushed on and I'd probably not catch them again.

With my tent pitched and my gear hanging in the wind to dry, I pursued the spring. It was three tenths of a mile across the meadow. When I returned, there was GQ and Walking Man, all set up. They had dipped into the shelter where I had told them I'd be stopping, and since I never showed up, they decided to hike on.

I thought morning would not come soon enough. The beautiful meadow turned into a wind tunnel between the surrounding hills. The soft breeze I welcomed for drying my clothes turned into a gale with dropping temperatures. I was wishing the tweezers was the only item I had sent home.

Back in Troutville, I had given all my cold gear to Bruce, believing spring had sprung. While I enjoyed my lighter pack, I did not relish the cold. That night, the meadow winds sucked the warmth right out of me.

As soon as there was the lightest glow on the horizon, I packed up and headed out. All I wanted to do was hike. I was always warm when I was hiking. It was the stopping that was cold. That day I worried. How was I going to keep warm for two more nights? I didn't have my wool PJs, down jacket, or even a sleeping bag. I only had my sleeping-bag liner.

That day while hiking, I was so mad at myself for trying to be too much of a minimalist. As I trudged along feeling sorry for myself, I found a fleece blanket lying on a rock next to the trail. I thought I was hallucinating. I sat next to it to claim it without really claiming it. I waited a while to see if its owner would return. Lucky for me, no one showed up. I rolled it tightly, then stuffed it into my pack.

It helped a little that night, but I was still extremely cold. It made me think of when we try to go it alone or follow our faith with minimum effort or none at all. Things don't always go as they should. When we reach our lowest point, we realize going without is dangerous. In my case, I was trying to have the lightest pack possible to make the hike easier.

We do the same thing spiritually; we don't want to follow rules and guidelines that are clearly laid out for our wellbeing. We think they weigh us down or stop us from having a fun life. But when we leave God out of our packs, life actually becomes too heavy for us to bear on our own. And while we are crying and moaning over our situation, God will drop us a safety line or blanket to remind us He is there.

The third night out was the worst. We were camped high up on a tree-covered ridge. I thought the trees would provide some shelter. Wrong. It was so cold that GQ warmed a few rocks by the fire and put them in his cook pot and slept with them. I was too proud to tell anyone what I had done.

I went to bed wearing every layer of clothing I had—which wasn't much. My pretty pink blanket provided very little protection from the mountain air. Part way through the night, I couldn't take it anymore. I was freezing, and this time I recognized the early signs of hypothermia. I emptied my backpack and stuffed my feet and legs into it. Because I'm vertically challenged, the pack actually covered my lower half. I would guess I am the only hiker who has actually used their pack to sleep in. I don't recommend this as a way of achieving ultra-light backpacking. But I can say I wasn't as cold. I wasn't warm, just not as cold.

My challenges did not end there. Along with ditching my cold gear, I had also shed all items I thought I would not need any time soon. Two days into my five-day stretch in the woods, Mother Nature busted through the door. Not having tools for tick removal or the right gear for the cold was bad enough, but then I started my period.

How could that be? I had just finished it a week ago. This made the third time in two months on the trail. But this time I was not prepared. I had no idea what to do. I had in my possession just enough tissue for normal use. I asked every female hiker I saw if she could help out. Usually females on the trail were scarce, but not those few days. There were more girls on the trail than guys, but not one of them had any feminine hygiene products. I resorted to collecting as much toilet tissue as I could from everyone I saw. Tampons were the first item on my pre-hike list, but I had failed to remember that.

On the fourth evening, we were sitting around a campfire; it was myself, GQ, Walking Man, and two new hiking friends, Still Bill and Wye Knot. The guys were enjoying beer, and I my Pepsi. I was the only lady, and I was short on very much needed supplies.

There is nothing like spoiling the mood, but I had to ask. I knew I couldn't make it to town the next day without more tissue. So I said, "Guys, I need help. Who has extra tissue or T-paper to help a girl in need?" Still Bill gave me a little, and I had to inform them I needed more. The look on their faces was priceless when I had to explain why it wasn't enough. Still Bill surrendered his entire roll, and Walking Man shared some wipes with him. Guys don't realize just how easy they have it hiking in the wilderness.

There was still more. The last night before we reached a town, I ran out of fuel. As I was boiling water, the flame went out. At my last resupply from the car, I had accidentally grabbed a partial can instead of a full canister of fuel. GQ was my hero that time and shared his hot water with me.

It was a week of struggles and challenges that ended in laughter. I survived. The guys frequently reminded me of that week. If only I had put into practice the key to success. Preparation prevents poor performance.

I made it through all the issues, and when Bruce rejoined me, I collected all my gear. That night, I was so hot I sweated.

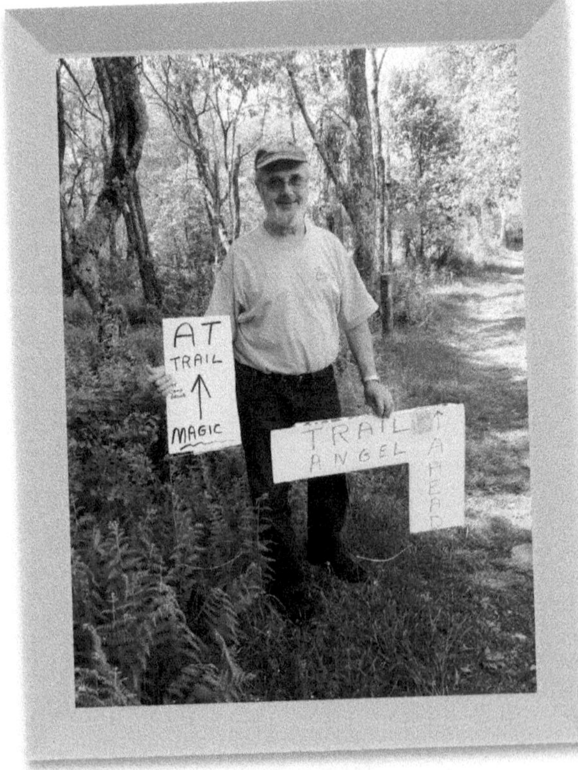
AT
TRAIL
MAGIC
TRAIL
ANGEL
AHEAD

18

Tequila

Waynesboro, Virginia, greeted us with open arms. It was another hiker-friendly town. I enjoyed camping in the small-town parks. The center of attention included a large gazebo with solar power outlets, porta potties, and even poles for hammocks. Located on the backside of the community, the park sheltered hikers from the hustle and bustle of town folk. But was only a short distance to eateries and the YMCA, where hikers could shower for free.

We had spent six of the last seven nights in the woods, hiking long days without a break. We were all ready for a zero day. After showers and a little R&R, we headed to an AYCE at Ming's Chinese Restaurant.

This was my first and only Asian cuisine I had on the trail. Chinese food does not mix well with my system, so I avoid it. Ming's came highly recommended, and since we were zeroing the next day, I took a chance. So glad I did. It lived up to its reputation and was outstanding. It's the only Asian cuisine I have ever been able to eat without resulting intestinal issues.

May 16 was a wonderful zero day in the park. I had my second shower in two days, resupplied, and relaxed. Best of all, Bruce was with me. I got to spend two nights in a row with him.

On the second evening, we were heading to the car to check out town when a young hiker passed us on his way to the tenting area. He started openly flirting with me and making suggestive comments that were more than a little unnerving. It didn't seem to bother him that I was with my husband. Bruce and I got in the car and laughed, wondering what that was all about.

When we returned, we noticed that the new hiker had set his tent up so close to GQ's that their vestibules almost overlapped. Space was not limited in the park. There were two acres of flat, comfy grass to pitch tents. It was a strange encounter for all of us. Now it was my turn to tease GQ. Girls were not the only ones who fancied him. But I reminded GQ that he was the strange hiker's second choice after I had shot him down.

Our zero day came at a perfect time, just before we entered the Shenandoah National Park. Skyline Drive follows the mountain ridges through the park for 105 miles. The Appalachian Trail weaves along and crisscrosses Skyline Drive over 20 times.

This made it very easy for Bruce to leapfrog ahead while I slackpacked most of it. In the beginning of the hike, I was a purist at heart. I was not going to slackpack one blaze. The pain in my knees and feet had other plans. Easy access to the trail for Bruce made it easy for me to shed whatever extra weight I had, then retrieve it from the car at the end of the day.

We entered the Shenandoah National Park on Sunday, May 17. The easy terrain and smooth path welcomed us. We had logged 20 plus miles for 3 days in a row. Without the weight loading me down, I was able to go farther, faster. But by that third day, my knees and feet were screaming at me. I just couldn't alleviate the pain. I decided I was going to stop 3 miles from our destination.

The campground right along the trail would also be handy access for Bruce to join me. Two and a half miles before the campground, the trail crossed Skyline Drive again like it had done several other times that day. As I crossed the road, a truck pulled up and out jumped an energetic man with two signs that read, "AT Trail Magic" and "Trail Angel Ahead."

GQ and Walking Man were behind me that day. They hadn't passed yet. I was with another hiker, Rerun. We were so pumped up to meet this man that we flew through the woods. At times, we were even running. I briefly ignored my pain and concentrated on the reward at the end.

It is amazing; when we have a clear vision of what we want, we will do almost anything to get it. The facts don't count. That is why it is so important to have a purpose in life. When we know what it is we seek, and we can see it in our mind's eye, or better yet, have it written down, we are more likely to achieve it.

When we arrived at the campground, there were four couples set up with their RV's, picnic tables, and food for galore. Bruce was also there. Once we claimed a tent spot and relaxed, I was beginning to regret that big push to get there. I could barely walk. I was suffering from some major hiker wobble.

Our trail angels were offering beer to the hikers who wandered in for trail magic. Since I don't drink beer, in jest I said, "Got any tequila?" The friendly trail angel who posted the signs disappeared into his RV and came out with a large bottle of agave juice. He poured shots for us, and I enjoyed the warm sensation as it flowed down my throat to my stomach. One was good.

A little while later, two other hikers entered camp. Maps and Moxie, two ladies my age I met back in Pearisburg, were lots of fun to be around, and it wasn't hard for them to talk me into a second shot of the nectar. One shot of tequila is usually my limit, but the second went down surprisingly easy and enjoyably. I now had a happy little buzz going on.

Another half hour or so later when GQ joined our group, he too partook in all aspects of the trail magic. I couldn't let this opportunity slip by. I had to have a shot with him also. So down the hatch went shot number three. Mmmm! Each one went down smoother than the one before. It wasn't long before I realized that my knees and feet no longer hurt. My scientific conclusion was that tequila works better than ibuprofen. Unfortunately, a bottle of tequila weighs more than a bottle of Vitamin I.

The Shenandoahs offered easy walking with plenty of chances to slackpack. Tourist rest stops known as waysides dotted the scenic byway. They were a disappointment, though; they were expensive, and, most of the time, lacked adequate amenities. Unless a hiker really needed something, I found stopping at a wayside to be a completely wasted effort.

My traverse through the park brought surprises. One day Bruce met me at a parking area, for a snack break. He suddenly heard the panting of an animal. I could not hear it, which was very unusual. He is normally the deaf one.

We both went to investigate. With my eagle eyes, I spotted the source of the heavy breathing. It was a mountain lion. How exciting—and terrifying at the same time! I was able to watch the huge cat climb out of a tree then disappear amongst the forest's undergrowth. That was amazing! Mountain lion sightings are rare. (This was before the influence of tequila.)

The other wildlife encounter was being stalked by a deer. Bruce and I were going to sleep near a shelter where the rest of my hiking friends were also staying. But when another hiker pointed out a black snake who had taken up residence in the shelter and then a crazy deer ran through the site almost throwing itself on the fire for venison stew, Bruce and I decided we'd set up our tent closer to the parking area.

As evening shadows faded and the night sky twinkled above, we stargazed as we lay in our tent. Since it was such a beautiful night, we left the tent fly off.

Soon our romantic evening was abruptly curtailed by a slow, methodical thrashing. We heard the crunch of leaves and branches… then nothing. Then more *crunch, crunch, crunch*, and… nothing. Our headlamps showed nothing, but after several cycles of these sounds, we decided to put the tent fly on. Not really sure what that accomplished, but it gave us a false sense of security, which was better than no security.

The *crunch, crunch…* nothing went on most of the night. It started downhill from our tent, headed straight toward us, then circled around the tent. It was really unsettling. Morning came, and I was exhausted from lack of sleep due to paranoia. When I exited the tent, a large deer ran off. It was so strange. Growing up, I spent a lot of time in the woods hunting, and I've never had an encounter like that before. It felt like I was the prey. Maybe it was payback.

The Shenandoah National Park was a gentle hike and a nice change of pace from the southern terrain. Views were limited, though. Skyline Drive offered spectacular panoramas and many hikers choose to yellow-blaze (road walk or ride in a car) this section just for that reason. But I was a purist, keeping to the white blazes, and I stayed on the trail.

Most of the time, the path weaved through the trees with little chance to see anything outside my canopied prison. I was not locked in by fences, bars, or armed guards, but rather by my decision not to quit.

The simplicity of the trail and monotony of doing the same thing day in and day out was initially very appealing and relaxing. But after three months on the trail, what I had first found enjoyable was easily becoming a boresome chore. Was this the Virginia Blues everyone talked about? If only my feet and knees didn't hurt so darn much. It took every ounce of physical strength and even more mental strength to endure the suffering. It would have been so incredible to experience SNP with healthy lower limbs.

But that didn't happen, and after hiking almost 300 miles in 18 days, I set myself free from the self-imposed imprisonment and quit on May 20.

A mile and a half before our designated stop for the night, Bruce met me to give me all my gear. He would join us for the night. Even with slackpacking, I couldn't take it anymore. Walking Man, GQ, Bruce, and myself had Pass Mountain Hut all to ourselves. It was God's way of letting me go down with grace. I was tired, sore, and the temps were starting to drop. I was so grateful that Bruce was there to help me. Despite that gratitude, I snapped at him ferociously, something he did not deserve.

After I cooked our packaged meals, I excused myself from my hiking buddies, explaining I was a grouchy bear and needed to put myself in a cage. Then off to bed I went to sulk. It was a nice shelter, but the guys chose to tent. They were probably afraid of the Black Bear already denning in the shelter.

Morning came, and it was a new day. Cold and rainy, but a new day. I slept well and woke up refreshed and ready to take on the 14.9 miles we had planned. It was a light day compared to the 20 plus-ers we had been doing. Just before heading out, I let Walking Man know I was no longer a grouchy bear but a happy bear. He looked at me, looked at the sky, and replied, "How can that be on such a shitty day?" I agreed, it was a shitty day weather-wise, but for the moment, my feet didn't hurt, and I was ready to start my AT hike again.

As always, a good day on the trail follows a bad day. The night before when I quit, I didn't really quit. Psychologically, I had allowed myself to quit so I could free myself. I knew that at any moment I could walk away from the trail and Bruce would take me back to the comforts of our home. But all I needed was just a little time.

All great accomplishments only come to fruition after long and arduous trials. If you have big dreams, you will also have to endure big challenges, and sometimes those hurdles will become overwhelming and you will want to quit. But quitting is seldom the right choice. Sometimes, all you need to do is step away and give yourself a time-out, a break.

The only way I could escape was to let my mind think I was done. Our subconscious does not know the difference between reality and fiction. So, I let it go where it needed to go. I retired that evening to my sleeping bag sulking, but more importantly, mentally and spiritually I had stepped away from the trail.

I could not really step away; there was no place to go. But after unleashing the Black Bear wrath on my innocent and wonderful husband, I knew I needed to be put in the naughty corner.

For me, I needed a little God time, so I retreated to the back of the shelter to be alone with Him. It was time for a checkup from the neck up and a chance to make sure the dream that was inside of me was coming from Him. Sometimes when life is difficult, it's because we chose a path that was not directed by God but by our own desires.

And when things are hard, you need to confirm that you are in fact on the right journey.

After my time-out, I decided I needed to slow down. I was approaching 1,000 miles and Harpers Ferry, West Virginia, the unofficial halfway mark. I knew what I should have done, but the reality was a different story.

Harpers Ferry is rich in history, and Bruce and I wanted to spend some time there. But he was on a tight schedule with work commitments and plans with our son Patch. With my new shoes and trying to maintain high miles, I wanted to get to the celebratory milestone before he had to leave. I actually was ahead of GQ and Walking Man by 10 miles.

Bruce and I were able to spend a few more days and nights together. He would leapfrog ahead and hike south to meet me. We would hike out together, then he would extract me and we'd go to a hostel or hotel. We stayed at the Bear's Den three times, once inside and twice camping on the lawn.

The Bear's Den is an old stone residence built in the early 1900s by Dr. Huron Lawson to replicate a medieval castle. The Appalachian Trail Conservancy (ATC) owns the property and jointly runs it with the Potomac Appalachian Trail Club (PATC). The AT is 150 yards from the hostel and is positioned conveniently for tourists to visit a popular overlook close by.

One night when we stayed there, it was crowded with view seekers. After dinner, one family asked if I was going to join them for the sunset vista. After all, it was only 150 yards away. I declined, and they could not understand why I did not want to walk a mere 300 feet. They had no idea!

During these few days, I received new shoes that seemed to work well and a new tent. It would make my third tent. It was an MSR Hubba single tent. I owned the MSR Hubba Hubba, my initial purchase. I'd tried it for a while, but it was too heavy. The second tent I purchased was the Echo II by Hyperlite Mountain Gear, the same as my pack. I liked the weight of the Echo II and the fact that it didn't absorb moisture, but it wasn't free standing. The design of the Hubba Hubba was awesome, so I wanted to try the single version.

Even with the new footwear and lighter tent, my feet and knees were still bothersome. I needed to slow down and drop the miles if I wanted to make it to Katahdin. The next couple days, I logged less than 14 miles. One of those days was over the Roller Coaster. As noted in AWOL's guidebook "the Roller Coaster is a 13.5 mile section of trail with tightly packed ascents and descents." Yay! just what I needed. My average speed on the trail was 2.0 mph. That day, it took me 7 hours to complete only 10 miles of the Coaster. It was a beast. That was the same day I passed the 1,000-mile marker.

Even with accomplishing those mini milestones, I did not make the goal of Harpers Ferry to match Bruce's time frame. We visited the historic town separately. He dropped in for a visit without me while assisting other hikers, and I hiked in with GQ and Walking Man, who had closed the 10-mile gap between us.

On May 26, the three of us made it to Harpers Ferry, Mile 1023. We had our photo taken in front of the Appalachian Trail Conservancy. The Conservancy recorded our numbers. I was hiker number 304 signing in at Amicalola Falls, Georgia; and in Harpers Ferry, I was hiker number 265.

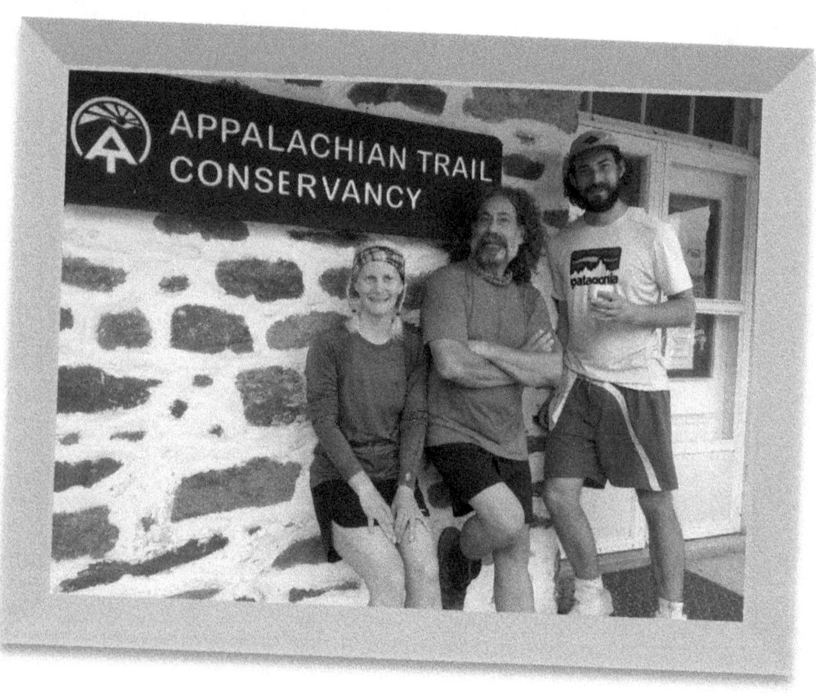
APPALACHIAN TRAIL
CONSERVANCY
patagonia

19

New Beginnings

Despite the smile on my face, sadness was overtaking me. I knew Harpers Ferry ended my time with Walking Man and GQ. My hiking family was disintegrating. Fruit Smoothie had to leave a while back, and Pumpkin flew ahead. Now it was time for me to separate from the father-son duo. They were much stronger hikers, and if I wanted to enjoy the trail and make it to the end, I needed to hike my own hike. It was time. I had to do what was right for me, even it meant saying goodbye.

In town, we did our own visiting and sightseeing. GQ and Walking Man went one way, and I hung around the ATC, waiting for Jim Fetig aka Sisu, the ridgerunner I met on my very first night on the trail back at Springer Mountain.

That first night on top of Springer Mountain, Sisu had informed me he also volunteered at the ATC in Harpers Ferry on Tuesdays. It just happened to be a Tuesday when I arrived. When I walked into the office, there he was, perched behind the desk. He reminded me of Captain Kirk from Star Trek.

He wasn't wearing a tight leotard, but he did have a commanding and professional posture that fit the bill. He recognized me right away and told me if I could hang around an hour and a half, he'd take me to lunch. What thru-hiker would refuse an invitation like that? I was quite happy to rest in the Conservancy's hiker lounge. I even snoozed on the well-worn couch.

Sisu took me to a little diner just down the road. He liked to frequent the diner for his lunch breaks and spoke highly of it. I was drooling just thinking of some good, home-style food. Unfortunately, the diner was closed.

Our choices were limited. The only establishment close was a chic little place with contemporary cuisine. I was famished. But my polite nature only allowed me to order a salad. It was way too pricey and I was not going to run up his tab. It was almost painful to eat a small salad that came with such a high price tag. All I could think of was, *You're not in Lowell anymore.*

The meal may have lacked in quantity and quality, but the company did not. We shared trail experiences and other topics of the day. What I found most interesting was the fact that for most thru-hikers who make it to Harpers Ferry, odds were in the hiker's favor to make it all the way to Katahdin.

The main factors usually preventing a successful completion from that point on were injury and lack of funds, not the hiker's prowess. Several hikers I had the fortune of meeting earlier on my hike were no longer on the trail for one reason or another. I felt special.

Bruce had helped two other hikers, Half-Blind and Cancer, get to Harpers Ferry, where they would end their thru-hike attempt. Cancer was worn out. His knees just couldn't take it anymore. He was hiking to raise money for St. Jude's. His trail name comes from his history of having cancer.

Half-Blind is half blind. He was leaving the trail because he had just had enough. He almost stepped on a rattlesnake because of his limited vision. He had fallen and broken ribs. When we met back up with him at the Bear's Den, he was suffering from norovirus. He was so sick that he was confined to his tent and the potty.

Lots of hikers out there had serious struggles. I tried to keep that in mind when my feet hurt. I could stop at any time to rest, and the pain would stop. For others, the pain will never go away.

At lunch, Sisu also shared his initial impression of me when we had met that very first day back on Springer Mountain. It had not been positive. Apparently, he had been concerned with my tenting skills, and he did not think I would make it. Huh, fooled him, didn't I!

How many times do we do the same thing to others? We prejudge them in a split second by the way they talk, look, or act. It is so easy to do. I do it. We all do it, but should we? If only we could look deep into a person's heart. Most of the time, we are too busy with our own concerns to take the time to understand others.

In Sisu's case, his thoughts of me did not hinder my well-being in any way, nor were they inflammatory. He was merely concerned for my safety. He was also kind enough to keep his impressions to himself. Sometimes, though, when we do share with others our prejudices about someone, we rob that person we're talking about of a fair chance and possibly of their dignity as well. It's always better to keep our lips zipped and not discuss negatives about our fellow folks. Who knows, that person who first made you think twice about a situation might just fool you, too.

Sisu needed to get back to work. And I needed to find GQ and Walking Man. I graciously thanked him for his generosity. I was in awe of his kindness. Trail angels are everywhere. Back at the Conservancy, we said good-byes and I headed north.

The trail continued through the little historic downtown of Harpers Ferry where I found my last two trail family members at a local pub. Where else would they have been?

Yay! They weren't ready to leave. I was so glad. I still needed to increase my calorie allotment before heading back into the woods. My stomach barely noticed the salad I had woofed down earlier. I ordered the usual: a jumbo burger and fries. No milkshake this time, though. It was time to celebrate. GQ recommended sangria, which became my new favorite beverage—after anything with tequila, of course. The three of us toasted our accomplishments; and, although it was unspoken, we knew it would be the end of our trio.

We departed the quaint little town, crossing the river from West Virginia and entering Maryland, our 6th state. We hiked our last 6.3 miles together to the Ed Garvey Shelter, where we spent our last night with each other's company.

I am sure the separation was harder for me than it was for Walking Man and GQ. They had each other and were probably glad to be alone. After all, they were on the trail to bond. The Appalachian Trail is a wilderness experience, but it isn't a secluded one. It is very crowded out there. I was more of a third wheel for them, even though they never once made me feel that way.

May 27, I started a new beginning—again. This Appalachian Trail journey had so many new starts. With each new beginning, a lesson was learned. When Andrew went home, I learned I would be okay. When I quit mentally, I learned that sometimes you just need a time-out. When I said good-bye to the guys, I learned to embrace the unknown.

The separation wasn't like ripping off a Band-Aid. We had that night together, and we hiked most of the last day in each other's company. It was an easy day, and the rhythm had us in step. At one point, we waited out a microburst storm.

Timing was everything again. We stopped at a tenting area with bathroom facilities complete with showers. I was the only gal, so I took full advantage of spreading out in the bathhouse. I showered, charged my electronics, and rested while the storm passed. The guys had to crowd in with several other hikers.

We headed back to the trail after the last roll of thunder silenced and the sun peeked out. I then had a left- and right-brain feud. The hemispheres of my mind had been arguing all day.

Left brain said, "Go, girl. Only 4 more miles, and you can keep pace with your friends!"

Right brain said, "You are no longer 26. Heck, for that matter, you are no longer 40, and you really should stop and rest."

Left brain said, "Yah, but…"

Right brain won, and I stopped for the day. Then I never saw the guys again.

I began my new hike with wide eyes and excited anticipation. As much as I grew to love hiking with Walking Man and GQ, I was letting that comfort stifle my growth on the trail. I needed to fend for myself now, and I looked forward to it. The next five days, I greeted each morning with a simple prayer: "Okay God, what do you have in store for me today?"

That simple act opened up a whole new way of looking at my future on the trail. Instead of being afraid, calmness and curiosity overtook me. I was quite happy and relaxed. I no longer feared the unknown.

That first night, I stopped at Raven Rock Shelter. It was a beautiful two-level structure, a log-home type with a side missing. The empty wall opened up to a large covered porch with a picnic table. This shelter even had a cot donated by a previous hiker. I claimed ownership for the night before anyone else could. I usually let others have the amenities, but that day I decided, "Why not me?"

The surroundings had multiple tenting areas, each with its own fire ring. Several hikers chose this little paradise as their day's destination. Voltron, Last Chance, D-Man, Divo and his dog Diva, and a couple others. Luckily, it was a large shelter.

Once settled in, I noticed a very large knife in a leather sheath, placed on the shelter's I-beam. I reached up, took if down, and asked if it belonged to anyone. They all denied possession. Then two young men came back from the spring. I inquired with them also. It did in fact belong to one of them.

The owner of the knife explained he thought he would need it, but it was too heavy and large to carry on such a long hike. My eyes widened, and I asked if I could keep the knife if he was just going to leave it. I only had three days to Pine Grove Furnace, where I would be meeting up with my sister Becky again. I did not mind carrying such a wonderful find.

For the next three days, I sported my Crocodile Dundee knife on my hip belt. I was one tough-looking hiker chick—so I thought. Every time I met new hikers on the trail coming the other way, I'd stop to give them the right-of-way, but I'd also turn ever so slightly to reveal my weapon. Not that I would ever use it, but they didn't know that. I did it to humor myself.

It reminded me that in my early planning for the hike, the main question I was asked each time I told someone about my upcoming hike was: "Are you going to carry a gun?"

An emphatic "NO!" was my reply. I was not going to carry heat, at least not in the form of a weapon.

If I had thought for one moment that most hikers would be carrying, I would have stayed home. In fact, I only met two hikers carrying a sidearm. I never saw it. One section hiker told me he had a gun on him. The other person was a thru-hiker I hiked with for a while, and I didn't even know he was carrying until over a year after the hike when we visited each other.

My oldest brother, John, was very concerned that I wasn't taking a gun. Heck, he would have preferred I had taken a small arsenal! He even offered to buy me one of my choice. After I refused countless times, he finally stopped offering.

My reasons for refusing a weapon were not that I am anti-gun. On the contrary, I believe in the second amendment and I am a gun owner. I just couldn't fathom carrying such a heavy item over so many miles up and down mountains.

If I had been smart, I would have let him buy one for me and pretended to carry it so I could have added it to my collection. But I didn't, and the only safety item I carried was the six inches of real estate between my ears.

I seemed to find things on the trail when they were needed the most. I had found GQ and Walking Man, the blanket, a few miscellaneous items, and now Rambo's knife. It came in handy the next day.

I had never seen a rattlesnake before. It was one of those things in life I wanted to see in theory but never really wanted it to happen. Just like tornados. It would be cool to see one, but not really. I like snakes, but in Maine they won't kill you. I even had a pet grass snake in college. The rattlesnake was something new to me. I had only seen pictures and heard scary stories of these vipers. Now, I had my own tale.

I set up my tent outside, under the picnic table awning. I didn't want to sleep in the shelter. Several hikers were also there relaxing when another hiker from their group approached and asked if we had seen the rattlesnake on the trail. We hadn't. I couldn't believe I had missed it; I had just come from the trail 10 minutes earlier.

We all walked back to the trail that crossed in front of the shelter and there it was, lying on a log in the middle of the path. We snapped photos as it moved off into the woods.

Resuming camp chores, we forgot about the snake. All too soon a hiker announced that the snake had slithered back to the shelter area. We tried to scare it back into the woods and move it with long sticks, but it kept coming back. I was a little scared because it seemed to like the area near my tent the best.

Securing my tent and gear, I headed to the spring. Before I left, I let the hikers know I had a large knife if they felt the need to use it for some reason and told them where it was. Upon my return, two of the hikers met me halfway and informed me the use of my blade was in fact needed—but not to tell anyone.

Apparently, rattlesnakes are protected in Pennsylvania. What about us? There were two dogs and three little kids in camp that night. I do not promote the killing of an animal unless you are going to eat it or if your safety is at risk. Since the snake kept returning, we felt we were at risk.

We were also going to eat it. I volunteered to skin it and cook it. I heard it was a delicacy. But that evening, the caretakers of the shelter dropped in for a visit, so snake-kabobs were removed the menu.

I was so much happier being on my own. Who would have thunk? I slowed my pace, but I was still making headway. On May 29, I crossed the Mason-Dixon Line—the 1700s survey line for a border dispute in colonial America. It divides the North from the South. In my blog, I posted, "This Yankee is one step closer to home." I had to add a note that I am actually a Red Sox fan. Being called a "Yankee" for a BoSox fan is just as bad as a Southerner being forced to live north of the Mason-Dixon line.

Besides being closer to home, I had seen my first poisonous snake; and by the end of May, I had also crossed the halfway mark for 2015, mile 1,094.6. It would all be downhill from there, I convinced myself.

At Pine Grove Furnace, Pennsylvania, there is an AT museum and a small country store. Arriving here, hikers have 1,102 miles down and a little less than that to go. Along with this accomplishment comes the challenge of eating a half gallon of ice cream to celebrate the halfway mark.

Of course, one has to hike those miles and then buy one's own ice cream for the sole reward of bragging rights, a souvenir wooden spoon, and signing the book. One must choose their flavor wisely. A flavor too rich and filling will surely end in failure.

I brought my Hershey's tub of chocolate to the counter. Thanks to inflation, a tub of ice cream is no longer a half gallon, so hikers need to buy a pint of hand-scooped ice cream to make up the difference. I requested butter pecan. The girl behind the counter informed me that hikers usually start with just the tub. Then they purchase the hand-dipped after they have consumed the tub so they do not waste any money if they can't finish it. I thanked her politely for the advice and said I believe in the power of positive thinking and doing it the way she suggested was setting myself up for failure. I took my frozen delights and a Diet Coke to the porch and began my eatery challenge.

I was 45 minutes into my tub when I began to feel nauseated. I only had a few more spoonfuls, but I didn't think I was going to keep it down. Was I about to commit the puke of shame? I sat up straight to catch my breath, and when I did, a deep, powerful burp rumbled from the depths of my body. It was so loud the civilians (non-hiking patrons) at the other end of the patio heard me, and they all gave a loud cheer, complete with applause. We all started laughing, and I finished my ice cream in exactly 60 minutes. It wasn't a record-setting time, but it did qualify. I gathered my empty containers and brought them inside to claim my prize, a small, flat, wooden spoon stamped cheaply with the words, "Member of the half gal club."

It was fascinating how much I could eat while hiking. It is the best weight-loss program ever! The hiker hunger took a few weeks to kick in. And when it did, I could eat anything. It was common for me to devour whole packages of cookies and chips in one sitting. After I finished the ice cream and soda, I ate a pizza. Then later that evening before going to bed, I had another snack. It was delightful.

Not only did I get to celebrate the halfway mark, but I was plucked away from the trail again by my Sister Bear Becky and her hubby Pat. Just like Mom and Dad, they, too, were on their northern migration back to Maine. They had purposefully planned their route to include helping me out. I love my family.

I spent six nights with Becky and Pat. They shuttled me to and from the trail as I slackpacked north. Pat worked out the navigational details while Becky took care of my laundry and feeding me. What a deal!

On the second day of slacking, it rained—and it was wonderful. It was a warm rain and friendly terrain, only a few minor inclines. I completed a not-so-whopping 46.8 miles in 6 days. During that time, I had two zero days and a hot meal every night, with snacks and sodas unlimited. They had a mini fridge in the RV dedicated to carbonated beverages with resupply cases next to it. The rule was if you took a cold one out you put a warm one in. A few times I did a 1:2 ratio. I did not want to run out of cold ones. Months after my hike, when reminiscing with Pat about my eating habits while I was on the trail, he said he couldn't believe how many sodas I could consume in one day.

Becky and Pat were not the only super-generous trail angels. Trail angels were too numerous to count. Several stick out as memorable, though. While I was a temporary resident of the RV with my sister and brother-in-law, I received mail. The real kind, snail mail. It was a package from Solomon, a hiker I had met a few days back.

He was on an overnight with his brother and their two sons; it was a guys' night out for them. We stayed at the same shelter area. I was tenting on a platform next to the young boys, and the dads each had a hammock close by. Their Gilligan-style sleeping quarters were protected by Tyvek housewrap. I was in need of a new ground cloth. Tyvek is very expensive to come by in small amounts, and I was quite interested in where they had purchased it. Solomon graciously said I could have his in the morning, since he wouldn't be needing it. Apparently, backpacking was not what he considered fun.

In the morning, I rose bright and early and the only sound from my four new friends was snoring. I left Bruce's contact information on a note tucked under a rock on the boy's tent platform. I let them know we'd pay him for his Tyvek.

To my surprise, while I was staying with Becky and Pat, a package showed up, overnight express, with the 8x10 piece of ground cloth. He wanted no money in return. The generosity of complete strangers toward complete strangers out on the trail was intriguing.

The news is filled with horrible acts and accounts of one individual against another or groups against groups. But out on the trail, everyone looks out for each other. It didn't matter what your skin color was, your background, or any other factor. The trail community is one of acceptance and communal support without people taking advantage of each other. Sure, there were a few scallywags, but they soon earned their just reputation and didn't last long on the trail. But the overall generosity and kindness of strangers put my faith back in humanity. Maybe humans are not doomed after all.

On another day of slacking, I pulled a typical Emmie-ism stunt. Since I was slackpacking, I emptied my pack of everything nonessential for the day's hike. You would have thought I had learned my lesson the last time I removed too many items. This time it was my wallet. Not only did my trail angels drop me off at the trailhead and rescue me from the rain afterward, they had to spot me for my groceries and lunch. Thanks, guys.

20

Time Heals

It was tough heading back to the trail. But I did. One step at a time. I was well fed and well rested. Oh, yes, and dry. All of which wouldn't last long on the trail. I was blessed to have my family and friends helping me along on this adventure. It was so much more fun sharing it with others. It was a fantastic day hiking, a great way to restart after two days of vacation from the trail.

It's weird to need a vacation from vacation. My hike was my getaway from the real world, but even something fun can be tiring and not appreciated when overdoing it.

It was an easy 11-mile day with a smooth footpath and no inclines. It was also my last slackpacking for a while. Becky and Pat dropped me off at Boiling Springs, where I had ended a few days earlier, and I hiked to the last pick-up point where they could assist me. They needed to pack up the RV and head north to Maine, my destination as well. I'd just arrive a few months later. I was anxious to see what the second half of the journey had in store.

Back to reality, and I was headed for my next small town, Duncannon, Pennsylvania. It would be a 16-mile day. I met a hiker on the trail who informed me that Duncannon was a nice hiker town. Being unfamiliar with the area, I was glad to hear this information. I guess my expectations were a little too elevated.

Soon after arriving, those expectations were pricked quicker than a water balloon thrown at a porcupine. Only one person said hi to me, a group of solicitors gawked at me, and another couple moved away from me as I walked by. So much for that "lovin' feelin'."

I marched through town with only a quick stop at the price-gouging convenience store, then continued on to the campground at the outskirts of town. It was a 2.5-mile stroll from where I exited the woods to the campground, making my 16-mile day stretch to 18.5. I was glad to finally finish so I could rest. Or so I thought.

Waterfront tent sites dotted the shores of a river, but hikers were not allowed to stay there. Instead, I was asked to stay in a section that was reserved for hikers. It was close to the bathhouse and abutted a long-term resident's site. I don't like to be judgmental, but my neighbor looked like he had just stepped off the set of a psycho-killer movie.

I positioned my tent as far as possible from him within the boundaries I had been given. I then checked out the facilities, and they were the perfect place for mid-night murders of the worst kind. I was beginning to think the campground was the set for a real-life horror flick, making a Stephen King script seem like a Disney production.

The place gave me more than just your average willies. After living in the lap of luxury for the past week, I was probably being a little too critical. Thankfully, just as I started to make supper, two fellow hikers showed up, Philamanjaro and Popsicle. They, too, had an unsettled feeling about the place.

Moments later, their friend Star Shine joined us, but she was being picked up by a friend. Star Shine felt our plight and asked her friend if we all could go back to his home for the night. The three of us repacked our belongings.

The next day, we were dropped back off at the campground for a 6:45am start. I thought that would ensure a successful long hike for the day, but a visit to the Hard Rock Café shortened that deal.

Did I say "café"? My error, it was Hard Rock Cliffs! This wasn't the name of the area, I dubbed it that due to the rocks, resembling a shark's mouth with bad dental work. A gigantic jaw of row after row after row of molars, bicuspids, canines, and laterals, all at funky angles, protruding every which way, just waiting to take a bite out of my feet. It was fun but very tiring. After only 9 long miles, my feet informed me they were not going any farther.

Not even to get water. I chose slight dehydration over a descent down 300 rock steps to the spring. Because what goes down also goes back up. I was slightly prepared. Some pre-reading in the guide book warned of Peters Mountain Shelter's water source, so I was carrying a little extra H2O from the last stream. That way, I would not have to descend and then climb those 300 steps at the end of the day.

The day's end had me with unfamiliar faces. My fellow hikers who had rescued me from a sequel to *The Shining,* lagged behind somewhere, and I never saw them again. I was in a new film with a new cast. We were just a bunch of vagabonds sharing communal space for the evening. We enjoyed the usual pleasantries and the stillness of the woods.

Before we knew it, it was morning and we were all on our own schedules and directions. For me, I was headed 17 miles north to Rausch Gap Shelter.

The hike was extremely long that day. With very little to see, even for myself who can find the greatest pleasures in the tiniest of details, I struggled. I wasn't even given my daily dose of a deer sighting. In the beginning of my hike, I didn't see any wildlife; but as I walked north with spring, creatures became abundant, especially deer. But this day, they were hiding. I was not graced with the white flag of a deer bounding off through the trees.

Water was also scarce. At one point, I could hear a stream in the distance and was anxious to camel-up; but once I came to the source, I was quite disappointed. The stream was bathed in bright orange, as if someone had spilled a can of tangerine-colored paint all over the ground.

The water was so rich in iron it looked unnatural. You could see that from the last rainstorm water had overflowed the little stream's boundaries and then receded, leaving behind iron deposits that stained the earth.

The day wasn't a complete bust. Thirteen miles into the hike, the trail opened up to the most unusual site—a mailbox on a post in the middle of the woods. Inside was a trail register that I gladly signed, proving my passage.

The clearing was the site of a historical coal mining settlement, Yellow Springs Village. As I sat on one of the logs positioned around a fire ring, I pictured the hustle and bustle of men and women working hard out in the wilderness to make a living and, for some, mere survival. Time separated our journeys. The once-thriving coal village was now silent, with only the rustle of leaves in the breeze and the occasional passing hiker.

As with all things, time heals. Years past, there was an industry here, complete with all the necessities to keep such a village running. Now Earth had healed herself with new growth and a thick forest. The only remnant was a mailbox to remind visitors of the once thriving village. The transformation took generations, but it had taken me only a few days to get over the separation from my wonderful hiking buddies, GQ and Walking Man. It wasn't nearly as painful as I had expected.

That was a recurring lesson I kept experiencing on the hike. I have heard the saying, "80 percent of the stuff you worry about never even happens, and the 20 percent that does happen is not as bad as you expected it to be, so stop worrying." I know worrying is a product of the devil. He feeds on our fears. But I still worry, and I usually worry in silence. I am great at helping others not to worry or fret about the unknown. If only I would listen to my own great advice.

The trail was teaching me to relax and to put my trust in God, where it belonged. This journey was a gift from Him that I was to cherish, and worry was only hindering my joy. I was prepared mentally and physically; I wasn't going out on blind faith. My only job was to seek out all He had in store for me, and the only way to do that was to stop stressing about the details. I was learning to do this with each new change or challenge that came my way.

The next obstacle to overcome was to beat a violent thunderstorm brewing in the distance. I had already been in a couple thunderstorms, and even with faith, they are pretty scary. I was not looking forward to another one.

I pushed hard to get to the shelter, and 15 minutes after my arrival, all chaos broke loose and Mother Nature unleashed her fury. I prayed so hard—not for my safety, but for all those hikers who had chosen not to remain in the shelter and were out in the elements. It was worse than most. Usually the storms would come in quick and disappear just as fast as they had arrived. But this one lingered for several hours, like a party guest who sticks around well past all the others.

I was joined by one other hiker. Within the three walls of the shelter, we were as protected as we could be from the lightning and downpour.

As I was preparing my bedding, directly above my sleeping bag was the biggest, blackest spider I had seen so far on the hike. (But each time I see one of those creatures, it's always the biggest and blackest.) Arachnid or lightning, I was beginning to think I had made the wrong choice. I started to panic, my normal response to close encounters with the eight-legged kind.

I asked Scavenger if he would do the brave honor of squishing the intruder. He obliged. But just as he was taking aim, I stopped him. I realized this was a great opportunity to fend for myself. I handed him my camera on video mode, grabbed my weapon of choice, my hiking pole, and went on the offense.

As I slowly inched the head of my pole handle forward toward my target, the enemy made itself larger than life. I swear the spider was the size of a dinner plate. Instead of being scared of my strike and retreating to the corner, it scrambled along the length of the wall as I jabbed continuously at it. I missed several times, despite the large target.

I finally connected with the spider's body. Well, part of it. I managed to dismember him just enough to tick him off, and he dropped to the shelter floor and scurried as quickly as his mangled exoskeleton could carry him. But his efforts were futile. He met his demise with one last fatal poke of my stick. Just to be sure he was not to be resurrected, I added several more flattening strikes. I was proud of my heroics, but was soon brought back to reality when I saw the video that told no lies. It showed my true fear and disgust of the ordeal.

The evening faded away with the roar of thunder and flashes of lightning. The shelter was free of uninvited guests, allowing slumber to take hold, making for an enjoyable night in the woods. The following day would be another long one, with 18 miles planned. But that was far from my mind as I drifted off to sleep.

Only a sunset and a sunrise separated me from my wonderful husband and one of our sons. It had been three months since I had seen Patch, our youngest. That was the longest separation ever from our kids. It would be another two months before I would see our oldest son, Stephen. It had also been a long stretch without seeing my Bruce.

The original plan was for him to see me only once a month while I was on the trail. That planned duration was shortened right from the get-go. He was having just as much fun supporting me as I was having hiking. We made a great team. Our marriage has always been strong, but this adventure was adding a whole new dimension. We are a firm believer in the couple that plays together, stays together. I was excited to bring him up to date. But first, before the sunset and sunrise, I had to tackle 18 miles.

The day cruised by with easy terrain and lots of enjoyable sightings of wildlife, which included deer and turkey. The turkey scared me half to death. Probably payback for what I did to the spider the night before. I never saw it until it flew away. It sounded like a herd of elephants rushing through the trees. I was surprised my bowels were still intact.

After securing my heart back into my chest and reassuring my imagination that I was not going to be swallowed by a Pennsylvania forest monster, I realized it was just a turkey. I started to head to the spot she flew from to see if she left any feathers. And there were three chicks looking dumbfounded as if to say, "Hey, mom, what about us?" I kind of had the same feeling when the guys hiked on. But that feeling was fading fast.

With 16.5 miles logged for the day, I was feeling great and was sure I was home free—until the trail set me straight. It snarled at me with its rock-infused path. I groaned, then slapped myself in the face, adjusted my attitude, and it was over before I could break a sweat.

At the trailhead, I was whisked away by two wonderful young ladies who shuttled me to a Girl Scout camp run by Michelle, Andrew's Mom. Andrew and I had made plans with his mom to stay at the camp when we came through. Even though he was no longer on the trail, Michelle was still gracious enough to host me for the night.

The Girl Scout camp was not open yet for the season. There were about 30 girls there for counselor training. They fed me supper, Taco Tuesday. We sat around tables seating eight campers each. The food was served family style. The girls politely ate one small serving each.

Not wanting to be rude, I followed their lead. But what I had eaten was barely a hiker's snack. Just before cleaning up, one of the girls asked if I wanted more because it was just going to be thrown away. Hallelujah!

"If you don't mind, I'd love more!" I cleaned up the leftovers from our table and amazed them with my appetite.

We gathered for the evening festivities, and I contributed by giving them a talk about my hiking, focusing it on setting goals. It was a humbling experience, giving back to them and being a role model. It was nice being amongst all the young ladies. The pavilion was filled with music, laughter, and giggles. You don't get that out on the trail where spaces are dominated by males.

Lunch delivery! Bruce and Patch arrived the next afternoon with food. A double dose of happiness. The two men were eyed affectionately by the all-female staff, especially Patch. Introductions and thank yous were quick, as the three of us headed to an empty picnic area so the counselors could continue with their training program. I needed to get back to the trail. I would be joined by Patch for a 9.5-mile trek, and it was already early afternoon.

It was a beautiful day with sunshine, blue skies, and no wind. I had been anticipating this day ever since Patch said he would join me. He and Bruce were returning from Florida, where Patch had attended a few days of lessons with his kicking coach. We had a great hike together. We saw baby birds in a nest, stopped at beautiful overlooks, and had some really nice Mama Bear and Baby Bear time.

It had taken me a few weeks to develop the ravenous hiker hunger. Patch was born with it. During his school years, I would make him huge lunches. By his junior year of high school, we bought him a picnic-sized lunch bag so he would have enough room for his food for the day.

One time, we received a call from a teacher who needed to conference with us. We were a little puzzled because Patch was a good student. At the meeting, his teacher, Mrs. Lammert, began by saying how she allowed the students to eat in her class because she understands that everyone's metabolism is unique and teenagers' needs vary. After a few minutes of small talk, Mrs. Lammert continued, "BUT, when Patch gets to class, he doesn't get his book out. He puts a five-course meal on his desk and eats." Bruce and I had all we could do not to laugh.

Before Bruce dropped us off at the trailhead, I double-checked with Pumpkin Bear (my trail name for Patch) that he had plenty of food. He reassured me he did. He had several snacks and another foot-long sandwich in the depths of his pack. He had just consumed one for lunch. So off we went.

We hadn't gone too far when he needed to eat. Patch just has a high metabolism and is very fit. To keep his furnace operating, the poor kid needs to eat often. We stopped for a quick snack. Then a little while later, he asked when we could stop and have our sandwiches. I suggested we wait another mile; the guidebook showed there was an outcropping with a view. He was cool with that and we hiked on.

When we arrived at the spot mentioned in the guidebook, there was a small clearing with a fire ring surrounded by several logs for sitting. We could see a side trail leading to the view. As we headed in that direction, another hiker and her three kids were coming from the area we were seeking. She confirmed there indeed was a beautiful spot. We were excited to claim a seat on the rocky outcropping to enjoy our second lunch while taking in the view. A reward for pushing on.

We began to follow the blue blazes to the scenic spot but were stopped abruptly as the hiker finished her sentence with, "Be careful of the rattlesnakes. There were two in the cracks right beside me, and I didn't even notice them until we got up to leave." So much for claiming our reward. We decided the logs around the fire ring would be just fine.

It was an easy day, with just enough small hills, rocks, and boulders to make things interesting. With half a mile to go, I realized we hadn't seen any white blazes. This is not a good sign. Pumpkin Bear was leading. Since I could hear the road and our ETA corresponded with my watch, I said, "Just keep going." Minutes later we intersected another trail, I peeked up that path and spotted the missing white blaze. We were on the wrong trail. I wasn't going to worry about missing those few white blazes since I didn't know I had missed them. No worries.

We found the car, and we were ready to get off the trail and get some more grub. Only problem was, Papa Bear was not in the car. He had hiked in to meet us. So back to the correct trail we went. We caught up to him at our wrong turn. So no white blazes were missed.

After a second consecutive night with a roof over my head, Bruce dropped me off at the trailhead once again. This time I was solo. Patch remained and I eagerly headed out, knowing I would be extracted by my family after I tackled 15 miles.

I quickly fell back into my hiking rhythm and was in my own little world. I liked being lost in my own mind out there. In the mornings, I usually started off with reflection and prayer time as I hiked, being swept away in the quietness of nature and God's beauty. This was one of those times. The soft morning light cast shadows through the trees.

It was peaceful, and I was oblivious to the details as I soaked in all the goodness.

All of a sudden, I felt a strange sensation and I was transported from my Garden of Eden back to reality. I looked up and saw a figure walking toward me on the trail. There was something not quite right about this hiker. His clothes were not of the normal hiking kind, he had no pack, and it seemed way too early for any day hikers to be out. As the space between us closed, his gait slowed. I became extremely anxious and reached for my SOS device, ready to activate the help button.

The man stopped about 30 yards away, knelt down, and started taking my picture. The shadows made it difficult to get a clear view. I was getting really creeped out. I kept going cautiously and just as I was ready to hit send on the SOS, I realized it was Bruce! I could have pooped my pants. What was he doing there? That wasn't the plan!

One June 12, I said good-bye to Patch and Bruce and continued my journey into the unknown. My destination was only 14.5 miles north at Hawk Mountain Road. I arrived at Eckville Shelter in late afternoon. The guidebook said the shelter had a shower, flush toilet, spigot, and enclosed bunkhouse. Sounded pretty nice.

Words on a page are just that sometimes. Reality was a different story. I am by no means a girly-girl, but I was not going to stay at that shelter. It was an old woodshed—which would have been fine minus all the cobwebs, ants, wasps, and spiders. Not to mention the fact that each bunk had some kind of cloth padding that looked like it hadn't been dry since Noah left the ark. My plans were to tent, anyway, so I could rise and shine early and not disturb the other hikers. I had already been yelled at for making too much noise in the mornings. The shower and bathhouse were not much better. I decided to fill my water bottles and then tent at the next tent site, only a half mile up the trail.

Those plans ended when I saw the site filled with four guys already set up. Three of them were running around in their boxers, and the fourth was chopping down a perfectly good tree, not your typical respect-nature kind of guys. A girl knows when she shouldn't stick around. I walked on and could feel them staring. I could also hear their whispers. I needed to get as much space and time between us as possible. They were weekend hikers out for a good time, and I wanted no part of it.

The next shelter was 7 miles out. No problem. I had plenty of daylight, and I felt great. I just needed to eat. After an hour of hiking, I came to a camping area and sat down to have a snack. While there, I noticed a deer bedded down in the ferns 60 yards away. He never left the whole time I was there. He was much more pleasant to look at than the rattlesnake I had seen earlier. Thankfully, Kilroy, a hiker I met just after passing the party guys, was ahead of the snake waiting for my arrival so he could warn me.

Kilroy and I played leapfrog a couple times that afternoon. I first met him shortly after my get-away sprint from the axe-wielding, half-naked lunatics. He was resting on the trail. It was a dreadfully hot day, and one look at his dripping shirt was proof. He was a solo hiker with the normal crazy hair and beard, yet I felt completely safe in his presence. I told him about my run-in with the guys and that I was distancing myself from them.

While I was enjoying a snack in the company of the deer, Kilroy caught up to me, and I was able to show him the bedding animal. We both agreed the furry creature was a better sight than the serpent.

The day was hot—not that I minded. The heat didn't bother me as much as the cold did, so I enjoyed being soaked in sweat. What did irritate me was that my short, 14-mile day was turning into a marathon of challenges. First was the letdown of the shelter, then the crazies running around in their skivvies, and now the trail turned into rocks.

It was by far the worst section so far. Small, jagged rocks strewn over the trail and large boulder fields went on for five miles, with the exception of one easy stretch for only a quarter mile. At one point during this stretch from hell, I rounded a corner, thinking the rocks would stop, and only more of the same dauntless course lay out in front of me. I broke out in hysterical laughter. I so wanted to break down and cry, but I knew that would only exhaust me more, so I started laughing. I thought for sure I was going crazy.

Before those miles were finished, I hiked along a 30-foot wall made up of rocks and ledge. I was thankful I didn't have to scale the natural barrier to get to the other side. The trail just followed at the base of it.

I arrived at the shelter exhausted, thirsty, and too tired to eat. Kilroy fetched my water so that I would have enough for breakfast. I did not mind taking advantage of his help that night.

Even a fish wouldn't get into trouble if he kept his mouth shut. The next morning's hike started out gradual with very little rockiness and smoothed into a level walking trail, the exact opposite of the previous day's trail. It meandered pleasantly for several miles. Then, when I thought things couldn't get worse than yesterday, they did.

I filmed an impressive 30-foot rock formation like the one I had seen yesterday and stated how nice it was that I didn't have to scramble up them. I turned the camera off so I could safely traverse the path that began to increase with rocks and hazards, and then the white blazes turned abruptly, disappearing into that rock wall. Wow! I had spoken too soon.

Unlike many of the other rocky, viewless climbs, this one provided a spectacular panorama. As I climbed through the ledge and crested the pinnacle, the valley spread out below under a magnificent blue sky accented with white, cotton-ball clouds and occasional feathery formations.

If it wasn't for the view to take my mind off the trail, I would have entered panic mode. But with almost 1,300 miles of hiking under my boots, my fear of heights was slowly waning. This section was called The Knife Edge, and it was every bit as tough and scary as it sounded. But it was super fun, and I had no problem, even though each step risked a fall that would end a hiker's journey.

The day continued with rocks and more rocks. Pennsylvania is known for its unforgiving trail. Many hiking shoes have been chewed up by the stony terrain. I prefer a trail with character over a trail that is easy, but enough was enough and there didn't seem to be any end in sight.

After a grueling stretch up and over an exposed power-line vista where there was no apparent best path and I just had to find what worked best for myself, there was an abundant spread of trail magic. I enjoy the heat, but the humidity zaps the energy right out of me, and this day was hot, humid, and still. The gallons of water, cooler of soda, and even a food bag hanging in a tree was an amazing act of kindness by a trail angel. It was just what I needed to stroll through the last part of the day, a calm before tomorrow's storm.

Along with my usual day's-end hiking chores of setting up camp, collecting water, cooking supper, and journaling, I would also take a sneak peak at the next day's terrain. I was at roughly 1,000 feet elevation. The next morning would drop me to below 500 feet then rise back up to just under 1,500 feet, all within 1.7 miles and with a mile of that being across a flat bridge and town roads. I was about to take on the only class III ascent south of the White Mountains on the AT. It would make The Knife Edge a couple days back seem like a stroll in the park.

Morning came, and I was out with hurried anticipation to greet the summit of Lehigh Gap. According to my AWOL guide, this section of trail is defined as a "Rocky, steep trail from Lehigh Gap. Deforested ridge due to zinc smelting from 1898-1980. Palmerton Superfund site."

The incline was intense. At one point, I needed to sit in a small protected area that was relatively flat to give myself a pep talk. It was probably the strongest self-talk I had with myself. The trail wasn't difficult. It was exposed and gave me a false feeling of falling. From my mini plateau, my next move required some hand-over-hand scrambling. I had one-inch finger and toe holds to lift me up over a rock that was taller than myself. I was told this was a class III climb. I didn't know what that meant, so I consulted my outdoor enthusiast niece, Stephanie, the night before, and she had informed me Class III means it's steep, hand-over-foot scrambling, but ropes are not required. Class IV climbing requires ropes since there's a high risk of falls, and Class V requires even more technical skills. Lehigh Gap may not have required ropes, but they sure would have been nice.

Climbing up the next section, I couldn't see where the trail went. It was just blue sky. It was the top; so once there, I bellied over it, too chicken to stand up and begin my descent.

The climb was magnificent! It would have been easy if I wasn't weighed down by a 30-pound pack. Once done, I realized I hadn't looked for snakes, not that it would have helped. My shaking nerves would have deafened any warning rattle from a viper sunning on the rocks.

I lost one of my bandannas that day. Not just any bandanna, it was one signed by students who were charting my journey. I heard a rattle in my pack and realized the sound should not be happening. I used one of my bandannas to keep my spork from rattling in my pack, but it must have fallen out at my last snack break. I dropped my poles, removed my pack from my shoulders, and leaving both on the side of the trail, headed back up the rocky path until I found it. There it was, just a few feet from my last resting spot. So glad I recovered it. Mrs. Gilman's class had signed it. Thank you, St. Anthony, patron saint of lost items.

Later in the day, I hiked into a blueberry patch loaded with succulent ripe wild berries like the ones we have in Maine. I stopped and was so excited to indulge in nature's treat. I didn't eat right away; I wanted to fill my cup first. A hiker went by, and I invited him to share my stash. He politely refused, reminding me the area was contaminated due to the zinc. Shucks, I had forgotten that minor detail. Too bad for the other hiker I had just given a large handful to who gobbled them down. I emptied my cup disappointedly. I felt like a kid in a candy store who had to put back all his chosen confections.

The day ended with, you guessed it, rocks! It took me ten hours. The morning's climb was fun and fabulous, but the rest of the day was just agonizingly slow and painful. I kept reminding myself that if it were easy, everyone would be doing it.

In the last few days, I had been blessed with trail magic at times when I really needed the extra boost. That day, I was able to give back. I met Peter, from Germany. We hiked about seven miles together. He had started three weeks earlier on a northbound flip-flop. We stopped together for a break, and during our chat, he expressed that he was getting low on snacks. I gladly handed over all my extra stash. I always packed too much. Besides, Bruce would be meeting me at the end of the day, and I could resupply.

Hubby Bear picked me up at 5:00pm. I took a hot shower after a soak in the hot tub, then ended the day snuggled in comfy sheets.

Morning came later than usual. We slept in. When we did crawl out of the rack, we headed right down to the hot tub again. What a way to start a zero day! And end one also. I was feeling like a girl again. In less than eighteen hours, I had two hot tub soaks and two hot showers. I even shaved. The day I was with Patch, he had asked me if I had given up shaving.

Our zero day was spent at the hotel, including our meals. We didn't go out to eat. I cooked up hiker food just as if we were on the trail. The only difference was that we didn't have to collect and filter water for cooking or cleaning. And we also were able to sit at a table instead of being hunched over the Jetboil on the ground.

It was relaxing and rejuvenating for me. Bruce, on the other hand, had to work. He has had the luxury of working from home when he isn't visiting customers. But at times that freedom means he is never really out of the office, since his office is mobile. So while I was taking naps and swimming, he was busy working on his computer. But we were together, even if it was in silence.

I loved it when a zero day was followed by a nero. The next day was an easy 8 miles of hiking. I crushed the rocks that day and barely noticed their usual annoyance. It's amazing what rest, comfort, and companionship can do to boost your morale. Plus, I knew I only had to hike 8 miles and I would be with Bruce again in a hotel. The novelty of camping had been lost about a month into the trip.

There was no way I was going to quit, though. It was all mental for me. My feet and knees gave me horrendous pain, but it was the mental anguish that was hardest to overcome.

I convinced myself I was out on short hikes. They just happened to be strung together one after the other to make up a thru-hike. Short hikes were fun. That was the key to my success! Instead of letting the magnitude of the complete trip encompass my thoughts, I focused on breaking it down into sections I could handle mentally. This allowed me to enjoy sections at a time without the burdensome stress of the bigger picture. But after this was finished, I never wanted to long-distance hike again.

Even though I focused on shorter sprints, I still had to manage pain and discomfort. There were few days on the trail that were completely pain free. I was either battling my fear of heights, my discomfort at being alone, or physical pain. Often, I was fighting all three. This short 8-mile day, though easy, was hard on the sore I had been nursing since the first week. Time may have been healing my separation from GQ and Walking Man, but it wasn't working for my toe.

21

Miles of Smiles

It started as a small blister on my second toe. The blister broke, and then, as the dead skin peeled away, a donut-shaped callus formed. The outer rim was hard, and the inner circle stayed raw. Some days, it hurt so bad I wanted to quit. I tried everything short of amputation: wraps, corn pads, tape, moleskin. Nothing helped except going barefoot. I was glad for the short day and the promise of hotel amenities.

The day was uneventful but was full of interesting sights. I saw lots of black and orange centipedes, two flowers I had not yet seen on the trail, and loads of caterpillars. Flowers always brightened my day. The pink, five-petaled bloom had a bright yellow fuzzy center. It was all alone, just like I was in the forest. The other flower was a cluster of red berries on a low-lying shrub. I did not recognize this plant.

For the past several days, the woods had been alive with caterpillars. There were so many, they made the tree trunks look like they were wearing fuzzy coats. A few nights before, I was hanging my food bag and tied the line off on a little sapling with a dozen or so healthy, fully leafed branches. This tree was also blanketed in those little creatures. The next morning when I retrieved my bag, the cute little tree was void of any green vegetation.

One night I spoke with a trail maintainer, discussing how numerous the caterpillars were. He made the comment, "Yeah, you can even hear their poop dropping from the trees!" I didn't register that fact until the next morning when a petite, green pea-sized drop landed on my arm. My first thought was *Just more of that mud that keeps landing on me and my pack.* Over the last several days, I had noticed lots of these spots on my pack and on the back of my clothes and occasionally on my arms. Then it dawned on me what the trail maintainer had said. Gross! It was caterpillar poop! Yucky, yucky, yucky!

I was glad to be extracted that day. Bruce was taking me to L.L.Bean. We found a store close by, and I was in desperate need of a new pair of boots. I started out with a pair of L.L.Bean Cresta Hikers, but they were a size too small for hiking. Hence, the blisters. At home, on short walks and hikes or doing chores, they were great, but not so great when I spent all day in them. I traded them out for trail shoes that were comfy but not sturdy enough, and my poor feet felt every pebble I stepped on. I went through two pair of those. At L.L.Bean, I purchased a pair of the Crestas one size larger than I normally take. I had to pay full price since I was no longer an active employee, but they were worth every penny.

I had my boots and was ready to go when Bruce received an urgent work call he had to take. I didn't mind. It gave me a chance to browse the store for anything else I couldn't hike without. I managed to find a few items I needed to help me hike better. That's my story and I am sticking to it. The next day, I sported a new hiking skort and tank top. Oh yes, and the boots! Because it's not how you hike, it's how you look when you hike.

The next several days flew by. I was enjoying solo hiking. My backcountry skills were growing; nearly 1,400 hiking miles had me whipped into shape. I no longer feared being alone. Each day brought new sights, smells, and acquaintances.

One day I met only women on the trail. It was girls' day out. Another day, I finished state number 7 as I said good-bye to Pennsylvania and all her rocks. Well, almost all the rocks; they spilled over into New Jersey for several miles, but who's counting? I saw Kilroy again. We hiked together briefly, but then he sailed on by.

One early morning when Bruce was taking me back to the trail, we had several animal sightings which included deer, birds, baby bunnies, red and gray squirrels, and a groundhog. The most exciting was a black bear picking through a "bear-safe" trash receptacle. So much for Don't Feed the Bears.

Step by step, mile by mile, hiking still made me smile. I was consistently logging 14-mile days. That seemed to be the magic number that kept my feet happy. I should have been satisfied with those figures; but after doing high miles in the past, cutting back to such a low number felt like a setback for me. I needed to remind myself it was more important to listen to my body. Too many hikers have gotten caught up in doing big miles too soon, too often, and too long, and then they burn out. Not me, though. That's why I was in a hotel again. No burnout here. Just miles of smiles.

June 21 came, and I decided to take a zero day. Not so much because I needed rest—the lower miles and rest in hotels had me in peak condition—but because it was Father's Day. I thought it would be nice to spend it with the daddy of my children. It gave me a chance to attempt to treat him for the day since he was spending all his free time for the last three months helping me.

Secretly, I did not want to be on the trail during that 24 hours. June 21 was the first day of summer, and on the trail there is an unwritten tradition I did not want to be a part of. It is solely by choice, and most people choose to abstain from the activity, but my wild side would have done it. So I stayed off the trail and saved everyone who may have encountered me from a hideous sighting of me in my birthday suit. Because you just can't undo seeing such things. Naked Hiking Day will have to wait for another time.

This zero day was a treat. Besides spending Father's Day with Bruce, I reflected on what a day in the life of a hiker was like. I was getting questions from friends and family on what I actually did "out there." So I wrote this in my blog.

Blog Post for June 21, 2015

Morning Ritual: Decide it's time to start the day. Let the air out of my partly deflated mattress pad and start packing my bedding. First my sleeping bag gets stuffed back into its compression sack and placed in the bottom of a dry bag followed by the mattress pad, then topped off with my interior ground cloth. After which I change into my usually wet and smelly hiking clothes and pack my dry sleeping attire into their own dry sack. If it is not raining, I place everything outside my tent, then take down my home away from home as it also goes into its own dry sack. If it's raining, while I am still inside my tent, I pack everything in my pack first to keep it dry. Then, I exit the tent and I stuff my wet tent into my pack last.

I have a quick breakfast, which is normally cereal enhanced with trail mix with dry milk. It is actually very yummy and nutritious. A great way to start a hike. If all goes well, I am on the trail by 6:00am or 6:15am. Sometimes if I am lazy, boots do not hit the trail until 7:00am.

Second breakfast, a granola bar comes about one and a half to two hours after I start hiking or sooner depending on how my feet feel. I usually like to hike a certain duration of time before resting. My normal pace on moderate terrain is 2 mph without breaks. So if I hike at least an hour I know I have covered about 2 miles or so. This helps me judge my progress and gauge my ETA based on the day's mileage goal.

Lunch hopefully happens around noon or 1:00pm and, with any luck, takes place at a shelter with a picnic table or a rock outcropping with a view. I am not always fortunate enough for this to happen, depending on weather, terrain, shelter spacing, and how I feel. Burgers and fries would be my preference, but I settle for pretzels and peanut butter, or crackers and peanut butter.

The afternoon is a rhythmical dance between hiking and stopping for breaks. They come more frequently in the afternoon. My best hiking time is in the morning. By afternoon I start to slow down and wear out. I like to arrive at my destination by 3:00-4:00pm. On some days I have arrived as early as 1:30pm. My latest ending time was 8:00pm. That was a long, rough, and tiring day.

Arriving at my home away from home is the beginning of the evening chores. Rest does not come yet. I lay claims to a spot in a shelter or a level place to pitch my tent. I must set up my tent and get everything pitched just right. I prefer tenting over shelters, so I have a barrier between me and all the creepy crawly things that are out there just waiting to freak me out.

When all the chores are done, I can think about eating. Supper choices have always been a challenge for me. At home I cook wonderful gourmet meals. Out on the trail I hate to fire up the Jetboil and prepare my trail dinners, not to mention cleanup. Many days I would just have snacks for dinner. When I head back to the woods tomorrow, I will not be packing out a stove. I will try just PB&J's for lunches and suppers. It will be much lighter and no clean up.

Hiker midnight is about 7:30pm. With any luck, that's when I can close my eyes. That doesn't always happen as planned. But I can always hope.

In between all the hiking, eating, breaks, and chores, there are those moments when I come across a fantastic view when the trees clear and the sun shines on the valley below. Or I stumble onto a black rat snake slithering across the trail, or enter a pond area in the morning fog, being serenaded by a chorus of frogs, just some of the reasons I keep putting on my boots and enduring the daily pain I experience in my feet. I never know what is waiting for me around the next corner or over the next climb. There you have it, a day in the life of a hiker.

It is a simple life. It's not an easy one, but definitely a simple one. The simplicity of the trail brought great joy, a deeper appreciation for my life off the trail, and personal growth beyond measure. I have a degree from the University of Maine, I read all I can about personal development, and I have a strong spiritual faith, but all that pales compared to what I had learned on the Appalachian Trail, and I still had over 800 miles to go.

The evening of June 21 to the morning of June 22 marked my eighth night in a row sleeping in a hotel. During that stretch of eight days, on the girls'-only day out, I met Squirrel and Spock, who were attempting to beat the mother-daughter AT thru-hike record of 126 days. Their goal was to do it in 99 days. The only record I seemed to be working toward was the most nights spent with a roof over my head that didn't involve a shelter or fabric. I never did see Squirrel and Spock again.

I was well rested and ready for big miles on June 22. I wouldn't be in a plush hotel at day's end, but I would be in a town. Bruce would slackpack me again and retrieve me from the trail at County Rd 517 in Glenwood, New Jersey. From there we would drive to Unionville, New York, and camp in the little town park.

It was a beautiful hike, with clear skies, easy terrain, and open fields at times. The added bonus came soon into the hike when I caught up with Kilroy. He was fun to hike with. His demeanor was calm and quiet, with an adorable sense of humor. He carried a very heavy pack and was more than happy to let Bruce slackpack him. At the end of my 18-mile day, Kilroy joined us in the town park.

Unionville was quaint and quiet but did not have too much to offer hikers. There was a small diner, but the menu was not gluten-free friendly. I managed with my trail food while Kilroy and Bruce dined on fresher goods. We were very grateful for the hospitality of using the town park and homemade treats delivered by the local girl scouts.

The peacefulness of this little town ended with the setting of the sun. The night in the park was not as restful as I preferred. Kid townies came in after 10:00pm, partying and carrying on. In between laughter and music, a midnight game of backyard hoops bounced until the wee hours of the morning. Five o'clock came way too early.

Thankfully, the start of the trail was inviting. At first, a wonderful boardwalk carried us over a marsh, much like the one in Bangor's City Forest back home. We traveled through the reeds and over a brook for about a mile before leading us back into the woods. At this point,

Kilroy and I said good-bye to Bruce. We would see him again seven miles out.

First, we had to climb the "Stairway" to heaven, a very steep and rocky ascent. It was a great leg and butt workout. Just another section prepping us for the White Mountains and Katahdin. It was challenging yet enjoyable.

The trail continued to be ambitious. The book of lies showed an unimposing profile, but the ups were abrupt and the downs were just as drastic. We journeyed along an exposed ridge that roller-coastered above and below tree line. When it peek-a-booed out of the forest, it revealed stunning 360-degree sights. Unfortunately, we could not take in the vistas as long as we wished. A violent storm rumbled in the distance and grew closer with each step.

The ride on the coaster went on and on, and with each summit we could see the clouds growing in size and darkening as they headed our way. With each dip below the trees, we thought we would reach safety; but just as quickly as we descended, we went right back up and were exposed again. I tried talking Kilroy into staying in one of the nooks, but he was sure we'd be fine.

I frantically moved forward. I was not going to huddle alone in the approaching storm. Besides, Kilroy was taller than me by eighteen inches and he was carrying a metal-framed pack. The odds were stacked in my favor. All of a sudden, the heavens opened and drenched us as lightning and thunder flashed and roared not too far away. Gone was our beautiful blue sky.

Finally, we dropped well below tree line. There we found a father and his daughter "safely" waiting out the burst. This time, Kilroy agreed that it was a good idea to wait for Mother Nature to calm her temper. So there we all stood, four drowned rats spread out under the trees, hoping the one we chose was not the tallest. Twenty minutes passed, and the storm was gone quicker than it had arrived.

With a group vote, we decided it was safe and we hiked on. It was a good thing we stopped when we did. In less than a quarter mile, we came to a section that looked as though artillery shells had hit the area. Debris covered the trail, and in several places, large tree limbs had fallen, making passage impossible. We had to bushwhack through and around them.

We had racked up another 18 miles, crossed another state line, and survived the worse thunderstorm I experienced on the hike. It seemed each storm became the worst yet. All in all, it was a successful day.

To top it all off, I didn't have to sleep outside. The three of us shared a motel room at Anton's on the Lake. It wasn't much, but it was dry, offered laundry, and it was cheap. That night, I lay my head on the pillow and the miles of smiles filled my dreams.

22

Sometimes Life Just Beats You Down

I was blessed to be born with a can-do attitude, a driven personality, or whatever you want to call it. But at times it can really get in the way. The last two days I had put in long, exhausting hikes. Mentally, I felt great. Even with the miles of smiles, I was physically beat. The days I did low miles, I felt great physically, but I beat myself up mentally.

I really wanted to be home by mid-August for Stephen's 21st birthday and for Patch's football season. Since I had come to the realization I couldn't keep doing high miles, I knew I wouldn't be home for either. I had a mental breakdown as Bruce was dropping me off at the trailhead.

I bawled my eyes out, big large crocodile tears with loud, snot-bubbling sobs. I was so upset and so tired of being in pain. As I walked away, tears flowed down my checks, blurring my vision, and all I could hear was, "I am so proud of you! You are doing great!" I hiked away in a flood of tears as my biggest cheerleader's voice faded with every step forward.

I proceeded up the trail for a mild warm-up, a nice time of transition for my anguish to slowly drift away. Then the trail went straight up. More hand-over-hand climbs, which I love. Walking hurts my feet, but rock scrambling was pain free due to the anatomical position used to make the climb; and those climbs were usually blessed with a view. The trail always seemed to give me what I needed when I needed it the most.

As I hiked that day, I could feel the love and support that seemed to gush out from Bruce. It was so amazing how much closer we had become while doing this hike together. It was like we were falling in love all over again. He would keep telling me, "It's your hike, do what you want!" But in reality, it was our hike. I may have been the one with boots on the ground, but he was the one that was making it possible in more ways than one.

He was strong enough to know what I needed to hear. He knew I didn't want to quit, but he also knew that I was suffering dearly. He held strong and didn't let my tears and babbling words weaken his support. When I was letting life beat me down, he picked me back up and helped me toward my goal. Together we hiked on that day; I was on the trail and he was in my heart, and I could feel his strength beating inside me.

I finished the day with a whopping 12 miles added to the captain's log. No records there, but I was pain free! I needed to stop beating myself up and get back to the reason I was out there. After all, my motto was Happy Hiking! The trail and my body had a conversation without inviting my prideful brain to join in. They decided my daily mileage needed to stay between 12-15 miles to keep me healthy. From that day on, I only had a handful of days when my miles stretched over 15; and most of those days, the extra mileage could not have been avoided. Consequently, the last part of the hike was my most enjoyable. Some lessons take a while to learn.

The days started flying by. No two were the same. Each one offered new surprises and escapades that were not for the faint of heart. I never knew exactly where I'd be, with whom, or what events would take place. I had a game plan of course, but it was just that, a plan. Over the next several days, I took a trip to Boston for the night, had a close encounter with a deer, squeezed through the eye of a camel, left the trail to help a fellow hiker, lost my poles, and slept with a stranger.

After our second night with Kilroy at Anton's on the Lake, we all realized we had two wonderful, restful nights of sleep but it was time to leave the comforts of plumbing and electricity and get back to the woods. Kilroy would be a day behind me. The day I headed out full of tears, he was back at the motel for a zero of his own. We wished each other well and went our separate ways, headed north.

I was in the woods by 6:45am and was thrown back into the trail full force, without the leisurely warm-up like the day before. The trail went straight up. I was headed to New York's famous Lemon Squeezer section. The trail sneaks through a narrow corridor of rocks that hikers must squeeze through. The rock hallway towered above an inclined path, so not only did I have to squish my way through the tight space, I had to climb upward. It was more fun than challenging. For the hiker who is more rotund, a blue-blazed trail leads around the Lemon Squeezer.

I lazily trod through the New York forest. The trees were incredibly tall and open, without any undergrowth. I felt so small and insignificant amongst the giant hardwoods. The day before had been so brutal, then this day was so wonderful it felt like a dream. The deeper I trod into the forest, the more I sensed God's presence. I didn't have any ah-hah! moments, revelations, or visions. But I did have a sense of peace. I let myself go, and as I did, I seemed to become one with the woods. I continued in that dreamlike state for so long, I thought I was going to float away.

All of a sudden, I was brought back to the trail with the sound of crashing and thrashing headed my way. I looked up just in time to see a deer dash across the trail a few feet ahead of me. I quickly hiked up to where she had disappeared to see if I could see why she was in such a hurry. Then there was more of the same ruckus, and I turned in the opposite direction to see a huge buck skidding to a halt about twenty feet from my position.

I asked him if he wanted to get by. When I spoke, he redirected his course and flew off, taking a wide berth in hot pursuit of his girlfriend. That was exhilarating, to say the least. That kept my heart beating fast for a while.

The day ended with another extraction by Bruce. This time we headed for Boston. Yup. I left the trail to drive all the way to Bean Town with my hubby for the sole purpose of returning the rental car he had and getting another one. Our plan was to get a van so we could sleep in it whenever he would meet me instead of getting a hotel or hostel. We did some crazy stuff on the trail. Most people would not even consider doing half the stuff that we did.

I never worried about the details. Bruce was the logistics guy. I just followed his lead, and he made things happen. It was awesome how our dynamics worked like a charm. I hiked, requested, cried, ate, and whined, and Bruce was my hero! He drove the miles, made reservations, dried my tears, filled my requests, ignored my whining, and even found time to work.

Our little excursion turned out to be not such a good idea. There were no vans on Emerald Isle for us to choose. The best we could do was a Ford Explorer. After the swap, we drove as far as a service plaza on I-90 and converted the SUV into our double-occupancy hotel suite. We looked like a homeless couple, if you overlooked the fact that we were in a fully loaded, sexy, black Ford Explorer. If we had to be responsible for the payments, we probably would have been homeless. Have you ever checked out the sticker for one of those babies?

We slept until 6:00am and I was back on the trail in NY by 10:30am. I will admit, the next day I was a little, well, a lot grumpy. Actually, I was a brat. I was not very happy I had chosen to ride to Boston, then had to sleep in the back of the small SUV instead of a van, and then be expected to hike the next day. I have no idea why I didn't just sleep on the trail like a real hiker. I may have thrown a small hissy-fit.

Praise the Lord! I ended up only hiking 4.3 easy miles that next day. I was aiming for 11.6. Despite the short and arduous escapade the night before, I was feeling strong. But I was more than happy to call it quits early. The hike up and down Bear Mountain was fun and comprised of mostly steps to make the venture enjoyable for touristy non-hikers.

Even without a guidebook, I could tell when the trail was approaching a tourist attraction. The trail before and after such places was always well groomed and engineered for about a mile in each direction.

The farther the path veered from a tourist epicenter, the more rustic and natural it became, until in places it hardly resembled a footpath at all.

On my descent of the mountain, as I enjoyed the perfectly placed stone steps and views being offered, I stopped to take a snack break. The Trailside Museum and Zoo was only a mile away. That was where I was meeting Bruce again. We were going to walk through the zoo and across the Hudson River together, then I would continue on.

Those plans changed when Wye Knot, a hiker I had met way back, contacted Bruce. Wye Knot was reaching out to trail angels he had met to see if anyone could assist him with a ride to the nearest REI store. His shoes blew out. So instead of me hiking on without knowing when they would get back from Yonkers, New York, I chose to end my day short and go with them. Obviously, I hadn't had enough punishment with my trip to Boston.

Bruce collected me at Bear Mountain Recreation Center, and we headed out to provide trail magic for someone in need. Wye Knot wasn't too far behind me. We found him at a road crossing with two other hikers I knew, Bud and Bud Light a couple from Germany who also needed a ride to town. We dropped the "Beers" off first, and delivered Wye Knot to his friend who would take him to REI.

I decided to head back to the park and walk through the zoo and then across the Hudson to get a few more miles in before camping at the Graymoor Spiritual Life Center in Grarrison, New York. The center provides a field with a pavilion, power, shower, and porta potty for hikers. Bruce dropped me off and he headed to the other side of the zoo to join me from the north as planned earlier. But those plans were foiled also.

I got back to where I had left the trail that morning, and that section of the AT was closed for the night due to a fireworks show at the park. The security guards said I needed to go around the building and pick up the trail on the other side. I tried to use my cunning charm. But that didn't work. Then I turned on the blondeness (which was actually more of a platinum gray). Still didn't work. They wouldn't let me through. They insisted I go around. "Nope, I can't do that! I have to follow the white blazes." I said. They thought I was nuts. The section I needed to do was less than 100 yards. Oh well, I will just start back tomorrow where I left off. There was no blue-blazing for this Black Bear.

We still were able to tent at Graymoor. It wasn't far from Bear Mountain Recreation Area, and I was able to return early the next morning. I followed the lake through the park, then used the restrooms before continuing. I never passed up an opportunity to use plumbing. It was quiet in the park so early; I was glad the facilities were open for use.

I reached the entrance to the zoo and it was closed. Great! The night before, the white blazes were closed due to fireworks; now the next morning, the white blazes through the zoo were not yet open.

Kilroy was close by, so we sent him a text to see if he wanted to join us for breakfast. We headed over to his hotel, and he had decided to have the breakfast buffet there since it came with his room. I went to pay for breakfast for Bruce and me, but the lady at the counter let us eat for free. Sweet deal! It's a grand treat to encounter an AYCE buffet and even better when it is compliments of a friendly hostess.

With our tummies full, we headed back to the trail. If only my hands were full also. They were empty. They should have held my hiking poles. Not realizing it, I had left them in the bathroom earlier that morning. When my error dawned on me, we made an attempt to retrieve them, but they were gone. We checked at the lost and found building in the park, and no one had turned them in. That was one very expensive bathroom break.

Bruce dropped off both Kilroy and I back at the recreation area, and I redid those blazes just to be able to stay with Kilroy. Then Bruce drove across the Hudson and walked back to meet us. It was a nice walk through the zoo. We learned an interesting AT fact from the guidebook as we strolled through the attraction. The bear enclosure is the official lowest point on the Appalachian Trail at only 124 feet elevation.

The walk across the Hudson was amazing for me. I had never before traversed such a large structure on foot. Kilroy was in the lead, and Bruce had my back. I relished the wind in my face, the rush of the cars as they whizzed by, and the openness of the water as we left the safety of the shore.

Rain was forecasted for that day. Every hiker we encountered had plans to cut it short for the day and to stay at Graymoor. We also had plans for a second night on the grounds of the monastery. After crossing the Hudson, Bruce drove ahead to meet us there. A huge field accommodates tents, but with the forecasted weather, space in the pavilion would be limited.

When the heavens opened, they spared no mercy. The rains drenched us. At least it wasn't cold, and we hiked on. With a half mile to go, we followed the trail across the junction of US 9 and NY 403. Conveniently located in the Y of the intersection is a store with hot food. Kilroy and I were not going to pass up the chance to get grub and to get out of the weather. Several other hikers took refuge inside the store. There was a guy I had not met, Fourteen. Kilroy knew him and did the introductions.

The half mile to Graymoor was over in a flash. Bruce was waiting for us. It was raining hard, and none of us were thrilled about tenting. Sleeping in the rain with the pitter-patter of droplets dancing off the tent's fly is quite enjoyable, but this was a downpour with the threat of another electrical storm. So Kilroy, Fourteen, Bruce, and I decided to split the cost of a room.

The storm was driving hikers inside, and we were in a tourist area. Vacancies were few and prices were at a premium. Fourteen found a place not too far away. We headed over to inspect.

For a lack of a better description, it was a hole-in-the-wall for a whopping price of $180.00 plus tax. Ouch! It had two double beds, dirty rugs, and a tiny bath. One person would have had to sleep on the floor, or the two guys would have had to bunk together.

Bruce travels a lot, and he knew a rip-off when he saw one, so he worked his magic and found a place for significantly less. The only problem was, it was over an hour away, but it offered an over-sized room with two double beds and a pull-out couch. The hotel had a hot tub and swimming pool; and because of Bruce's elite status with that chain, he had access to a club lounge with free food and beverages. We let Fourteen and Kilroy know what we found. Before Bruce could finish explaining all the amenities and the distance, they were all in. So off we went.

My wonderful husband drove the three of us wet, smelly hikers to the lap of thru-hiker luxury. Once again, my hero came through, and it didn't bother him one bit that we would be sharing a room with two other guys, one that we had just met a few hours earlier.

Bruce and I let the guys have the beds while we put the mattress from the pullout on the floor and topped it with a cozy comforter we found in the closet. I was singing the zzz's in no time. I slept straight through until morning, something I rarely do even on a good night.

The rain stuck around longer than predicted. We didn't mind. The Sheraton was a wonderful place to enjoy an impromptu zero day. Fourteen thought he had died and gone to heaven. He was fully enjoying all the amenities. He especially loved the free food in the club lounge. We all did; it was a free hiker resupply. The room was large enough to give each of us our own uncrowded space to dry our soggy gear. If we desired even more room, we had the rest of the establishment to roam. I was quite content at staying put. I soaked my feet, napped, and repacked my gear after it dried.

We were refreshed and ready to go. Bruce drove us back to the retreat center where he had retrieved us. I had a 15-mile day planned, and Kilroy was bumping his mileage up. He wanted to get his northern section done to finish his flip-flop in time for his ticket to St. Martin for a restful, post-hike, Caribbean getaway.

Hiking with Kilroy had been a hoot. He was a gentle giant with a kind soul. We were an odd hiking pair. He was young; I was less young. He was tall; I was vertically challenged. He was quiet; he probably wished I was quiet. The one thing we had in common was our day's-end music ritual. We loved our music to power us through the last two miles of a day. We summoned the help of Aerosmith, Asia, Black Sabbath, ELO, and other artists I'd never heard of.

Everyone I met on the trail eventually hiked on and I fell behind. It no longer bothered me, though. What I thought was a curse in the beginning became a blessing. My slower pace and the need to rest my aching feet caused me to fall into a variety of hiking bubbles. This was not a curse, but rather a gift. I had the chance to encounter hikers of all ages from all walks of life. Earlier, I would pray for my feet to be better, but those prayers were never answered.

The song titled "Unanswered Prayers" by Garth Brooks held true here. I wanted healthy feet, but if they would have been fit earlier on, I would not have gotten a chance to meet my favorite hiking buddy, Kilroy. It was a lesson I learned and relearned over and over again on the trail. Things would be okay, I should not fret, and I should just relax and enjoy the journey. After 1,400 miles I was finally putting it all together and was at peace with whatever the trail offered me.

I still wanted feet that didn't hurt, so on the first day of July, my fourth month on the trail, we headed to REI, an outdoor specialist store. I wasn't sure what I was looking for, but I knew I wanted something. It was in Hartford, Connecticut. On the trail, I was still in New York, but New England was just next door.

Rain was forecasted, so Bruce and I decided to head on over to the outfitter for some equipment adjustments. I knew I needed a new sleeping pad. The one I had was leaking. The pad I wanted was out of stock. They offered me a heavier one, but I decided to tough it out with my deflating pad. I would be in the White Mountains soon, and extra weight was not going with me.

My new boots were helping some with my metatarsal pain, but the donut sore between my toes was not getting any better at all. As I was cruising the store to see what treasures I could find, I noticed toe socks. Hmm? Andrew had worn toe socks, and he didn't get any blisters. I grabbed a couple pairs of the Injinji brand, and we were off.

I wasn't expecting any miracles from Injinji. I was doubtful such a simple little item could help the pain I had been experiencing since week one. But sometimes when life just beats you down, you finally decide to try something new.

23

Ba Ba Batman

New York was my favorite state to hike in so far. I was just as shocked at that fact as my husband. I thought New York was all city, crowded, and dirty. I am probably the only person I know who has no desire to ever visit New York City. After hiking the woods in New York State, I now know better. New York has a lot more to offer than the glitz and glamour of Fifth Avenue and Broadway. I still do not want to go to the streets of NYC. But I will wander through the state's woods any day.

New York ushered me out with a fabulous 16.7-mile stroll. It was time to say good-bye to the Empire State as I entered Connecticut.

The beginning of July was like Christmas for me. Along with my new toe socks, my new poles arrived, and Bruce surprised me with new Dirty Girl Gaiters, patterned in a patriotic field of blue with white stars and red trim. They went perfectly with my flag-design do-rag I had found weeks ago. I was all ready to celebrate in style. Like I say, "It isn't how well you hike on the AT, it's how well you look while you hike."

I had just finished a break on the side of the road, compliments of a trail angel, and I headed across the street to finish five more miles. As I crossed, a day hiker jumped out of his car, wrestled his pack to his shoulders, and yelled to me. We exchanged pleasantries and continued up the trail. My sixth sense jumped a little but vanished when my phone rang. I wasn't on the AT to stay connected, but when I was close to town or near an extraction point, I would turn it on. It was Bruce, and he wanted to know where I was. Luckily, he was only a couple miles from my location. I said bye to the day hiker and turned back to the road to meet Bruce.

We rendezvoused at the crossing I had just left, and he gave me my new items. Then Bruce had to drive around to where I was ending for the day; and I, well, I had to hike. Off I went. I didn't hurry; it was a nice day and the trail was easy. After a mile or so, I caught up to the day hiker. He was slowly weaving back and forth on the trail, going more side to side than forward. He was engrossed with taking pictures.

I startled him as I approached, and he said, "Oh, great! You caught up!"

He had been really excited to meet me out by the road. The feelings were not mutual. I hoped he was way ahead since I had gone back to meet Bruce. I exchanged a friendly greeting and meaningless chatter. I tried to be nice. The last thing I wanted was to upset him. He didn't seem normal. I don't know what it was about him, but something was off. He reminded me of the character George in Of Mice and Men. He was big, tall, and cumbersome.

When George stepped aside to take a photo, I went ahead, slowly increasing my pace in a way that wasn't obvious I was escaping. But he soon came hobbling down the trail to catch up. I slowed again, thinking he would sail by. Nope, George also slowed. My sixth sense turned to paranoia, and I tried texting Bruce to let him know what was going on. But cell service diminished once I got in the woods, and I was on my own.

I kept my SOS device handy. I could not shake George. I went fast, and he all but had a heart attack keeping up with me. I dragged, and he matched my slowness. I thought for sure he was going to grab me so he could hug and pet me until he squished me to death. It was the longest five miles of the journey so far, but finally Bruce showed up. George continued on and I never saw him again.

That evening while enjoying fire time with fellow hikers, I retold the George story. The consensus was that I was just freaking out like I usually do. Then I started to feel really bad. I went to bed thinking I was a mean person and how could I have profiled that day hiker just because he was different? The more I thought about it, the worse I felt. But deep inside, I could not change my gut instinct, no matter how guilty I felt.

It wasn't until several weeks later when I was talking with Bud and Bud Light who also experienced an uneasy event with that hiker. They shared with me a conversation they had with George. During their chitchat, George found out Bud and Bud Light were from Germany, and he digressed into a long monologue about how he loved Hitler and how great a man he was, just misunderstood. YIKES! I instantly had no more guilt.

The next day was Independence Day, the birth of our nation. Usually we spend July 4 at home on the lake. This year, the plan was to find a place to camp near the road so Bruce could join me and have trail food. We didn't mind, since we would be together. The place we had picked out was "the pits" once we got there.

No other options were open to us, so we resigned ourselves to the fact we needed to find a relatively safe place and sleep in the truck. Before we could find a home for the night, we also needed to pick up Wye Knot. He was just a little way behind me, and he had reached out again for a shuttle.

Two other hikers were with Wye Knot. Lucky for us, they knew of a lady who was letting hikers tent in her backyard for the night; she was also serving a July 4 trail-magic barbecue. Good goes around. We committed to help Wye Knot, he in turn had told the other two hikers they could tag along, and we all had a place to call home for the night. The trail really does provide.

It was a fabulous barbecue with scrumptious food, and when the sun set, the fireworks began. I didn't stay up to watch the pyrotechnic display. I was tired and retreated to my tent to enjoy the laughter and partying from my own space. Just before climbing into my Hubba Hubba shelter, I recognized the flip-flop sound of a hiker's walk.

At the tent city the previous night, well after all hikers were sound asleep, I was awakened to the sound of flip-flopping all around our tents. It was strange, and I thought someone was searching for what they could claim as their own while we all slept. My tent vestibule was open, and I could peer out. A lone hiker just stood there, looking lost. Seeing he was one of us, I went back to sleep and forgot about it until I heard the distinctive flip-flopping again. This time, I asked if he had been with us last night and explained my story. He proudly boasted that he was the guilty one up that late. He had gone partying and was having difficulty finding his tent.

We were up bright and early despite the party atmosphere the night before. I was in New England now, I could see the end, and the trail was calling. I had to contain myself often so as not to sprint too soon.

We dropped Wye Knot off first, then headed out to my location. He had taken a respite at Harpers Ferry, West Virginia. Enjoying 11 days of R&R had put him behind me for a while, but he was a machine and now we were back together.

Our plans were to stay together. He liked to hike fast and long. I liked to hike medium and not too far. So we would see. Our goal for the night was the home of Maria in Salisbury, Connecticut. She is a sweet little old lady who takes in hikers to help supplement her income. Going to her house was like going to Grammie's house. It had all the charm and character of your typical grandmother's home.

Before we went to Grammie's, we were blessed with more trail magic. Red Panda, a fellow thru-hiker, lived close to the trail. She took a few days off and convinced her family to throw some trail magic. Her family was large and generous. We feasted, then feasted some more. We were at the picnic for over an hour and half. Finally, Bruce said to me, "Shall I get your boots?"

I replied, "I suppose I should get hiking."

Then he added, "If you want a pillow tonight, you must hike!" I thought Wye Knot and Hoosier Mama were gonna fall out of their chairs laughing. Hoosier quipped, "There's a little tough love!"

Hoosier Mama was new to my hiking family. Wye Knot and I met her just prior to the barbecue, and the three of us instantly clicked.

With that suggestion from Bruce, I strapped on my footwear, and Wye Knot, Hoosier, and myself went off merrily to Maria's house.

When we were close to the day's extraction point, I told my hiking buddies I needed to call Bruce to inform him we were almost out. Simultaneously, Wye Knot and Hoosier Mama excitedly yelled, "He needs to have the trail name Batman!" They were hysterical about this suggestion. Up until this point, Bruce did not have a trail name. I tried to give him one, but he hadn't approved any of my names for him.

I couldn't figure out why my hiking friends thought of "Batman." I am not a superhero follower, and I did not understand the connection. I was aware that Batman saves the day like Bruce did for me, but I wasn't feeling their enthusiasm. Then they educated me on the fact that when Batman isn't being Batman, he is Bruce Wayne. OH MY GOSH! I loved it. It was perfect. While I was hiking, he was working and carrying on business as usual—until he got a call from me or another hiker in need. Then he turned into Batman.

And he has been Batman ever since.

July 6 was an unplanned zero day and became a lesson from legends. On the trail, sometimes you have to push through and sometimes you have to listen to your body. Wye Knot and I decided—actually, our knees and feet made the decision—to lay low at Maria's house.

This lady was amazing. She was 85 years old and had been taking in guests and hikers for sixteen years. She was witty, lively, and feisty. Being widowed twice and outliving three other proposals would send anyone else over the deep end. Not Maria. She was full of life and kept going. Even the Everready® bunny got out of her way.

Maria's mind was as sharp as a tack, and she was quite the flirt, especially with Wye Knot. She teased him about being blind, which legally he was. And Wye Knot dished it right back to her about her being deaf. She told us a story about one hiker who asked to go smoke over on the grass, and she told him sure, as long as it was way away, because it made it hard for her to breathe. But, she added, with her deafness, it could be that he had asked, "May I go over there and smoke grass?" She slapped her hands onto her lap and laughed.

We spent the afternoon under the canopy visiting with Maria and Lorraine, her neighbor. The little anecdotes and life lessons they had for us were amazing. Maria and Lorraine were from another era, and the stories they shared connected our generations with valuable life lessons.

We asked her if taking in strangers was risky business for her. She said when she started her hiker B&B, her family was worried. But she said she has been so blessed. In the winter, when it is cold and lonely, she pulls out her hiker albums and recounts all the memories. She said she can only remember a few hikers who took advantage of her generosity, and when word spread about it one time, another hiker stepped up and took care of the financials, so Maria didn't have to bear the burden.

As our social time with the great ladies came to an end, I commented that I wanted to grow up to be just like them. Lorraine said, "All you have to do is to have a good sense of humor, keep moving, and be nice." Wow, that seems easy enough. What great lessons from two great seniors!

Maria was teary-eyed as we said goodnight. She really did make us feel like family, and just like my own grandparents after a visit, she cried. Maria was not a morning person; she knew once we went to bed, we wouldn't see each other again. Our hearts broke as we could see the love in her eyes and feel it in her warm embrace. This was one gift I had no idea I would receive when I decided to hike the Appalachian Trail.

How many Marias are out there in our own neighborhoods that we take for granted? One day they will be gone, and the wisdom, the knowledge, and the love from a bygone error will disappear as well. We were too busy with our day-to-day lives to even give them a second thought. Just think for one moment how much better our world would be if we sought the resources of an elderly neighbor rather than Google.

Today made the first full day of hiking with Wye Knot. We were quite the combination. He was legally blind, and I was legally ditzy. He liked to hike in front of me for my safety. He stumbled often, and he didn't want his forward momentum crashing into me. One injured hiker was better than two. He did not need help by any means. Wye Knot had hiked 1,500 miles so far on his own, and he had done just fine, minus a few bumps, bruises, and a sprained wrist. He was a tough nut, and nothing was going to stop him.

Since we were together, though, my job from the caboose was to help eliminate any possible threats of injury. I would let him know of low hanging branches and trees, knee bangers, toe stumblers, and ditches ahead of him. Most importantly, I would call out if he started to veer off trail. The trail was obvious, but for someone with limited peripheral vision, the trail and a drainage ditch looked the same.

I would yell "Left!" or "Right!" depending on which direction Wye Knot needed to correct. For someone with normal intelligence, this would work fine. But we were talking about me. After a few misguiding directions, I confessed to Wye Knot that I am directionally challenged. I get my left and rights mixed up. Several laughs down the trail, with left meaning right and right meaning left, I learned to focus clearly and give accurate directions. At one point when we came to an exposed ridge, I concentrated so hard to get it correct that I gave myself a headache. At least, I didn't send him over the edge, physically anyway.

Despite the rain and humidity, it was a day full of laughs, three small inclines, and a new state line, Massachusetts, for a total of 13.5 miles. I fell, my first real fall in 1,500 miles. I had slipped off the trail once, way back in the beginning, but this was a fall that could have caused damage. It didn't, though. Wye Knot fell twice. For the record, neither time was due to my misdirection.

The dampness from the precipitation and humidity made the rocks greasy. On one particular loss with gravity, Wye Knot slid down a slippery section of ledge and fell off the lower three-foot drop, landing splayed out on his pack so hard that he bounced up, flipped over in the air, then landed on his belly with arms and legs spread wide. His face was down in the ground, and his leather, down-under brimmed hat covered his head. He looked like a corpse resting upside down.

I was so scared. My breath stuck in my throat, and I couldn't breathe. I was reaching for my GPS to signal an emergency when I heard him laugh. It wasn't until he rolled over with dirt on his face and his Crocodile Dundee hat still on, that I took my next inhale of air. Then we both roared with laughter. I'm not sure if he hurt from the fall or from laughing so hard. It reminded me of a story called Things That Go Bump In The Night. Only this version was "Hikers that bounce on the trail." It was a close call, one we will never forget.

Massachusetts was over before we developed hiker stench. We didn't set any records with only 90 miles completed in 6 days. Can't say we enjoyed every step either. Massachusetts is nicknamed Massa-ROOTsetts. In many places of high traffic, the sod has eroded away from the trail, exposing tree roots that resemble viper pits and are every bit as dangerous, just waiting to grab, twist, and wrench the feet and ankles of careless hikers.

In areas without roots, we were waddling in mud, tons of it, dirty, slippery, slimy mud. There was black mud, brown mud, red mud, and watery mud. With all that mud came mosquitos, hungry swarming, biting little demons. Massachusetts was a mixed bag of nuts.

We had good weather mixed with the wet yuck. We had good accommodations and a night with Nurse Ratched. That was a real treat. The guidebook made note of a retreat center. Sounded good to Wye Knot and myself; it would be a chance to wash off some mud and bug dope. It was the worst experience so far on the trail. Retreat center? Yeah, right.

The kitchen consisted of a coffee pot and a one-burner hot plate. The beds were mattresses on the floor, no big deal there, except the fact that the room was damp and moldy. The bathroom was not much cleaner. And to top it all off, "laundry amenities" meant wearing your clothes in the shower, wringing them out, then putting them in the dryer. But wait! It gets worse. Nurse Ratched only allowed the dryer to run once, so we had to wait for the other hikers who were coming to "wash" their clothes so they all could be dried together. EEEEWW-WWW! If I would have known that, I would not have "washed" my clothes. Keep in mind, we were paying the going rate for what we had been paying at nice hostels.

After our night at the insane asylum, we were hosted by Fruit Smoothie and Pumpkin Butt's parents, Mr. and Mrs. Birrell. I hiked with the sister and brother duo back in the beginning. It seemed like ages ago. As we were getting close to Smoothie's place, I reached out. She had to get off trail due to foot issues, but Pumpkin was cruising and in Maine by now. Batman had planned to join us, but instead he dropped us off at our home for the night then headed to help out Ryan, who was again hiking with GQ and Walking Man.

In 24 hours, we went from filth and slime to glitz and glamour. After 1,500 miles and four months on the trail, it took more than a little bad weather, biting insects, and crotchety people to get me down. It was all part of life on the trail. With the good comes the bad, and it's in the bad that we figure out what we are made of. And with the bad we learn to truly appreciate the generosity of strangers like the Birrells and others we meet along the way. I would need a whole chapter just to list them.

The Cookie Lady and her husband were another such couple who opened their place to hikers. They had a working blueberry farm and country house 100 yards east of the trail. She grew veggies, berries, and raised chickens. But her specialty was cookies. In the afternoon, she offered free homemade cookies to hikers who were also welcome to tent in her yard. The owners' only request was a helping hand mowing the lawn. I attempted to mow the lawn the morning before we hiked out, but I could not get any of the mowers to work, and Mr. Cookie Man was nowhere to ask for assistance.

For the last two hiking days in our eleventh state, we meandered through Dalton, Massachusetts, where the paper for the U.S. currency is made and then up and over Mt. Greylock, the highest peak in Massachusetts at 3,491 feet. On the mountain, we stayed at the Bascom

Lodge, which sits just below the Veterans War Memorial Tower that stands at the summit.

I had reached mile 1,586.3 of this 2,189.2-mile journey. In 10.4 miles I would enter the beautiful state of Vermont. The view from my bunk was perfect; rolling hills disappeared into a misty fog. Experiences such as this were what kept me pushing on when the hiking was tough, hard, painful, and challenging. Listening to my favorite songs, like "Days Like These" by Asia, helped me to push through and overcome any challenge that might have prevented me from enjoying the good that was right in front of me.

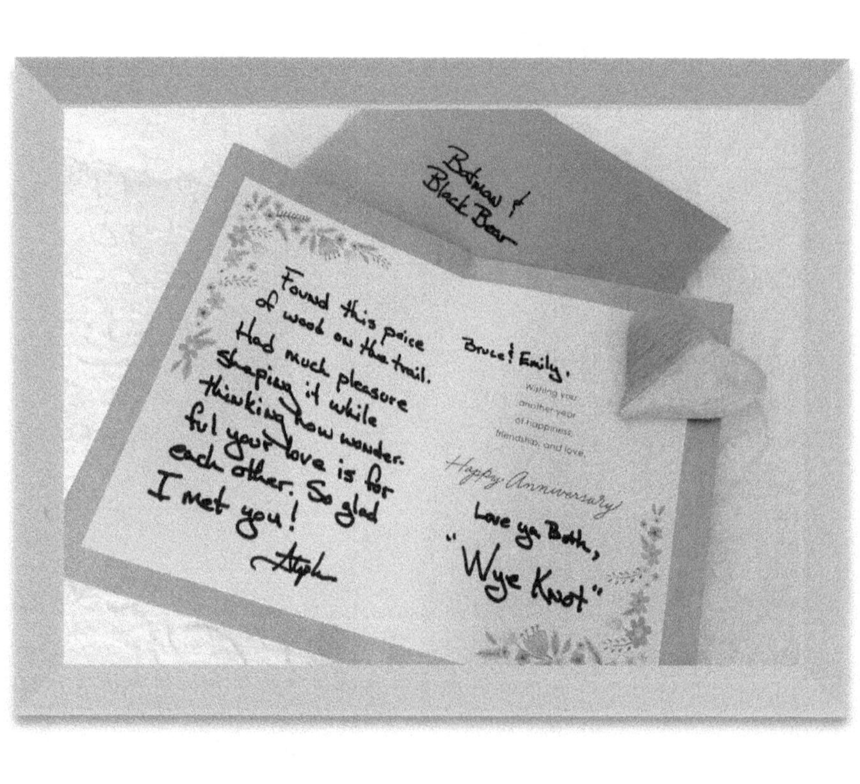
Batman &
Black Bear
Found this peice
of wood on the trail.
Had much pleasure
shaping it while
thinking how wonder-
ful your love is for
each other. So glad
I met you!
Bruce & Emily,
Wishing you
another year
of happiness,
friendship, and love.
Happy Anniversary
Love ya Both,
"Wye Knot"

24

Happy Anniversary

By mid-July, I had slowed my pace and lessened the distance for each day, which rewarded me with feet that did not hurt. It was a little miracle. I can't even begin to express my appreciation for feet that didn't scream at me with every step. I stopped complaining about it because everyone had sore feet. But mine, I do believe, were out of the ordinary.

The last few days had been pain free and I was loving it. It was a good time to have happy feet because I did push on for one last 20-miler. I needed the stars to align if I wanted to be able to spend a night in a hotel with Batman for our 25th anniversary.

In order for that to happen, Wye Knot and I had to do 20.5 miles to reach Congdon Shelter. That would allow Batman to hike south to meet us for a nero out. We were off to a great start in the morning; hiking was easy. We even took time to enjoy a snack at the small vista on top of Mt. Prospect. It was an easy half-mile climb from a road we had just crossed.

After our power snack, we were off again. I was in the lead. Several steps down the trail, I realized we were on a blue-blazed trail. No worries, it was only a few yards. So we backtracked to the vista and headed in the correct direction. The descent from the top was just as easy as the climb up. Fifteen minutes later, we reached a road. My pride sunk deeper than the valley at the bottom of the vista we had just enjoyed. I had led us half a mile south on the trail.

Wye Knot was so mad at me. Thankfully he didn't stay that way for long. Forgiveness is easily given among hikers. Neither one of us had recognized the trail from the opposite direction. Back up Mt. Prospect we went for the second time. That's just what we needed, more distance on an already long day. That morning, we were the blind leading the blind.

The mud increased as we continued. We had been warned about the mud in New England, especially in Vermont. Several states have nicknames and Vermont is known as VerMUD. We were not quite to the state line but close enough for the mud to smear its way over the border, just like the rocks of ROCKsylvania didn't stop at the border of Pennsylvania but continued up the trail for at least another 30 miles into New Jersey.

Our leisurely morning hike increasingly became a mud pit, slowing us down. When we arrived at the shelter, all available tent sites that weren't covered with deep black mud were taken. No worries. Wye Knot used a hammock, and Batman had planned to show up early to have my tent set up. That was the deal for me doing another 20-miler. But where was my Batman and my tent?

Not set up! I found him in the shelter. He had mixed up the flies for the tents. We have two tents, a single and a double. When he was drying them out the day before, he accidentally mixed up the rain flies. With rain forecasted, we couldn't tent without it, so he set us up in the shelter.

I don't usually like shelters unless they are new, and even then, I prefer to tent. To make matters worse, this shelter was awful. It smelled like stale farts stored in a frat house. Around the base, dangling wire caging meant to keep the porcupines from chewing the wood, pricked the back of our legs when we sat down. We could see mice activity, and the hikers already inside were quite annoying.

Inside, I was so mad; but I wouldn't let my face show it, because, after all, I didn't have to carry my tent or sleeping bag that day. It was a mistake easily made, and how could I be mad? If I was really going to be mad, I could only be mad at myself for not taking responsibility for my own things. If I hadn't slackpacked, then I would have had everything I needed.

Who was this person thinking with such reason? Pre-hike, if something like this would have happened, I would have pouted for hours and let Batman know it was his fault. Being on the trail and going through challenges of all sorts had made me realize that blaming anyone was a waste of time and energy. First of all, when I point a finger at someone, there are three other fingers pointing back at myself. So for every one incident I want to blame someone for, there are most likely 3 other events where I am at fault. Just that day, I led Wye Knot a precious extra mile off course. Crap happens. Sometimes you are at fault, sometimes it's someone else's responsibility. Deal with it and move on. Doing anything else is a waste of time and energy.

Sleeping in a shelter is risky business. After a rain, bugs are out in swarms, and you're sharing space with mice, other rodents, and hikers. Thankfully, the night came and went without so much as a nibble from flying creatures nor the fury scurriers. Wye Knot also had an uneventful rest in his hammock. We were packed up and out early so we could make the most of our nero day.

Back at the car, we were excited to get to our accommodations, the Hampton Inn in Bennington, Vermont. A pool and soft beds with crisp sheets awaited us.

First stop was breakfast at a roadside diner, Papa Pete's. It didn't look like much from the outside, and the inside had even less appeal, except for the decorations. There was something for each season. They had the whole year covered: nutcrackers and ornaments for Christmas, hearts for Valentine's Day, shamrocks for St. Patty's, flags for the Fourth of July, and miscellaneous other seasonal displays. No time wasted each month on sprucing up the place. It was time well saved. We knew right where they used that time—on the food. The meals were generous and delicious, a great way to start our nero and Batman's and my 25th anniversary.

Twenty-five years ago, I married my best friend. It was a perfect day. Family and friends came from near and far to share it with us. This year, we celebrated at a Hampton Inn with only our new friend Wye Knot. After breakfast, we did the usual hiker chores of resupply, laundry, eat more, and rest.

Once our tasks were done, the three of us hung out at the pool. Wye Knot claimed a chair across the pool from us, working on a project I thought was for his feet. Bruce and I played musical chairs between the hot tub, the sauna, and the pool. Once we had our fill of relaxing—which came way past hiker midnight—we headed up to the room.

Wye Knot handed Bruce and I something. It was a beautiful anniversary card. Inside was a hand-carved piece of wood in the shape of a heart.

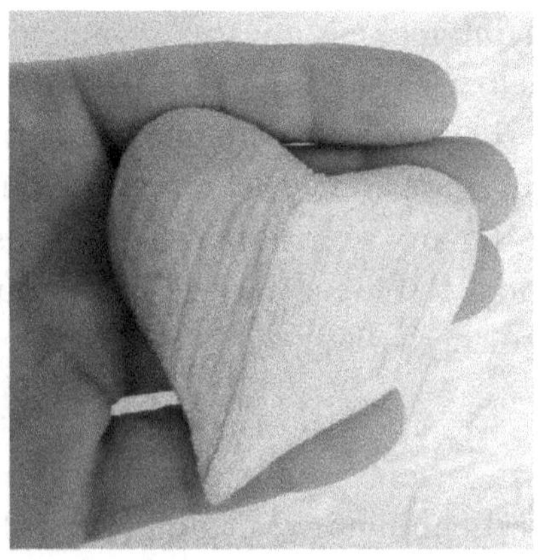

When I saw it, I teared up. I knew exactly where it came from. On the previous day's hike, we came upon a felled beech tree alongside the trail. Someone had attempted to chop the log in half without much success. Their chipping away exposed the inner beauty of the hardwood. The chopping had spewed small pieces of wood around like puzzle pieces scattered on a carpet. For a brief moment, we both had stopped to enjoy the markings carved out by the hacker. I remember running my fingers over the wood and saying what a shame this tree couldn't be hauled out to be made into something beautiful. Little did I know, someone was carrying a sample out to do just that. Wye Knot secretly grabbed a piece of the puzzle and created his own masterpiece for us. Just another form of trail magic.

Wye Knot and I were melding nicely as we continued up the trail. I no longer felt the need for security in another hiker, but it was nice to have him around. We were developing a brother-sister bond that was filled with teasing, taunting, and caring moments. I teased him about being blind, he teased me about other things, but we took care of each other.

After a few days, Wye Knot was trying to walk off a rolled ankle when he decided enough was enough. It was time to have it checked out. Batman and I reached out to various family members who were in the area. My big brother John and his wife, Elizabeth, answered the call. It's so great to be out on the trail, living life on your own, experiencing things you have never done before, but when it is all said and done, nothing beats family. And it was family that was there when we most needed it. Bruce drove us the extra-long distance while Wye Knot and I took advantage of the down time and rested in the vehicle.

Once at John's house, we did the usual hiker chores. The next day, Bruce took Wye Knot to a clinic and I made a spaghetti sauce. John and Elizabeth love my sauce. It was the least I could do to repay them for the impromptu visit.

Wye Knot's diagnosis was a sprain. He decided one day's rest was enough. We were back to the trail in no time.

From that point on, things began to change. Our charming teasing became more like an old married couple's bantering. I began setting out earlier without him in the mornings, and that was okay. I needed earlier starts to get the miles in, and he needed more daylight to see. I liked our friendship, and I didn't want to ruin it by forcing trail compatibility. So we hiked on separately, meeting up at breaks or at the end of the day, and sometimes not at all.

Vermont wasn't all bad. Yeah, there was the mud. Yes, Wye Knot and I grew apart, but there were nice hostels, nice venues, and the awesome country stores, little hidden treasures in the middle of nowhere. One particular place was On The Edge Farm, a little market with fresh treats, beverages, and ice cream.

Two older gents I had met earlier in the day told me about the store. I didn't usually go off trail. My feet didn't like to do any more than what was needed. But I convinced myself the ice cream would be good for the pain. I thought a scoop of the creamy indulgence would be just what the doctor ordered to get me through the day.

When I finally left the farm, I had consumed only one scoop of strawberry ice cream topped with fresh raspberries, but I packed out a Milky Way bar, fresh wax beans, Doritos, and 8 ounces of habanero cheese. I put back the soda. With a little over a month to go on the trail, I was already trying to eliminate poor eating choices. Soda was the first to go, so I thought.

That good choice didn't last too long. Later in the afternoon, we had to cross a stream and our prize on the other side wasn't just being a few yards closer to Katahdin. It was a bucket of stream-chilled sodas. My willpower was left on the south side of the stream. I enjoyed every ounce of the cool, bubbly, caloric, quick energy.

When I got to camp, I went right to work setting up. I had to cook. I hadn't done so in a while. I ate mostly cold meals. I did not like the task of cooking in the evening after a long hike; and with the little sidetrack to the market, I arrived late for me, after 5:00pm. I went right to work cutting and cleaning the beans. They cooked while I set up my tent and did my other chores. I feasted on cheesy green beans and rice as the sun set. GQ would have been so proud of me.

Exiting Vermont was easy. On our last morning in the Green Mountain State, there were four of us now kind of hiking together, Wye Knot, the two gents, and me. Our preplanned early start was stalled by a soft, constant rain. I lay awake in my sleeping bag longer than usual, listening to the pitter-patter on my tent.

We planned to hike out to meet Batman so that we could all slack-pack to the New Hampshire border and then start our zero day. The morning rain slowed our start, but we eventually headed out. It was a wonderful hike, even if the vegetation was all wet. In places where the brush grew close to the trail, it felt as though we were going through a human car wash. We all needed a good rinsing, anyway. Five miles into the hike, we crossed the White River.

On the bridge, we heard the sound of a dinner bell, and just like Pavlov's dogs, we drooled. We had been told about Linda and Randy, who cook for hikers. The two watch for hikers crossing the bridge, then sound the bell and beckon them over for a hot meal.

We were ushered in, dirty boots and all, to Linda's kitchen, where we sat at an oversized island while plates of pancakes, eggs, and sausage were passed around. When we had our fill, we dismounted our stools just in time for the next round of hungry hikers making their way to the island. It was awesome! The generosity of strangers was amazing, and I never once took it for granted. They never wanted payment. Just a smile and/or a hug was all they charged.

Batman was parked across the street from Linda and Randy's place. He was taking our gear so we could enjoy yet another day of slacking. I joked how I am a not a "fisher of men" but a "fisher of hikers" who I bring over to the lighter side.

We all threw our gear in Batman's vehicle; even Wye Knot caught up to us with his later start. He was in that next round of hungry hikers. The gents and I headed out; we hiked slower than Wye Knot. New Hampshire, here we come!

Seven hot and sweaty miles later, we exited the woods at Elm Street. This was the beginning of a 3.7-mile road walk, the longest road section on the entire AT. The first driveway we came to was stocked with coolers of soda, snacks, and miscellaneous hiker needs. We reclined with beverage in hand as we geared up for the last section of the day, which included crossing into New Hampshire.

As we relaxed, a car exited the driveway. We thanked the driver for his gifts, but he was not the homeowner. The driver explained that he lived next door, but if we were interested, he and the homeowner in whose driveway we rested did take in hikers for the night—at no charge. That was the end of our day. The gents canceled their hotel room and made reservations for the free stay as well as reserving a spot for Wye Knot. I chose to go to a hotel with Batman. New Hampshire would have to wait one more day or two.

I enjoyed my night with Batman. We had a nice dinner, did laundry, dried my gear, and slept in the next day. I was worn out and tired. The weeks had been tough, the climbs longer and harder. But that seemed to be the norm. Apostle Paul even wrote in his book *Hiking Through* that "The climbs are either getting tougher or I am getting weaker. I am 63 miles from Mt. Washington… I don't know how I will feel when I am closer to being done with this hike, but right now, I am so ready to be done. I am just completely worn out right now. Some good news though, only 398.5 miles left. Just a little walk in the park."

Years separated my hike from Apostle Paul's, but our feelings were mutual. Since quitting wasn't an option, the only thing to do was to take a break. If a zero day wasn't possible at the moment, I would quit at the end of the day. I'd just start back up in the morning as if it was a new beginning.

Bruce had to head off for a business trip. After our relaxing morning at the hotel, he dropped me off back at Elm Street with the gents. I spent the night there, relaxing more and reviewing some of my reasons to remain on the trail. During my pre-hike planning, someone had advised me to make a list of why I wanted to hike. If I was going to make it to Katahdin, that "why" had to be more important than anything else in my life at the time.

I had never thought my why was really important. I just wanted to do it, and then once I say I am going to do something, I do it. It was really that simple. As time went on, that was still my driving force, but other reasons became strong contenders. The biggest one was that this hike was no longer about me, but for my followers.

I had many friends, family, and strangers reading my blog and living life on the trail vicariously through me. There was no way I was going to let them down. If I didn't finish, they didn't finish. I was not going to do that to them. Day after day, I would dig deep to find the strength and grit through the pain and tiredness to make it through the next day so I could write the next post. It was no longer my hike; it was our hike.

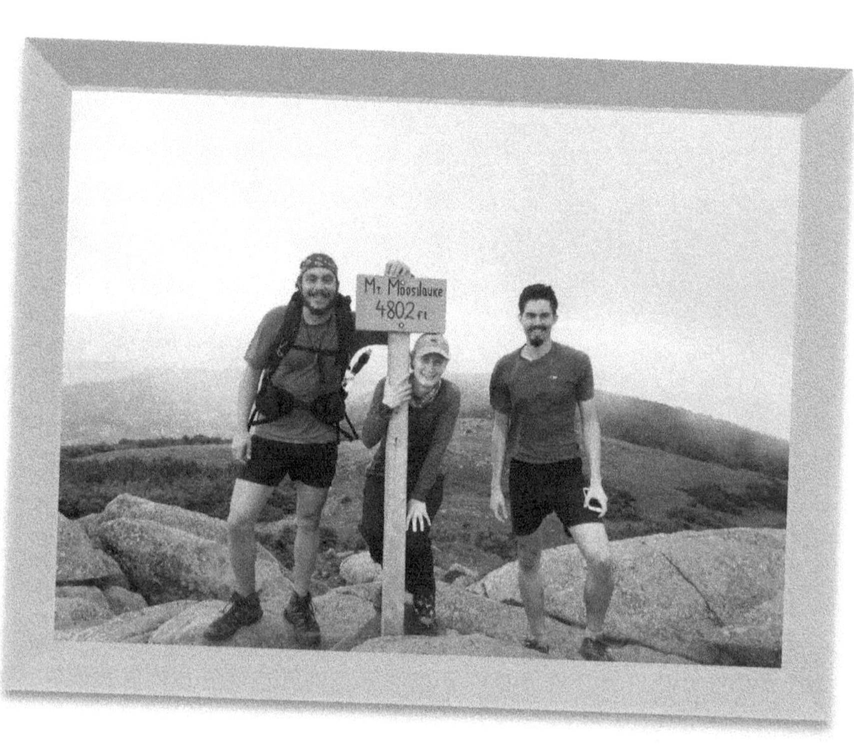
Mt Moosilauke
4802 ft

25

Live In The Moment

July 28 was another new beginning. I was refreshed and about to enter my thirteenth state. Wye Knot had left the day before, so I didn't get to see him. The gents and I headed out early in the morning but not so early that we missed the sunrise over the Connecticut River, the border between Vermont and New Hampshire.

We took our pictures and continued the long road walk to Dartmouth College, where we stopped at a diner for breakfast before finishing our stroll through the college town. Then we were back in the woods, where we would stay for a couple days until we met back up with Batman.

One of the gents was starting to get on my nerves. I couldn't quite put my finger on the aggravation. My sixth sense was acting up again. I didn't know if it was me being tired and annoyed easily, or if it was something else. I ignored the feeling for the time being.

During the next two days in the woods, I met up with Maps and Moxie. I thought they were way ahead of me. They were strong ladies my age who were rocking it on the AT. But a few weeks earlier, Moxie had fallen on a privy's steps and injured her bum. It sounds funny, but it wasn't. She had a dangerously large hematoma the size of a soccer ball on her buttocks. She had to take time off the trail. When I saw them, they were just out for a day hike to help Moxie get her legs back, but the injured area was still pretty swollen.

I hiked the rest of the day with the girls. At one break on top of a peak, we were laughing and catching up. As we were doing so, the gents also caught up to us. Next Time made a very sexist, rude comment about us ladies that only he thought was funny. Even Apples seemed to be embarrassed by it. I was waiting for Moxie to throw Next Time off the mountain. But she didn't. I guess she was being nice since she thought he was my friend.

The girls and I continued to the next road, where Batman was waiting. We parted ways. They had a few more miles to their car, and I had to wait for the gents. I was getting tired of waiting for people. I liked to help out, but now it was becoming a hindrance when it slowed me down.

During our wait, nature called. No big deal. I had been living in the woods for months. I disappeared into the thicket to take care of business, but that was a bad choice. The place was swarming with mosquitos. I did not notice them until it was too late. I could not stop mid-stream or mid-deposit. I tried to pee faster and push harder, but nothing helped. My poor fanny was exposed to the bloodthirsty day-vampires. Bruce heard me screaming and had no idea what was wrong. I came stumbling out of the woods with my hiking skort halfway down. I could not get my sweaty bottoms up fast enough, so I just ran out half-dressed. By the time I had finished, I had bites in places I didn't know insects could reach. It was awful! All because we were waiting to help others. No good deed goes unpunished.

The gents finally showed up. Bruce was taking us back to a hotel where we would share a room—the same hotel where Bruce and I had stayed a couple days before. We were way too nice. I was beginning to regret the offer to share. Next Time was really beginning to creep me out. Apples was cool. But Next Time's true colors were coming through.

First of all, he kept calling me by my real name. Real names were reserved for only your best of hiking friends, and he was not one of them. Plus, he kept winking at me. Eew! He even winked at the guys, so I didn't think I was special. But just the same, it creeped me out. We should have backed out of our arrangement, but I felt bad for Apples. No reason for him to suffer because his hiking buddy was a turd.

We made it through the night. I was only assaulted by Next Time's eyes a couple times. I let Bruce know how I was feeling about this hiker, so he did well to keep between me and the voyeur.

August 1 began a new month on this awesome journey and also a very exciting section of the trail, the White Mountains. The Whites are known for their treacherous terrain and sometimes deadly weather. I was extremely excited to be entering the White Mountains. Most hikers moan and groan about them, but to me they were just another challenge that would make me stronger. And I had heard that if Mother Nature was cooperative, the views were jaw-droppingly spectacular.

Several hikers chose to slackpack over Mt. Moosilauke, the first big mountain in the Whites. Thankfully, the gents chose this option. Slacking required being dropped off north of the mountain and hiking south back to the hostel. My hike only allowed me to travel in one direction. I did not blue-blaze and I only traveled north.

I left the Hikers Welcome hostel in Glencliff, New Hampshire, at 6:20am, hiking solo with a pack weight of only 27.5 pounds. It had taken me 1,790.5 miles to tweak my gear to only necessities. Mt. Moosilauke would be our highest and steepest climb in a while at just under 5,000 feet. I was the queen of slackpacking, but not on this day. Even though I knew this mountain would be tough and slacking would be nice, I wanted all my gear. I wanted to have options in case I needed to spend the night.

I may have headed out solo, but I wouldn't be alone. The hostel was full of hikers, mostly NOBOs (northbounders) who chose the slacking option like Apples and Next Time. We would pass on the trail again at some point, they going south and me headed north.

Wye Knot had zeroed at the Hikers Welcome the day before and I was sure he would pass me. He might have been visually impaired, but he flew on the trail. I sure did miss him. I would have given anything to have his bantering instead of Mr. Creepy Eyes. You never know what you have until it's gone.

After hiking an hour and a half, I was already on my second break and enjoying the solitude. Hiking alone did have its advantages. I loved my hiking buddies, except the ones so noted, but I also loved hiking alone. Solo, I could do whatever I wanted, hike at whatever speed I chose, sing out loud, talk to the trees, break as often as I wanted without feeling like I was holding someone up or annoying them. If anyone heard the conversations I had with squirrels, I surely would have been locked up. But when I hiked alone, there was no one to catch me. I could let the craziness out. It was just like Alka-Seltzer: "Oh, what a relief it is!" Everyone should try it; just let loose. In this world, we all have to do so much, act a certain way, be politically correct, don't do this, don't do that. You would be amazed at how talking with the squirrels can make you feel so much better.

About 75 yards from the summit of Mt. Moosilauke, I could see Turbo coming from the opposite direction. He was slacking with Peacedog. They were two super-friendly young hikers I had seen from time to time on the trail. They had also spent the night at the hostel. The three of us arrived at the summit together. At the top, we congratulated each other with hugs and high fives. We were separated by a generation and opposite social habits—they loved their cabbage and spirits, and me, not so much—but out there we were friends, respecting each other's choices and truly enjoying the journey together. And if they did see me talking to the animals or hear me singing out loud, they would not have judged; they probably would have joined in. Boy, I loved it out there.

The day was splendid, and to top it off, Wye Knot caught me toward the end of the day. We kept each other company the last couple of miles and finished the hike with some surprise trail magic at a parking lot. We had our fill of food and drinks, thanked our trail angels, and hiked a mile north, where we stealth camped. It wasn't much of a spot, just barely large enough for my tent and his hammock. Sleep came fast.

The next morning came even faster. As tired and worn out as I was, a new round of adrenaline was seeping into my blood. I had made it to the Whites, and each morning brought the excitement to get going, as if it was the first day on the trail.

The hike from NH 112 to Kinsman Pond Shelter was every bit as beautiful as it was challenging. It began as a relatively gentle push up and over Mt. Wolf.

My lunch was at Eliza Brook. I cooked a large lunch while I soaked my feet in the cool, refreshing stream—downstream, of course, from where anyone would gather drinking water. I could count on one hand the number of times I cooked at lunch, but since we had been blessed with trail magic for supper the night before, I had extra food and I did not want to carry it up Kinsman Mountain. I ate my normal lunch and the food I would have had for dinner the previous night.

After dressing my happy feet and packing up my smorgasbord trash, I headed up the trail. A lovely stream escorted the trail on the left. The path slowly inclined. But the stream stair-stepped its way, creating small, stagnant pools at the base of mini waterfalls. It was aerated by the churning cascades and as clear as a glass of water drawn from a tap. Small pebbles lined the base of each pool. It was so inviting.

I passed the first pool five minutes after my very long lunch. To swim or not to swim? I hiked on. Two more minutes of hiking, another pool. To swim or not to swim? I hiked on. A few more minutes of hiking, and I couldn't take it any longer. The summit could wait. Sometimes you just have to live in the moment.

I stripped down to my skivvies and was getting ready to go au naturel when two young guys paused their hiking a few yards away. I kept my bikini base layer on and told the guys not to worry, I was just going for a swim. That was so kind of them, to be considerate.

They wanted to swim, too, but hiked on to keep on their schedule. After the refreshing dip, I redressed into my sweaty clothes and continued up the path. It wasn't long until I heard some hooting and hollering from the two guys who had just passed me. They had thrown their agenda over the cliff and also enjoyed the refreshing pools.

I arrived at the shelter before Wye Knot. In the Whites there are huts, tenting areas, and shelters. The shelter was only $8, but I wasn't sure if I wanted to hike on or stay. I chose to stay. The shelter was a nice, three-sided log cabin next to a pond. Wye Knot showed up later and decided to stay also. I didn't really want to stealth; it is discouraged in the Whites. Plus, the terrain wasn't suitable for tenting; there were too many rocks, and if it wasn't rocky and steep, the ground was too damp with moss.

The next morning, we had a slow start. We were not in too much of a hurry. Batman couldn't meet us until late morning, and we had less than a 5-mile downhill hike. Never underestimate the downhill hike. Descents are many times harder than the incline, and so was this one.

Two miles out, we came to our first hut, Lonesome Lake Hut, run by the Appalachian Mountain Club. The AMC owns and operates nonprofit, self-sustaining huts throughout the White Mountains. They are hiker-luxurious cabins in the woods with electricity, running water, and hot meals for paying guests. The price is $180 per person, and most hikers think that is outrageous. It is pricey, yes, but if you consider what it costs to provide such amenities in the middle of nowhere on top of mountains, it's a pretty sweet deal.

We stopped at the hut for a break. They sold beverages and home-baked goodies to visitors. I had a lemonade. I needed the sugar to power me down the mountain. I also packed out a whoopie pie for Bruce. He loves treats.

The 5-mile descent seemed more like 20. We were glad to be out, and once again we were whisked away by Batman. He dropped us off at The Notch Hostel, run by a young couple. It was another wonderful place to stay, and Wye Knot and I planned to rest up for a couple days. His ankle and knees had been sore, and my feet could always use a rest. The gents were still hanging around. But they were not staying at this hostel.

Two days of rest and calorie-loading was just what I needed. I was lazy. Even though I had access to a full kitchen, I did not cook. I consumed a box of Fruity Pebbles, Snickers, Milky Ways, a package of gluten-free Oreo knockoffs, a half gallon of milk, Doritos, Fritos Scoops, and almost a gallon of Moxie, the drink. (Not Moxie, my friend.)

The second night at the hostel, I overheard a hiking friend, Mr. Peanut Butter, say, "I'm going to town to get a Black Bear Special…" That grabbed my attention, and I inquired what a Black Bear Special was. He replied, "Doritos, a Milky Way, and a 2-liter bottle of Moxie." He had seen me eating those things earlier and decided he needed some of the same.

At home, my diet was healthier. But out on the trail, I ate whatever I wanted and all I could get when the getting was good. I called it the 2189 diet. Hike 2,189 miles and eat whatever you want and still lose weight. It's a blast!

Six of us were in the 7:30am shuttle. We were all headed up Franconia Ridge, a 2-mile section of AT above tree line. Two hiked on, while four of us started out together—Wye Knot and me, joined by Mr. Peanut Butter and Iron Maiden. They were a young married couple who were so kind and humorous and a joy to be around. As we hiked, the gaps between us widened, and at times, we played leapfrog as one of us would overtake the other while they were on a break. It made for a fun day.

At one particular snack time when I stopped for a rest, the ground was steep and covered in wet, mossy undergrowth. There was no suitable spot for hanging out. I decided to drop my pack and straddle it like a horse. I had never sat on my pack before, but I had seen other hikers do it all the time. It was quite comfy.

I wasn't down but a few seconds when I heard, *BLEEEEEEP*!

Oh, no! I had just activated my SOS signal. Again! I didn't mean to do that.

I frantically tried to cancel the call, but I could not see the screen. I unsuccessfully dug through my pack for my glasses. Thankfully, Mr. Peanut Butter came down the trail to my rescue and canceled the SOS.

About ten minutes later, I heard a helicopter. *No way!* I thought, *That can't be for me?* It came to my location and then went away. A coincidence for sure, but one that had my heard pounding and kept Bruce on the lookout for a bill to arrive in the mail. The bill never showed up.

I was glad the call didn't go through. I had already sent one accidental SOS back at Neel Gap that had sent my family into a panic. I didn't want to do that again. Mr. Peanut Butter had come along at the perfect time.

That was the last I saw of any hiking pals for a while. There was no more leapfrogging. I worried about not seeing Wye Knot but was so glad the gents seemed to be gone.

I knew there was one more possible encounter with Apples and Next Time. Batman still had some of their gear they didn't want to carry. He had made arrangements to meet them at Crawford Notch to give it back to them the morning of August 8. I was also meeting Batman for a nero day to resupply for my traverse of the Presidential Range.

It was a short 3-mile hike out from Ethan Pond Campsite to the rendezvous spot. I hadn't seen the gents for a couple days. I exited the woods into the parking area and proceeded to walk down the short, paved driveway to US 302. I rounded the corner and could see the gents at the batmobile with Bruce. I doubled back so they wouldn't see me and walked back to the trail, where I tried to text Batman.

No signal. Frantic, I didn't know what to do. I really couldn't handle seeing the creep again. His winking, wanting to give hugs every time he saw me, and his constant talking about how he loves his wife, were wearing my patience thin. And, dude, if you need to keep repeating how much you love your wife, then who are you trying to convince? Not me; maybe yourself.

One of the last times we had hiked together, Apples was ahead several yards and Next Time was behind me. Out of the blue, he started telling me in graphic detail how he had told his son about the birds and the bees. It was quite uncomfortable and inappropriate. I tried to pretend to be interested. Sometimes on the trail, one must tread lightly. You are alone in the woods with people you hope you can trust. You need to be nice, hoping not to make them angry enough to want to hurt you. My tactic was to be nice, then avoid them by hiking off.

I couldn't hike off just yet. I needed them to leave Batman, but I was afraid they were all waiting for me. As I sat there on the verge of tears, another young hiker who I hadn't met before came strolling along. Relieved, I asked him if he had a minute. I explained to him what was going on a couple hundred yards away. He agreed to secretly let Batman know I was there. The young hero and I walked together a few paces, then I dipped into the trees and hid.

The message was delivered. The gents hiked on, and I made it to the car. Phew, I escaped that one. Batman and I could start my nero day.

So much for those plans. Little did I know that Batman had offered to take the gents' belongings to Gorham, where they would be staying in a few days. He didn't know what strong negative feelings I had about Next Time. Anyone reading my blog would have thought things were hunky-dory, but that's because I didn't want to offend Apples. He had given my blog address to his wife, and I was afraid if I wrote anything bad, it would get back to the creep; and I didn't want to deal with that out on the trail.

So my nero day was spent riding in the car 2 hours to help someone who was annoying me and probably taking advantage of Batman's kindness. Bruce and I tried to focus on the fact that we were also helping Apples.

After our goodwill delivery, Batman and I enjoyed some ice cream and a Moxie before setting up our tent just in off of US 302. Pitching a tent so close to high-traffic areas is not recommended, but there wasn't enough daylight left to hike in farther. Batman was spending the night with me before he had to head off to work again. It was our routine. He met me to help resupply, then sent me off for a few days to hike north while he went to work. A pretty good partnership, I must say.

Whoo-hoo! I was sleeping single in a double tent. It was like the Taj Mahal. Of course, I'd rather be with Batman, but since he wasn't there, I was enjoying the extra space.

I had started out five months before with a double tent by Hyperlite Mountain Gear. I loved the weight of it, and it did not absorb moisture. But it didn't have enough headroom for me. There was plenty of space left-to-right and head-to-toe, just not enough space to sit up. I switched to a double Hubba Hubba by MSR, but then I wanted something lighter. So I had switched to a single Hubba. I had more tents now than I had underwear for the hike.

After being cooped up in the single for a while, I was back to the double. By now I was fit as a fiddle, and I didn't even notice the difference in weight when I went back to the two-person tent. The extra space was worth the extra weight.

Extra space wasn't the reason I switched gear, though. My niece Stephanie was going to meet me to hike the Presidential Range. I told her I'd carry a tent for both of us. She was an experienced hiker and one of my biggest fans on this adventure. I was so happy to have the privilege of her joining me. Other friends had offered to meet me and I had declined for a host of reasons, but I had no reservations about Stephanie tagging along. In fact, I had encouraged it.

The weather was starting to change. Early August in the mountains brought cooler temps. It was great for hiking and sleeping but made set up, break down, and snack time a bit chilly. At 3,800 feet, the cool morning air kept me in my cocoon a little longer than normal. I also chose to eat inside the hut. I had tented, but after a brisk time packing away all my gear, my fingers were already a little numb. So instead of eating breakfast as I hiked, I decided to take advantage of the warmth inside the hut.

I was truly living in the moment. Sleeping in and eating before I hiked were things I rarely did, but this morning, I did both. The door to the hut hadn't even closed when I saw Maps and Moxie in the dining room, packing up their gear. It was meant to be. The trail will provide.

We had communicated with each other, trying to meet up; but with lack of cell service in the region and schedules being so different, we never made a connection. But now, here we were, together by chance—or was it? Just the day before, Bruce and I had said a prayer for my safety.

The Presidential Range is the longest above-tree-line section of the entire AT. It includes Mt. Washington, where the worst weather in the world has been recorded. Some people would call my meeting with Maps and Moxie a coincidence, others would say it was luck. I think it was maybe a little of both and a whole lot of faith.

After our very excited reunion, we got busy checking the weather. A storm was coming in, which meant I had to make a quick decision. Do I keep my plans to meet Stephanie to do the Presidential Range in two days? Or do I put on my big-girl boots and do the range in one day to beat the storm? The three of us decided it would be safer to traverse the Presidentials as quickly as possible and avoid bad weather. That meant I needed to contact Steph, and cell service was spotty at best.

Little miracle number two. I was able to get a call out to her. Stephanie was able to adjust her arrangements also. So Maps, Moxie, and I hiked off to tackle the Presidential Range in the White Mountains of New Hampshire.

Up, down, over, up, down, and over we went. The AT didn't actually summit all the peaks. Instead, the trail skirted most of the summits.

Stephanie joined us on top of Mt. Washington. It was a great meeting place. We waited inside the visitor center and had hot food. While we were there, we ran into other hikers. Wye Knot, Iron Maiden, and Mr. Peanut Butter were also there. I didn't know what was more amazing, the incredible, endless views the Presidential Range offered us or the serendipitous way we were all reconnecting.

Once again, we girls, four in number now, went up, down, and over.

Stephanie was a peakbagger, so she would blue-blaze to the summits and meet us at the northern trail junction. We finally made it to Madison Springs Hut, between Mt. Adams and Mt. Madison, the last peaks in the range.

Stephanie had attempted Mt. Madison in the past and for whatever reason wasn't able to add it to her accomplished 4,000-footer list. With the change of plans and worsening weather, she, too, had to make a decision whether to continue north with us to claim Madison's summit, then hike back down and out her exit trail alone and in the dark, or to leave Madison again for another day.

We all have to make choices in life. Sometimes you have to buck up and go for it, and sometimes you have to know when to say, "Not today." For Stephanie, Madison would have to wait. Maps, Moxie, and I would continue north without her, but we were three strong and didn't have as far to go. The White Mountains are not to be toyed with, and it takes a strong person to put safety over pride. Madison's summit was one of my favorites on the hike up to this point. When Stephanie finally is able to claim her prize, it will be one worth waiting for.

After goodbyes, Stephanie went her way and we went ours. Madison Springs Hut sat at the base of Madison Peak. We had no problem scrambling the half-mile, 600-foot elevation gain to the marker sign. As much as we would have loved to have stayed and enjoyed the sunset, we needed to make tracks and get back down to the tree line. There was a campsite 3 miles from the hut, but we knew we would be doing good just to make it back down to the safety of the trees.

The one-mile descent back to the dwarfed spruce trees gave us little hope of finding a place to set up for the night. We were still at about 4,800 feet elevation, losing daylight with every second as well as our stamina. We passed one spot right next to the trail that was not even large enough for two tents, let alone three. The trees were barely seven feet tall and about the diameter of baseball bats. The ground was steep and rocky.

We had almost given up hope of stealthing when something to my left caught my eye. There was a different feel to the surroundings. I stopped and concentrated my sight to the west of the trail, and twenty yards away through the toothpick forest was a small clearing.

A not-so-visible trail led to the clearing. It was such a tight squeeze through the path that we had to take our packs off and carry them in front of us so we wouldn't snag them on the branches.

Once inside the clearing, we had the most perfect spot a tired hiker could ask for. It was flat, rock free, and had room for two tents. Maps and Moxie doubled up, and I enjoyed another night in my Taj Mahal.

A 2,000-mile thru-hike offers many experiences, some good, some great, some bad, and some you wish had never happened. As wonderful and/or not-so-wonderful the memories are, it is impossible to remember every detail. But I will always remember my 13.5-mile traverse of the Presidential Range with Maps, Moxie, and Stephanie, from the moment I walked into Mitzpah Hut to the last ray of sunlight before I closed my eyes in our hidden site among the dwarf trees high in the sky.

We may have been below tree line, if you can call it that with the trees barely reaching over our heads, but we still had 6 miles of hiking to get to Pinkham Notch before the storm. We rallied early, beating the sunrise. We were not messing around. We wanted off the mountain before any rain hit.

It was the trail that seemed to never end. I don't know if it was because we were tired, if it was the challenging ground, if it was the stress of beating the precipitation, or a combination of all the factors, but the trail seemed to go on and on and on.

We were elated when the path dumped us behind the visitor center at Pinkham Notch and even more excited as we stepped under the porch and the heavens erupted without warning, unleashing a torrential downpour. Not one drop touched us. Again, we lived in the moment. Maps, Moxie, and I did a little dance and shouted out. Bystanders looked as us strangely, but we didn't care. We had just spent the last 26 hours pushing ourselves to the limits over some pretty spectacular terrain, testing our endurance, determination, and will. We felt like we had won the Olympics; only in this case, we all stood on the winner's platform.

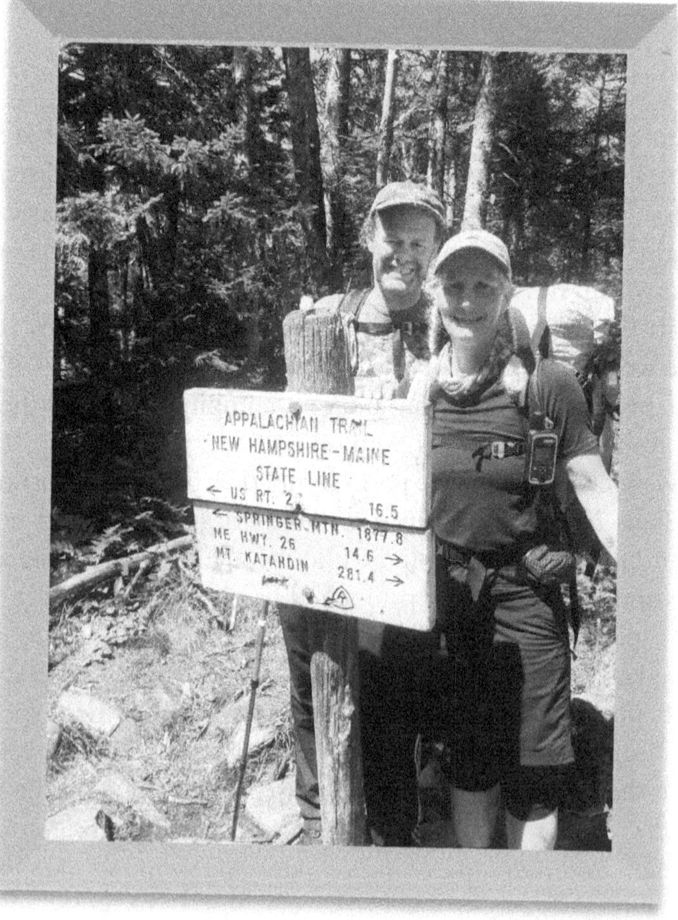
APPALACHIAN TRAIL
NEW HAMPSHIRE-MAINE
STATE LINE
← US RT. 2 16.5
← SPRINGER MTN. 1877.8
ME HWY. 26 14.6 →
MT. KATAHDIN 281.4 →

26

Maine - The Beginning of the End

We waited at the visitor center for the shuttle Batman arranged for us. We had no cell service, but thanks to my satellite device, I was able to send a text to Bruce, who was in Alberta, Canada, and he made the arrangements. Even across the border, Batman came to our rescue.

Maps, Moxie, and I headed into Gorham, New Hampshire, to rest up. Gorham had a couple hostels and a few hotels. We chose to stay at The Barn which was part of a very nice bed and breakfast. The B&B was exquisite; The Barn, well, it was a barn. The owners had converted the downstairs into a makeshift living/kitchen area, and the upstairs had 10-15 beds on the floor. For the price, it would do. It was dry and kind of warm.

Hikers were only allowed in The Barn and could not enter the B&B for any reason. To use the hikers' bathroom, we had to pass the side entry to the main house. Through the window, we could see the plush antique accommodations in stark contrast to our own. For a split second, I felt worthless. That thought made me realize how we so often place our worth on external circumstances.

We let what happens to us decide our moods. Just hours before, I was unstoppable; and now in the midst of peasantry, I was not feeling so worthy. I brushed those useless thoughts aside and focused on my internal well-being. Not being able to afford better standards did not make me less off, nor did accomplishing something great like I had just done, make me any better. It was a great lesson in just being. Being in the moment good or bad, seeing what it really is—just a moment, and it too shall pass. It does not define me. Only I can define me.

While we all took turns showering, we plunked on our barn beds and began our chores. Our spots were located at the top of the stairs, so all hikers passed by our location, and we could not hide unless we dove under the covers. I wasn't paying any attention but felt the presence of someone staring at me. I looked up and there was Next Time. Oh, my gosh! My stomach knotted up and I thought I was going to be sick.

I gave a quick head nod and pretended to be extremely busy with my tasks at hand. He didn't get the hint and proceeded to question me about my behavior toward him the last several times we had met up. I gave him a brief response, and when he pushed, I said I didn't need to explain any further. He carried on and chose a bed three down from mine.

We picked The Barn over the nicer hostel because I was under the impression the gents would be staying at the nicer one. That is where we had dropped off their gear a few days before. I asked the girls to come downstairs with me and I reminded them of who Next Time was. I could not stay there. They were in agreement; they didn't like him either. We had already paid for our beds though.

We checked other options and found a room at a nearby motel. We booked that. I decided to speak to the owner of The Barn. I explained my situation of not feeling comfortable around that man and asked if we could get a refund. The bed and breakfast owners were a couple, two wonderful men who were furious someone was behaving like that on the trail. I had all I could do to keep them from having a "discussion" with Next Time. I felt like I had just been given two big brothers. They were so kind and graciously gave all three of us our money back.

Safely in our own space, we spread out our gear, resupplied, ate, and rested. Morning came, and none of us wanted to head back to the trail just yet. Luckily, we were able to book the room for another night.

We spent a second day just chilling. All our chores had been done the day before. It wasn't a five-star hotel, or even a three, but we had our own room, we were dry, we had access to lots of food, and we had each other. Couldn't ask for anything else.

Rest was over and it was time to head back to the trail. Our shuttle dropped us off at Pinkham Notch where we had been picked up two days ago. We were heading into the Wildcats, the last set of White Mountains before entering Maine. We couldn't wait. We had rocked the rest of the Whites, including the Presidential Range. Nothing was stopping us now.

We tamed those Wildcats. It wasn't easy, and to be honest, we were all a little surprised at the difficulty. No one talks about the Wildcats of New Hampshire. The focus for that state is always on Mt. Washington. The first day back after our break, completing 8.5 miles took us a whopping 9 hours. But we did it! With each grueling climb up and over Wildcats E, D, C, and A, we cheered in victory and were rewarded with spectacular views. We wondered where peak B was but were happy it wasn't an added waypoint.

Maps, Moxie, and I found a stealth camp close to the trail where we quit for the night. We may have tamed the Wildcats, but it wasn't without a price. We were exhausted; and for the first time, we worried if the rest of the trail was going to be this hard. But that was a fleeting moment, and at the same time, we felt exhilarated by our accomplishments.

Morning came and we were packed up. After 1,800 miles of backpacking, breaking down camp was so easy we could do it with our eyes closed. I had a routine I followed every time. I set up and took down in the same order. This allowed me to know exactly where my gear was at any given time. In the middle of the night when it was dark, I could put my hands on whatever I needed quickly and quietly. During the hike, breaks were more efficient because I knew where my snacks were and more importantly, my rain gear. I also only lost two items—a hat on day two and my hiking poles way back in New York, and both times that was because I had done something out of my normal routine.

Twelve and a half miles later, we were back in Gorham, the same town we had left two days ago. But this time we did not need a shuttle. The trail exited the woods 3.9 miles east of the town and only a tenth of a mile from the White Mountains Lodge and Hostel. We joyfully walked the short distance, knowing we would be meeting up with Batman again. Wye Knot, Mr. Peanut Butter, and Iron Maiden were also there. We had not made plans to meet the latter three. It was always a surprise how the ebb and flow of hiker reunions up and down the trail brought reencounters, most of them welcoming, unlike the one two days before at The Barn.

Our town day was the same old, same old routine: shower, laundry, resupply, and eat, and not much time for rest. The living room at the hostel was comfy and cozy. We all hung around, chitchatting as we melted into the couches and chairs. It was all too surreal. In a day and a half, we would be entering Maine, the beginning of the end. It was something we all longed for, and now it was within our grasp.

Mixed feelings were creeping into my head. Before too long, trail life would be over, and I would be back to the real world. I wasn't sure I wanted to go back. I was tired of backpacking; I even hated it. I just wanted to be done. But the thought of reintroduction was a little scary.

After a wonderful breakfast cooked by our hostel host, the five of us took to the trail once again. Batman joined us. From the very beginning, he had planned to cross the New Hampshire - Maine border with me. But work called, and he could only do a five-mile stroll with me and then headed back out. Wye Knot, Maps, Moxie, and I continued north, and Batman went to work.

The next day was our big one. We would finally step foot into the fourteenth and final state. Our goal was to get within five miles of the state line so it would set us up to have lunch there. But just like Batman's plans changed, so did ours.

An unexpected storm was fast approaching, and we made a quick decision to set up camp before the heavens opened up. No time was wasted, and we were all snug in our tents and Wye Knot in his hammock. Shortly after, the pitter-patter of rain turned into buckets. We were very grateful we had made the decision not to push on.

We all had reached a point in the hike where we were just plain tired of being wet and miserable. In the beginning, getting caught in the rain was kind of fun. You dealt with it, joked about it, and even welcomed it on hot days. But not now. We were tired, getting worn out, and we still had just under 300 miles to go. We chose dry over extra miles.

The storm didn't last long, just long enough to lull us to sleep. It rolled out as fast as it rolled in. We were happy with our decision to stop early. Even our tents dried overnight. Not having to carry or wear wet gear up and over the roller-coaster ascent of Mt. Success was sweet. The big treat was at the border, though.

Batman came through again. He managed to take care of work all while he slept in a Walmart parking lot, drove around to a side trail, then met us south of Mt. Success. From there he hiked to the New Hampshire - Maine border with us. At the border, we stopped for the typical state line photos and took a little break. While we were doing so, Batman pulled out a bottle of wine and cookies. How awesome was that!

Bruce, Batman, whatever we call him, is one incredible man. I am the luckiest—more like blessed—woman to be married to him. Sorry, ladies, I don't share. I may have walked the miles, but he was the one to make it all possible for me. He not only financially supported me on this endeavor, he physically and logistically made things happen for me that would have been very difficult for me to do on my own. I have always loved him with all my heart, but a deeper love that I didn't think was possible grew while I was out there. Wine and cookies at the border; it doesn't get any better than that.

Maine, here we come!

I finally made it to Maine. If anything happened now, I could still say I had walked from Georgia to Maine. All four of us had overcome our own unique challenges to make it this far. Wye Knot had his vision and injuries; Moxie had her fall she needed to recover from; Maps struggled with the realization that this hike was temporary and she would have to go back to the real world; and I had my feet to deal with. I wasn't anticipating anything going wrong at this point, but I did feel that if something did go wrong, I would be okay with it. I was in my home state now, and the pressure was gone.

The five of us were going to hike on together, but as Batman likes to tease now, we wimped out. Which meant he had to continue without us to a side trail in order to get back to his car. We admit, we were tired and tried to blame it on the wine, but that was just a small nip. The real culprit was the tough climbs and drops we had been doing for the last week.

The exit from New Hampshire and the entrance into Maine was no picnic. We were seasoned hikers, and in the last three days we had only covered 30.5 miles. A little discouraging, even though we had been warned that was the norm for this section. We could not do the upcoming triple threat, Goose Eye west, Goose Eye east, and Goose Eye. So, we quit early, and Batman hiked on.

The sun went down and came up even faster. My body was not getting rested at night like it had been a few weeks ago. Up until that point, I was amazed at how tired, exhausted, and sore I would be at the end of the day, but come morning, I was refreshed and ready to go. Was it burnout? Was it lack of nutrition? Was it the terrain, or a combination of everything? No matter the cause, the not-so-restful nights were exhausting and worrisome.

That was not the day to wake up tired. We had the three peaks to do and Mahoosuc Notch. The Notch is highly anticipated by most hikers. The guidebook describes it like this: "Most difficult or fun mile of the AT. Make way through jumbled pit of boulders." Sounds like a giant jungle gym to me. I couldn't wait to do this section, but first I had to shake off the morning slug.

The Goose Eyes took most of the day to do, and by midafternoon we finally reached the south end of the Notch. The average time to navigate from one end to the other is about two hours.

Maps, Moxie, Wye Knot, and I took a break to hydrate and fuel up before tackling the infamous mile. The trail only dropped 300 feet over that one mile, so there didn't seem to be any incline or decline. The challenge was pulling yourself up, over, around, and even under the bus-sized boulders that had fallen into the notch when it was formed. We were having a grand time, each of us hiking our own speed, then catching up to one another at different times. We even met up with Mr. Peanut Butter and Iron Maiden at one point.

During one of the leapfrog sessions, Moxie jumped ahead while Wye Knot, Maps, and I stayed together. All of a sudden, Wye Knot fell, wedging himself in a deep crevice. His fall was so loud, we could hear the thud and the air escaping from his lungs. I was horrified. I was sure he had clocked his head and died.

Maps and I rushed to his aid. He couldn't move. His pack had him stuck tight, and his feet had no support. He was suspended in mid-air between the boulders. We managed to wrestle his pack off while he clung to the boulder. Maps then braced herself against the rocks, providing a bridge for Wye Knot's feet as I lifted him up. It took every ounce of strength I could muster from my emaciated thru-hiker frame. He winced in pain with every move.

It was harrowing, but we did it! We got him out of the crack and onto a large boulder. We sat there for quite a while, gathering our wits.

After that scare, we sandwiched Wye Knot between us. Maps took the lead and gave verbal directions from the front. I took up the rear and did the same from behind. I think we drove him batty by mothering him through the rest of the mile, but Maps and I had been so frightened; we didn't want that to happen again.

The Notch took us three hours to complete. We didn't set any records, but we made it.

At the north end, the four of us took a much-needed break. We sat on the trail next to the brook that flowed through the Notch and under all the rocks. You could hear it babbling at times but couldn't see it until the very end. At one time, we could see a spot that was full of ice. It was mid-August and there was still ice; that's how cold it was in there. It was like having natural air-conditioning.

We filled up on calories and ice-cold water from the brook, then headed up and out of the Notch. We only had 2.4 miles to go. Our destination was Speck Pond Shelter and campsite.

We hadn't gone long until we all were throwing out "F" bombs, even me. That wasn't unusual for the other three, but I seldom if ever used that word. But it was flying free that afternoon. The climb out was intense. Maine just kept throwing more and more at us. It was grueling. It was steep. It was never-ending. We thought for sure our 50-something-year-old bodies were no match for this section. Then, sketched in a rock on the trail, was "F*** this trail!" We all felt a sigh of relief that it wasn't just us who felt this way.

Over a mile straight up and 1,100 feet of elevation later, we came to the summit of Mahoosuc Arm. We were all astonished that certain parts of the trail like The Smokies, Mt. Washington, Mahoosuc Notch, and the 100-Mile Wilderness get notoriety, but none of us had ever heard about the difficulty of the Wildcats or the descent or ascent of Mahoosuc Notch. Not counting Wye Knot's fall, the Notch was fun. It was the climb down to it and the climb out that was hard. But once again we prevailed. After 1,900 miles of hiking, we should have known better. Any place with the name Gap or Notch is the low point between two mountains and never a walk in the woods.

We may have made it out alive, but that was as far as we decided to go. We cut it short for the third day in a row. We had only hiked 7.7 miles. But those miles were some of the toughest we had seen on the whole trail. Today we were even more discouraged than before. Each day our mileage was declining, we were getting tired, and our good friend had a terrible fall.

The summit had an open, slanted area of exposed ledge. There was not enough flat space to set up two tents, let alone three. Wye Knot attempted to hang his hammock in the shrubby alpine trees to no avail, so we all just unrolled our pads and sleeping bags on the open ground. This would be the first time and only time I cowboy camped.

It was a beautiful night. The sky was crystal clear and there was no wind. It couldn't have been more perfect. But we couldn't fall asleep, even though we were so exhausted. The sun set the sky on fire, then it finally burned out and left a deep and endless sea of nothingness. One by one, the stars broke through the vast, empty space and filled it up. We lay in our cocoons on the hard rock, eyes fixated on the nighttime sky, not wanting to miss any sights. We searched for space debris, satellites, and meteors. Sleepiness eventually took over, but I fought it hard as I struggled to keep my eyes open on the grandness. One eye closed, then the next, and I was asleep at last.

I didn't think anything could top our Presidential Range traverse, but the night after the Notch was the best night I had ever had. Was it because we had worked so hard to get to that place? Everything had lined up. We had been discouraged about our lack of performance and shortened miles over the last several days, but if we would have stayed the course and not taken that extra day in Gorham, or pushed on to the next shelter another day, we would not have had the experience of that starry night.

I could have done without Wye Knot's fall, and I am sure he would have rather stayed upright. But there is a silver lining to everything and ours was that magical night on top of Mahoosuc Arm.

The next day we had a 5.5-mile hike to Grafton Notch State Park in Maine. There we helped Wye Knot hitch a ride to town. He decided he needed to get checked out and let his ribs heal. The girls and I hiked on to Frye Notch Lean-to for the night, then to Andover, Maine, where Batman would pick us up the day after that.

All things are possible through Christ, who strengthens me. Well, most things are possible with Batman, who rescues me. We took a zero day in Freeport, Maine. What a wonderful place to take a zero. The only downside is that it is 75 miles from the trail. But that is not an issue when you are married to Batman. After showering, we headed over to the L.L.Bean flagship store. Moxie needed some new shoes. Her sneakers were literally shredded. That is one of the never-ending and expensive challenges of the trail—gear wears out.

Maps and I didn't need anything, but we did not come out of the store empty-handed. We saw these matching slackpacking packs. We had to have them, so we each got one in a different color. They would come in handy the next few days as we dumped our gear with Bruce and only carried a day's worth of food, water, and a raincoat.

Zero day completed, and by late afternoon we headed back to spend the night closer to the trail. We rented a camp. What a pit that was! I don't mind roughing it; I grew up spending every fall at a friend's hunting camp that was very primitive, but it was clean. This place was barely habitable. We went from staying at the Hampton the night before, with clean, crisp sheets to a cabin that had mouse turds on the soap bar in the bathroom. The worst thing was that we had rented the place for two nights.

We slackpacked the next three days. We looked quite comical. There we were, three grown women on this grand adventure with matching packs. Moxie had green, Maps sported orange, and I had my signature color, black. We looked more like children setting off for their first day of school.

The first two nights we went back to the pit of a cabin we had rented. I don't know why we didn't just eat the $60 rent and go someplace else. In the whole scheme of things, what's $15 each versus risking TB or some rodent-carried disease?

The third day of slackpacking brought us to Rangeley, Maine. This was a special night. Our son Stephen drove over to spend the night with Batman and me at the motel. It was Stephen's twenty-first birthday. I hadn't seen him since I left home in March. This was the longest I had ever been away from him. It was so good to see him.

The three days of a light pack had me liking backpacking again. For quite some time, I had not wanted to be hiking. I loved being outside, but I was tired of hiking, setting up camp, tearing down camp, getting wet, and getting cold. I just wanted to be done. I wasn't going to quit, but I was not ever going to backpack again. A lighter pack and sleeping inside was turning my frown upside down.

Stephen dropped all four of us off at the trailhead the next morning. Bruce was out for a couple days with us. I remember when we were first married, he had no desire to go camping, and backpacking wasn't even a fleeting thought for him. But he supported me on my dream, and it didn't take long until he fell in love with the sport. As he was falling in love with the sport, I was falling ever deeper in love with him. I didn't know that was possible.

I also learned you can love someone deeply and at the same time want to kill them, figuratively of course. It was a long, hot 13-mile day. The humidity and air were so thick you could cut it with a knife. We camped just south of Oberton Stream. We had wanted to hike a little farther, but the climb out of the stream looked steep, so we decided to fill up our water and backtrack 100 yards to a stealth site we had marked out as Plan B as we went by it.

It was a small, flat knoll nestled right next to the trail. The only thing we needed to do was clear away the tons of moose droppings before setting up our tents. There was only room for two, so the girls shared Map's double tent, and Batman and I shared ours.

Soon after setting up camp, we retired for the night. I could hear the girls laughing while one was cursing the other in fun. One of them had made a smelly in the tent. I thought that was hilarious. A few minutes later, my breath was stopped mid-inhale and I, too, was gagging. It didn't seem so funny now. Bruce had let out a silent but ever-so-deadly fart that just hung in the tent. I gasped for air, unzipped the tent, and hung my head outside. But that did no good. The air was so thick from the humidity that nothing was moving. To this day, I don't think I have ever smelled anything so vile. What was it with him and potty issues on the trail? It was a good thing I love him.

The next day was filled with more ups and downs. We trudged on, and with every step we grew closer to Katahdin. We couldn't see her, but we were beginning to feel her. She was tugging and pulling us along like an invisible lifeline.

The girls and I stopped north of the Carrabassett River ford. Bruce hiked on. We had met a section hiker from Canada who had his car close by. The hiker was heading back to Rangeley, where our car was parked. Bruce had planned to hike to Stratton with us and hitch a ride back to Rangeley, but this seemed more logical and a sure thing. So off he went with a stranger from north of the border.

Being flexible is not one of my strongest attributes, but on this hike I learned to be more fluid. It is almost a necessity in order to thrive on the trail. It is important to have a plan, but it is even more important to recognize when to make alterations to your plans. Things come up. Sometimes a clear plan can avoid most issues, but not always, and a strong person can recognize when changes are needed. So Bruce once again became the hero and hiked ahead so he could go get the car. We would meet back up with him once we hiked to Stratton the next day.

When we left Stratton, we had 188.2 miles left to reach the summit of Katahdin. Worst case scenario was that we had only eighteen days left on the trail, not counting unforeseen injuries. In reality, we probably had fewer days than that.

We could break the remainder of our hike down into three sections: get to Caratunk, get through the 100-Mile Wilderness, and climb Katahdin. It was just a matter of time and putting in the last effort.

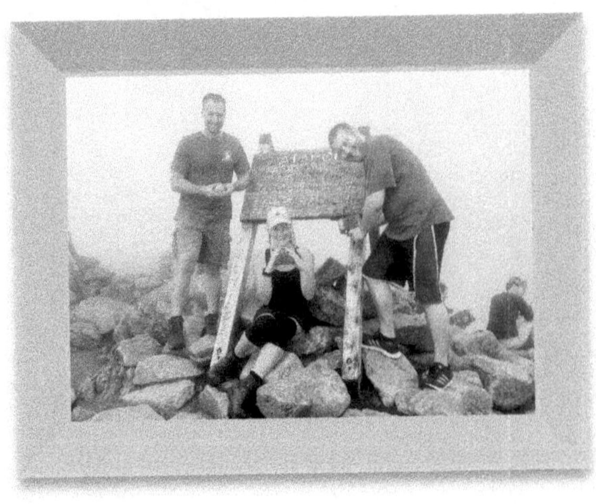

27

The Final Push

Caratunk, Maine, was the next goal, but first we had to traverse the Bigelow range, a popular tourist attraction for outdoor enthusiasts seeking a rugged backpacking weekend. There are three main peaks, South Horn, Bigelow west, the tallest at 4,145 feet, and Avery peak. Our goal was to get up and over these peaks and camp someplace on the north side. But Mother Nature had other ideas.

Along with a dramatic drop in temperature, a storm blew in, wedging us between Bigelow and Avery peaks. We were able to make it to the fire warden's cabin, but it was locked up tight. We even tried jimmying the doors and windows. It was tighter than my mother's wallet. The storm was brewing fast and hard, so we quickly threw up my two-person tent and the three of us gals climbed inside and waited out the weather. It was snug with all our gear, but we were dry and warm at 3,800 feet. We laughed, sang, and told stories. The time passed surprisingly fast. Most gratefully, though, no one farted.

Once the rain stopped, we were not sure we could make it to the next campsite with what daylight remained, so we stayed put. Maps and Moxie set up their own shelters, then we huddled under the eaves of the warden's cabin for protection from the wind and cooked a hot supper and tea.

The previous days had been hot and miserable, and with one quick mountain storm, the humidity left and we were now cold. There is no happy medium out on the trail; it's always extreme, too hot, too cold, too wet, too dry, always hungry, or stuffed from town. You learn to make your own middle ground. Dwelling on what you prefer instead of living in the moment robs us of the present. I would often say, "A bad day on the trail is better than a good day someplace else I don't want to be."

The Bigelows were quite spectacular, with over a thousand-foot climb from our lowest point on the trail to the Bigelow Mountain west peak, the highest at just over 4,100 feet that is sandwiched between the two lesser summits of 3,800 feet for the south horn and 4,000 feet of Avery peak. The hike covers 2.8 miles of alpine trail, some above tree line and some below. Traversing the three tops was like a little game of peek-a-boo. First, we were in the trees, then out, then back in, and out. It made for an interesting journey, with ever-changing views.

After Avery peak, we dropped 1,800 feet rather fast, then went back up another 800 to the mile-long flat top of Little Bigelow before dropping another 1,700 feet again to our rendezvous spot with Batman. The best roller-coaster engineers could only dream of making a ride half as entertaining as a walk following the white blazes. Another section of trail logged in the journals as we continued being tugged north by our lifeline—Katahdin.

Maps planned a surprise. A few days before, on one of our town days, we retrieved a package she had shipped ahead of time. It was filled with birthday goodies for Moxie. Batman secretly also bought a cake. Wine, cookies, shuttles, hotels, slackpacking, birthday cakes—there wasn't much Bruce couldn't do, all the while maintaining his 50-plus-hour work week that often required travel.

At the car, we grabbed a comfy piece of ground and had a break. It was no ordinary stop. This involved birthday cake and trail margaritas. The recipe for such a concoction on the trail is simple. All you need is a travel packet of your favorite sport drink or Kool-Aid (lime flavor works best), mixed with 6 ounces of water, and a single-shot bottle of tequila. It can be a recipe for disaster if you are not careful. You can't tell you are drinking alcohol. We were careful, I think, can't really remember. These items pack well in a hiker's pack without much added weight, but we had Batman, so we didn't have to carry it.

We would have liked to have stayed with Jose Cuervo in Margaritaville, but we still needed to hike 2.8 miles before calling it quits. Luckily, we could slack it. Batman was going to drive around to Long Falls Dam Road and pick us up again to take us to Flagstaff Lake, where we would spend the night. The same spot a year earlier I stayed with Jimmy, I Believe, and Owl Bear.

The three of us were comfortably numb as we left the parking lot and headed into the woods. It wasn't the smartest thing to do; either one of us could have easily twisted an ankle. Sometimes you just have to let loose. At least, we didn't have to carry our packs. We went slow, enjoying our inebriation as we walked the gentle, wooded trail to the next road.

Jimmy Buffet songs were not the theme of the next day. We needed something with more attitude as we rocked out 16.4 miles, half slacking and half with full packs. That set us up to be within half a mile of the Kennebec River crossing. This spot is the only section of trail that you can't hike. You must use the canoe ferry service provided by the Appalachian Trail Conservancy.

In fact, there is even a white blaze painted in the bottom of the canoe to make it official. The river is wide and most of the time lazy. But at unscheduled times, the hydro dam upstream releases water, and the river rises rapidly and without warning.

Several hikers have died by trying to swim across. There is only one guide, and during peak season, there can be a wait to cross. Wanting to beat the rush, we planned well in advance. This time, our preparations were successful. Weather and conditions were optimal, and we were at the river's edge just after sunup, a good two hours early, guaranteeing we would be the first hikers to be shuttled across. We did not mind the wait one bit. We saved breakfast to enjoy by the water as we waited for the guide to arrive and start his day.

Dave the ferryman was right on time. He has been shuttling hikers across the Kennebec safely for nine years. He was a friendly chap, and you could tell he took pride in his work.

Once we were across, we could begin our nero day. First stop was to check into the Northern Outdoors, a sporting resort that caters to outdoor enthusiasts such as rafters, ATVers, and snowmobilers. Tired, dirty, and hungry hikers make up a small percentage of their guests.

The place is spectacular. I have visited this secret gem tucked away in the Maine woods a few times. It has something for everyone's budget, from tent platforms to hotel rooms to cabins. Batman booked us a room in their logdominium. It had a kitchenette, dinette, living room, bedroom, bath, and a loft sleeping area. In the main lodge was a restaurant and bar with a ten-person hot tub right outside. You didn't even need to get out of the hot tub to order drinks. We were there less than 24 hours, but it was well worth the price.

This journey was coming to an end faster than I expected. I was ready to be done; but at the same time, I couldn't believe it was almost over. Only 151.2 miles remained. At the beginning, it had taken me thirteen days to do my first hundred miles. Now I could do those miles in less than half that time. I had grown so much, not just physically, but mentally and spiritually also.

So many thoughts were running through my head. I was so done with dragging my stuff through the woods, over mountains, and down into valleys. I was tired of being wet all the time from either sweat or rain or both. I was sick of having enough dirt under my fingernails to plant a garden. I was ready to not have to drip dry because I ran out of toilet paper. Packing and unpacking my crap just so I could eat and or sleep was now a chore. If I did not ever see another jar of Jif, it would be too soon. The list could go on and on. But with all that yuck, there were greater joys that prompted me to stay.

Back to the trail we went, bright and early as usual. We had an 18.8-mile day planned. We hadn't done that many miles in over a month. Thank goodness for Batman. We were slacking half of it.

In the morning, we cranked out our miles to Moxie Pond, where Batman had a Moxie soda waiting for us. We snacked up, hydrated, and collected all our gear for the push up and over Moxie Bald.

We were running on autopilot now. We crashed at Moxie Bald Mountain Lean-to and did the same thing again the next day, just in reverse order. We were fully loaded to start the day, then dropped our full packs with Batman at Shirley-Blanchard Road, grabbed our L.L.Bean matching slackpacks, and continued another 6.3 miles on to Monson, completing another big day of 17.9 miles.

Making it to Monson, Maine, is a huge feat. Hikers who make it this far have journeyed through 13.5 states and done an elevation gain and loss equivalent to climbing Mt. Everest 16 times. They have endured snow, rain, wind, blood, sweat, and tears. It is the beginning of the final push. When hikers leave Monson, there are no towns or services until they reach Abol Bridge Campground in Millinocket, 100 miles away. There are only miles and miles of dirt roads sporadically cutting through the wilderness.

Shaw's Hiker Hostel located in the small town just east of the trail provides one last respite for hikers to rest up, refuel, resupply, and plan their trek through the great North Woods. Maps, Moxie, Batman, and I took advantage of this stop.

The warning sign at the trail entrance suggests that hikers carry ten days' worth of supplies to safely pass through the 100-Mile Wilderness. Six days of food is a lot to carry; carrying ten days' worth would be a burden not welcomed.

For supper, the four of us went to a local establishment, where Batman struck up a conversation with a local who provided food drops for hikers on this wilderness stretch. Shaw's also would make arrangements for hikers. The fee is hefty and even more if you want it personally delivered rather than left in a tree at a predetermined location. We had Batman, and he had his trusty Maine Gazetteer; but even better, the polite and generous local man wrote out a two-page set of directions for all the road crossings where Batman could slackpack us each day. What a gift!

Excited and pumped up with the information, we planned out a six-day schedule to complete the 100 miles. We would be able to slackpack all but one and half days of the infamous 100-Mile Wilderness. That was unheard of. Some hikers caught word of what we were doing and snubbed us in their not-so-polite way. We didn't care. We had nothing to prove. We walked the miles. We weathered the storms. We beat the heat. We could have done it fully loaded; it's not like we had never carried our packs before. I think they were just jealous because they didn't have the same opportunity. We were not about to let anyone dampen our spirits over something so petty.

The plans were made, and we were ready to go. After a good night sleep of course.

Earlier we had thought we were on autopilot and the days flew by. Sometimes it was hard to remember when one day ended and the next began. It was all becoming a blur. Now we were on cruise control. Batman dropped us off at the beginning of the 100-Mile Wilderness.

We hiked 14.3 miles to Long Pond Stream. On the other side of the stream sat Batman, waiting for us.

We forded the swift, thigh-high water with the help of a rope tied between two trees on either side of the stream. Once we were safely across, Batman escorted the girls half a mile along an unmarked trail to a small, dead-end parking lot where the car and our gear waited. I stayed back to rest my feet. Hiking high miles had brought back my foot misery. They gathered their gear; Batman grabbed ours and a pizza he had brought from town. Not only were we slackpacking, we had pizza delivery in the 100-Mile Wilderness.

The next morning, we did it all over again. We packed up, took our stuff back to the car, grabbed our slackpacks, and headed north. Sixteen miles later, we were at West Branch Pleasant River. This area is called Gulf Hagas, a popular hiking destination for locals and tourists. All the tent sites were full. Maps and Moxie managed to find a spot just inside the woods off the parking lot. Batman and I pitched my tent in front of the car in the parking lot. The sun went down and morning came.

Third day in the wilderness, and we were still slacking. This time, we only did 14.4 miles to Logan Brook Road. Again, Batman met us. No pizza this time. Subway sandwiches were on the menu. We must have been the best-fed thru-hikers on this section of the trail. Batman couldn't stay this night. He was headed out to watch our son Patch play football for UMaine.

The girls and I stealth camped just off the road in the woods next to the trail. It was a peaceful place with tall hardwoods and leaf-littered, soft ground, and no one else around. Even though we were slackpacking, we were still tired at the end of the day, and we all fell asleep quickly.

I was snoozing quite well, which was not the norm for me, when my dreams were interrupted by a familiar and unsettling noise. In the daytime, I would have welcomed the intruder, but not at night as I lay helpless in my tent. Spending many years in the woods in the fall at this exact time of year, I knew all too well what was headed for my tent. A moose!

I knew I could not survive the massive animal stumbling on me as I was lying down, so I sat up quickly. My air mattress is the lightest one on the market, but that lightness comes at a price. It is also the nosiest pad. When I sat up, the pad, sounding like a potato chip bag, scared the poor creature and he took off. I braced myself for impact as I heard hooves scuffing the leafy ground and antlers clanging in the trees. I do believe my heart stopped for a brief second, and I only breathed once I heard Maps and Moxie yelling from their tent, "BLACK BEAR ARE YOU OKAY? WHAT THE H**L WAS THAT?"

That, my dear friends, was your Maine moose!

We could hear the monster trotting up the road, then it came back down the road. Only once silence could be heard for a long time did I dare attempt to drift away. I never did make it back to la-la land. I couldn't relax enough to fall asleep soundly.

In the morning, I investigated the events of the night. I discovered my tent was in the middle of a well-worn animal trail. I guess I had it coming. There were moose tracks and leaves kicked up less than 5 feet from my head. It was by the sure grace of God that the beast did not get tangled in my guy lines and land on top of me. Further discovery showed where he had run up and down the dirt road. My presence must have confused him even more than his meanderings scared me.

Day four, we were packed up and ready to go, this time with all our gear. The terrain for the day looked pretty mild, and the weather looked even better. With only one little bump, less than a 700-foot climb, we were ready to go from cruise to overdrive. We had 18 miles to cover to keep the pace for our itinerary. Before we knew it, another day was in the journal.

Waking up next to Jo-Mary Lake was a wonderful way to start the next day. The sun's golden rays bouncing off the ripples of the lake's surface was an invite to get going for another wonderful day on the trail. This time, we had 19.2 miles as our goal, bringing us to Pollywog Stream, where we would be reunited with Batman.

We arrived just in time to set up camp along the stream and cook dinner on the bridge as the sun went down. We finished our hiker meals aided by our headlamps and were serenaded by a cricket orchestra. Who needs $100 tickets to a concert when you can enjoy dinner and a show free of charge in God's country?

The sixth and final day in the 100-Mile Wilderness meant I was on the final spread of my guidebook, The A.T. Guide by David "Awol" Miller. The book was 223 pages of everything we needed to know to thru-hike the Appalachian Trail. When I first received my copy, I was a little overwhelmed with all the information it contained and the sheer magnitude of the trail. And now on this day, I could open it up and see the end.

As much as I wanted to be done, I had a flickering thought of climbing the summit in two days then turning around and doing the book backward for a southbound hike, also known as a yo-yo. But that's all it was, a tiny flicker of thought that burned out as fast as it ignited. At that moment, though, through all my misery, I now understood why some hikers actually do just that.

Pumped up and ready to go, Maps, Moxie, and I once again gave our gear to Batman and donned our schoolgirl matching daypacks.

We headed off for our final day in the wilderness, with only 17.2 miles to go. It was another beautiful, hot sunny day in the Maine woods. So hot that we went swimming in Rainbow Lake.

I was always up for a dip in the cool waters. Maps and Moxie were more reserved. But this day was extra hot, and the crystal-clear lake was just beckoning us to take a plunge. The only dilemma was that we didn't have our full packs, so we didn't have any dry clothes. We were not about to hike in wet ones. We hadn't had any chafing on the trail yet and weren't about to get any for the last days, ruining our summit climb. So the only natural thing to do was to skinny dip. Since we had entered the 100-Mile Wilderness, we hadn't seen any other hikers during the day. We figured we were safe.

The trail followed the lake, and we found a spot with a large, flat rock surrounded by a few smaller ones. We undressed and enjoyed the freedom from our sweaty clothes. There was no easy access to the water, and as we were trying to figure the best way to lower ourselves into the water from the rocks, we heard an engine.

For real? We were out in the middle of nowhere!

We looked up, and just over the tree line on the opposite shore came a float plane, and it landed right in front of us. What were we to do? We couldn't dive in. Too many rocks. We couldn't slide in fast—rug burns, ouch! So we waved, then continued safely getting into the water to cool off. I do believe he tipped his wings.

The swim felt so good, we didn't want to leave, but we still had about 8 miles to go. We hopped out of the water, each claiming her own rock to dry off on. We had our little camp towels, so we weren't completely unprepared. We needed those to dry off our feet after all the water fords. Maine doesn't build bridges of any sort across the brooks and streams. I am not sure why, but my guess is the spring run-off from the snow melt would probably just take out any bridge.

None of us were dressed. We were still toweling off when we heard *clink, clink, clink, clink*, the distinctive sound of hiking poles on rock! No way! Not another person coming! What were the chances of that—first, a plane lands, now a hiker! We hadn't seen anyone on the trail in days.

I grabbed my skimpy towel and held it over the important parts. I looked up and saw OSHA, an older gentleman we had been leapfrogging up the trail in the past. I grinned and said "Hello, please just keep hiking." He said nothing as he clinked along with eyes straining to keep forward.

A few miles later, we climbed Rainbow Ledges. At the top was OSHA, having a break and enjoying the view of Katahdin. Being the shy character that I am, I asked him, "Which view was better, this one or the last one?"

He replied, "This one." He didn't get my joke; I was referring to the view of us naked girls. He quickly then said with a sly grin, "Oh that one. No, that last view was definitely better!"

OSHA left, and we snacked while enjoying the view of Katahdin. This was the second time we saw her. We had been view-starved for a few days while we were in the lowlands. There were plenty of lakes, streams, ponds, and woods to enjoy, but no mountaintop vistas.

Three days before when we climbed White Cap Mountain, there was the normal shrubby alpine growth and rocky top. Off to the left, barely visible, was a trail carved through the stunted, shoulder-height trees. In the beginning I investigated all I could but after hiking 2,100 miles, I seldom went off trail to chase extra sights. My feet did not want to do more than necessary, but that day I pushed my way past the trees.

A force I had no control over nudged me to scope out where the hidden trail was leading. On the other side, I was caught off guard by my first view of Katahdin. I yelled to Maps and Moxie to come and see. It was unbelievable. There she was off in the distance, standing solo, the highest point on the horizon, and she had called me to her. I felt the dampness of a tear trickle down my check and the salty taste on my lips. They were tears of joy and overwhelming accomplishment mixed with tears of sadness that it all soon would be over.

This second view of Katahdin didn't have the power of the first but it was still impressive. At almost a mile high, she stands taller than any other peak in Maine. Katahdin seems to rise up out of the ground with a presence all her own, dwarfing anything around her. Percival Proctor Baxter said, "Man is born to die; his works are short-lived. Buildings crumble, monuments decay, wealth vanishes. But Katahdin, in all its glory, forever shall remain the mountain of the people of Maine."

Refueled from our snack break and refreshed from our swim, we took off to finish the last six miles of the 100-Mile Wilderness.

Batman hiked in to meet us as he had done other times whenever he could. He was simply amazing. He would leave us at point A, then do whatever he needed to do to navigate his way around back roads and through small towns to point B. If there was time, he would hike south and join us on the trail.

I never grew tired of seeing his smiling face and his camera pointed in our direction to capture every moment possible. Right before we reached the Golden Road, he ran ahead so he could capture us exiting the 100-Mile Wilderness. The hoots, yells, and cheers together with the clanging of our hiking poles were loud and proud! We did it! Another milestone on the Appalachian Trail completed.

We walked the short distance on the Golden Road, a dirt logging road in the north Maine woods, to Abol Bridge. The bridge has one lane for vehicles with a divided section for snowsleds and pedestrians. The bridge is an iconic structure crossing the west branch of the Penobscot River. In the middle, a broad view of Katahdin can be seen jutting above the trees. From where I stood on the bridge, a mere 16 miles separated me from Baxter Peak. Another sobering thought reminded me the journey was coming to an end.

That night we camped at Abol Pines along the shore of the Kennebec River. It was a quiet night. Not much talking took place. I was lost in my own thoughts of the last six months. My guess was, so were Maps and Moxie.

Morning came, and we were our lively, sparky selves again, ready to tackle another day on the trail. It was an easy, short 10 miles from the campsite to the next campsite at the base of Katahdin in Baxter State Park. We enjoyed our daypacks again as Batman took our gear and met us on the other side one last time.

The hike was like being in a fairy tale where everything is perfect and pain free. It was the sweetest hike. We followed the river for a while and another stream whose name I cannot pronounce, Nesowadnehunk. Then more streams. We passed Big and Little Niagara Falls and Daicey Pond and eventually ended at Katahdin Stream Campground. The hike was so easy; even with frequent stops to enjoy the trail, we had a full afternoon to rest up before our big summit day.

Most hikers stay at The Birches Lean-to, reserved for thru-hikers for a nominal $10 fee, but we had reservations for two private lean-tos at Abol Campground two miles east of the trail. We didn't want to rely on space at the Birches, and it is only for thru-hikers, so Batman wouldn't have been able to stay with us. We also had more guests. My friend Justin and my nephew and godson, Sean, were joining us.

Bruce picked us up at the trailhead and drove us back to the campsite. The girls grabbed one of the lean-tos with their friend Penguin, who we met up with. Batman and I set up our tent, saving the other lean-to for Justin and Sean. I set right to work building a fire. Shortly after, the park ranger visited us to let us know we could not tent at the lean-tos. Thankfully, there was an empty lean-to next door, so the girls rented that one and Batman and I moved our tent into the lean-to.

Justin and Sean showed up close to sunset with Subway sandwiches and margaritas. It was going to be a great night. Alcohol is not allowed in the park, so we kept it very low-key and respectful. Sean took a seat next to me at the picnic table, and I told him I had a story to tell about his aunt once Justin joined us.

A few minutes later, Justin sat down and I proceeded to tell them about our skinny-dipping excursion with the plane and the hiker. I spared no details. When I finished, Sean laughed and confessed he already knew.

"How is that possible?" I asked.

He proceeded to tell us that he and Justin had stopped at a store in Millinocket for a few last-minute items, and they spoke with a hiker who told them about hiking upon three naked women—and one of them was named Black Bear. I guess it isn't true that what happens on the trail stays on the trail.

A bottle of tequila and two bundles of firewood later, we all retired to our spots for one last night on the trail.

We were up before sunrise and signing the trail log just as the sun started to break the darkness. The girls cruised ahead, and I didn't see them again until later that evening to deliver their gear. I was a little sad at first that we had been through so much together but didn't summit together. But that was okay, too. Things work out for a reason, and the day couldn't have been more perfect.

Justin, Sean, Batman, and I made our way slowly to the top. Batman and I could have easily pushed forward and kept pace with Penguin, Moxie, and Maps, but Sean and Justin did not have hiker legs hardened by almost 2,200 miles. We took frequent stops and relished the relationship we were building as they joined me on this climax of my trip. Justin likes to do an annual hike of Katahdin, but Sean had never summited her, even though he had attempted a few times in the past.

We also had another job to do while hiking. We were honored to be carrying two important articles. When I first thought about doing the hike, I wanted to do it for a cause. I was so bogged down with information overload of planning that I didn't have the brain power to also think about a cause outside of myself. When I met Andrew, he had heard about a program where you can carry a rock in memory of a fallen military hero. But that did not pan out, either. So I invited a couple schools I was affiliated with to follow me. At least, that gave me a sense of helping in a different way.

But on this day, it all came full circle. The night before as we sat around the fire, Justin had showed us a surprise. He had two stones of two fallen heroes from The Summit Project. The Summit Project is a living memorial for fallen Maine heroes who have died in the line of duty since September 11, 2001. It was the same program Andrew had told me about. The stones were for Bret Emory and Joel House. They were young men from our area who had been killed overseas.

I couldn't say a word. All I could do was cry. Justin hadn't known my desire to do something like this, and here he was, presenting us with the memory stones to be a part of my final summit. It was more than I could handle. Once again, the trail provides.

Our job was to ensure these Maine heroes are not forgotten by carrying their memorial stones to the summit and talking about their lives to other hikers we met along the way. Justin carried one, and Sean and I shared the responsibility for the other. The particular stone we had was a little heavy. Just when I could feel its weight start to be a burden, I quickly remembered the struggles the young man and his family went through giving his life for other's freedom. The weight I carried became trivial.

Our hike was shrouded in clouds all day. Visibility was at best ten feet. The downside was that we were working so hard climbing the mile-high mountain without the reward of a view. The upside was that we concentrated on each other. We didn't have to fuss over getting that perfect panorama because there was nothing to see. Our focus was on helping one another navigate the rungs and scrambles. We rested on each other as needed and told stories about the memorial stones.

This wasn't my first time up the Mountain, so I knew when we were getting close to the top. I could feel my excitement growing. A hiker descending asked if I was Black Bear. I affirmed I was, and he then said, "There's a welcoming party just up ahead for you." I started to hyperventilate. I knew who it was.

My niece Stephanie, who joined me for the Presidential traverse was meeting me at the top with two of her children, Brady and Kyla. The previous summer, we had all hiked the mountain together. We were going to descend by way of the knife edge, but my fear of heights had caused me to chicken out. We had to backtrack and go down the same way we had come up. Little Brady said to me, "Don't worry Auntie Em. I'm young, and I can do it another day." Words from the mouth of babes. They had driven from southern Maine, arriving late into Millinocket the night before and spending the night at a hotel, only to get up early to reach the summit before me.

The cloud cover was so thick we still could only see a few feet in front of us, but it wasn't thick enough to muffle the sounds of Brady and Kyla calling to me from the mountaintop.

"Auntie Em, Auntie Em, you are almost there!" It sounded like angels guiding me home. I could not see them, but I could hear them plain as day.

Then there they were. Excitement got the best of them, and they ran down the trail to meet me. My little niece and nephew appeared from the smoky fog like a dream in a fantasy movie. They threw their arms around me and hugged me tight.

I was almost there, just a few more yards, but I didn't want to move. Excitement as well as sadness took control. I had all I could do to keep from melting into the rocks that made up the mountain. I was so moved by the sincere joy those two kids had for me. Joy and sadness were ripping me apart from all directions.

It was all about to end. My brain knew it. My heart knew it. But my soul had not yet accepted it. On the trail, I was Black Bear, a fictional character I chose before the hike who became real over six months of hiking. Once my ears heard the cry of "Auntie Em," my soul flipped. I hadn't heard my real name much in the last six months. I didn't want to go back to being her. Yes, I still wanted to be a wife, a mom, a friend, an aunt. But I had also become so much more, and I didn't want to lose that.

By now I could hear Stephanie and the rest of my entourage. I finished my hug session with Brady and Kyla, and we headed to the finish line. Several steps later, there it was. First, I saw the sign, then Batman, smiling, with the camera in position, just like all the other times he had met me.

I had just walked 2,189.2 miles to reach that sign, white blazes guiding me north with each agonizing step my feet could endure, Katahdin pulling me toward her like a giant magnet. The goal was the summit, to accomplish something great, to kiss that sign.

But it wasn't the sign I went to. It was Batman. It was Bruce. It was my husband, the man I fell in love with all over again, the real hero of this journey who I went to first. Nothing else mattered.

We descended the mountain, said good-bye to our friends and family, then drove to Millinocket to deliver Maps and Moxie their gear. Just like that, it was over. After two years of planning, six months of hiking, and countless memories made, Batman and I headed home.

An hour later at 9:00pm, we arrived at my dad's house, where he and my brother were waiting for us. Dad had made his famous shrimp salad, hamburgers, and hot dogs. He made extra for leftovers, but little did he know how his little girl's appetite had changed. I let round one settle; then after sharing a few stories, I went back and cleaned up whatever food remained.

Batman and I left Dad's and drove the short three miles to our house. It was late, and we were exhausted mentally and physically. It was the first time I had ever been away from home for so long. The boys were away at college, and the place seemed so huge, empty, and unfamiliar yet comforting at the same time. It was a strange feeling I could not explain. But I was finally home. I enjoyed my adventure, but I was never, ever going to do any long-distance backpacking again.

We left the unpacking for the next day and went right to bed. I didn't even shower. I knew I could do that as long as I wanted, as often as I wanted, the next day. Sleep was needed. Uninterrupted, worry-free, alarm-free sleep was all I wanted to do.

It came fast. I fell into a deep sleep, the best sleep yet, but soon after drifting away, I woke up in a panic.

"Oh my gosh!" I screamed. "Bruce, there's an animal on my leg! I can feel its fur on the back of my ankle! I don't dare move! What do I do?"

I was so alarmed. It was the most frightened I had been on my entire thru-hike. I was in deep, peaceful sleep but was abruptly awakened by something furry rubbing back and forth against my exposed ankle. Thoughts raced through my sleepy, terrified brain. I tried discerning the danger I was in. Was it some carnivorous creature of the night looking for a midnight snack, or worse? I was frozen in fear. What if it were a skunk and we'd be sprayed? Okay, maybe being sprayed by PePe Le Pew isn't as threatening as having my leg gnawed off. But when you are terrified and you have no clue where you are, your reasoning skills are non-existent. My mind raced with horrendous scenarios playing out in a split second.

Bruce sensed my terror and calmly said, "Em, it's okay. You're at home, in your bed, and it's the cat."

I was completely disoriented and had no clue where I was. It took me a few seconds to process this new information. After I was sure what was fact and what was fiction and that the danger had past, I burst out laughing. It was my first night home from my adventure. My mind had adjusting to do.

I was home for two and a half weeks and settling into home life was much harder than I first thought it would be. The first days, I have to admit, were quite stressful and full of anxiety as I readjusted to life off the trail. Adapting to trail life at the start, something I had never experienced before, was a breeze and easier than I had expected. It was actually quite enjoyable. I slipped right into the routine of walking all day. My only concerns were food, water, shelter, and safety from the elements. It was routine and very peaceful. It was hard to believe that now it was all over.

Now that I was home, everyone expected me to carry on like before. But I couldn't. I had changed, evolved. I was still Emily, but with a huge dose of Black Bear. I had learned to live simply, love more deeply, appreciate everything, and other things. I went back to work right away and fell into the old routine of my domestic chores as well. There was so much to do, so many commitments, and not any time to just be. Black Bear was slowly going into hibernation.

I never have been one to like crowded or small spaces, noise, or other over-stimulating situations—except for outdoor sporting events. Now I started having more frequent panic attacks. Routine trips to the big city of Bangor, population 35,000, would have me riding in the car with my hands over my eyes. Walking into Walmart, Bruce would have to hold my hand and keep me calm as the masses zoomed by me with their carts and screaming kids.

Is it any wonder that a year later, when Sharon asked if I wanted to hike the Appalachian Trail again, I said yes?

Epilogue

The Trail Giveth and the Trail Taketh Away

Even before I stepped one foot on the Appalachian Trail, I had heard the old adage, "The trail giveth and the trail taketh away." Being slightly educated (which is a dangerous place to be, specializing in nothing and knowing just enough to get into trouble), I thought I knew what that meant. My definition was: "You give some and you get some." Simple enough. In reality, I had no clue until I became a part of the Appalachian Trail cult.

"Yikes! What is she talking about, cult?"

I know, the term cult dredges up images of religious fanatics and mass suicide, but don't worry, that isn't how I use it here. According to the Merriam-Webster dictionary app on my phone, a kinder and gentler description of the word is: a usually small group of people characterized by such devotion. Like all things one devotes to, there is give and take; and so it is with hiking the Appalachian Trail.

Throughout Happy Hiking I wrote about finding things on the trail, from items needed to friendships to spiritual gifts. From almost the moment I started planning my hike, I was a recipient of serendipitous items.

When I was done writing and re-writing my story as much as I could without professional help, I sent it away to my editor so she could work her magic. The next day, I started picking up my notes, drafts, and miscellaneous materials for Happy Hiking that I had scattered on my writing desk for over 4 years. As I was doing so, a blog-post dated April 02, 2015, fell from a stack of papers as I moved them. At the top of the print, written in my scribbling with very large letters was: "Put this in the book way later." This is what my blog post said for that day.

The Trail Giveth and the Trail Taketh Away
April 02, 2015

The first thing the trail took from me was my bright orange UMaine Black Bear hat. I lost it the second day on the trail. It was going to be my signature hat.

I have been a recipient of serendipitous items from the trail several times. The main thing I continue to be given from the trail is change. I find it everywhere. I think I am the only hiker who actually carries change. I collect it and drop it in the next tip or donation jar I come to when I enter a town.

My really nice find was a square foam seat that Gilligan found and gave to me. It was just lying in the middle of the trail. I like to take lots of breaks, and that makes it nice to sit on and is light.

Several smaller things like a twist tie to hold my cords so they don't become tangled in my bag. One morning when packing up, I said to myself I needed to get twist ties next stop in town. That night when I set up my tent, there was a large one on the ground. The trail giveth? I know it is really God who giveth.

The largest item the trail took from me happened about 4 days ago. The trail did not provide for my hiking buddy, Andrew, so he decided to go home. I cried for two whole miles. Then I was sad the whole day. I get so emotionally attached to people I care about. He and his wife have a special place

> in my heart. I know I will see them when I get home, but the first day on the trail without him was so hard and lonely. I wish him well.

That post was written very early in the hike. Those were not the only examples of the trail's give and take. Goodness and sadness continued to follow me north.

When I discovered my omission, I dropped what I was doing, sat down, and read the sheet of paper I had printed from the internet and had written the note on so as not to forget it, which I did forget. As I was reading it, my mind went in a totally different direction. I had written the post with less than a month of trail experience under my boots. When I reread it, I was a full-fledged AT cult member with a different set of processing tools.

The second paragraph mentioned continuing to be given change. I did not read that as money, but rather as the verb—change. I said to myself, "That is so true even today when I am back in the real world. The trail changed me and continues to do so, even though I am miles away from it." It wasn't until I continued reading that I realized back then I was talking about money. But my brain wouldn't let go of the thought about the trail providing change in me.

Most of the time when a hiker says, "The trail will provide," they are referring to unexpectedly receiving something at a time when they most needed it, usually in the form of food, water, a ride, or some other physical item or service. But the intangible is seldom mentioned, and that realization didn't dawn on me until I reread the post that slipped from my pile.

Change is a huge aspect in a hiker's experience when they embark on the journey from Georgia to Maine, Maine to Georgia, or any other direction they choose to hike. Thru-hikers are not the same when they finish mile 2,189.2 as they were at the start of mile zero. Something happens to them in between. Yes, they lose weight. They grow hair. They get fit. They make new friends. Those things are obvious.

What isn't obvious is the change that takes place in the hearts and minds of those unsuspecting 25 percent each year who actually complete a trek of the Appalachian Trail. That change is different for everyone. We all start with different stuff, and we all end with different stuff.

A friend of mine, Eric Lorrain, a thru-hiker in the class of 2014, called that stuff "the beast." He blew his knee out hiking through the Lemon Squeezer in New York. He was not about to quit, but the pain was ruining his enjoyment of the hike. He wanted to be present and enjoy the hike, but he couldn't get past the agony in his knee. He had to learn to deal with it, to figure out how to hike and live in the now. His pain and all the other stuff (the beast) he worried about were stealing the joy of his journey.

One day as he was hiking, he discovered his knee had stopped hurting as much and that it coincided with having a smile inside his heart. He was choosing to focus on the nice things around him, the now (the smile). He discovered the more he stayed in the now, his knees didn't hurt, his leg didn't hurt, and other worries didn't occupy his mind. It was because of the smile.

For Eric, the trail gaveth to him a strong heart and a strong will to see what was right in front of him, and the trail tooketh away his beast. For me, the trail did that also, and so much more.

I had a multitude of beasts I didn't even know lived in my being. But the trail stripped me down to my most vulnerable state and clothed me in a new way for which I will be forever grateful. Today, five years later, I am still learning how I have changed. Sometimes it is obvious, and other times it is subtle.

As I hiked north, I morphed into a better person. It wasn't like I was a bad one to begin with, but there is always room for improvement. What does "better" actually mean? My better will be different than your better. For me, I guess, the biggest change for the better in me was the trail tooketh away my pride. I didn't even know I had it.

I tend to be a very high "D" personality, everything had to be my way, or take the highway; and it was important that everyone know I am right and that I never ever showed weakness. I loved to win and usually did not have fun if I came in second. That was pre-hike.

Post hike, I couldn't care less what people think about me, right-wrong-indifferent. As far as never showing weakness in public, well, I don't care about that either. I still like to win; I am working on that. But the gist of it is, the trail changed my attitude and gave me a sense of freedom. With each mile I hiked, certain stuff—the beast—became less important to me. Once I stopped fretting about things that didn't really matter, I could focus on what was important.

Who would have thunk a long-distance hike could change someone? When AT thru-hiker-wannabes take that first step on the trail, the last thing in their mind is, "Oh, how will I learn and grow as a person mentally, physically, spiritually as I embark on this quest?" Yeah, right. We are wondering where the water source will be. Did I pack enough food? Did I pack too much food? Will I be bear food?

But once we devote our heart, mind, and soul to the cult of the Appalachian Trail (for lack of a better term), miracles happen. Sometimes it is finding a blanket when you send your cold gear home and the temps drop unexpectedly. Sometimes it is having a view of a summit all to yourself. Sometimes it is meeting up with hikers you haven't seen in a while to traverse a treacherous section with so you don't have to go it alone. Sometimes it is coming to a stash of water left by a trail angel when all the streams have dried up.

But the biggest miracle, or taketh and giveth of the trail, is change. It takes away the beast within us and replaces it with a smile within the heart of the AT thru-hiker.

Many Thanks

Thru-hiking the Appalachian Trail is not an easy accomplishment, but it sure was easier than writing this book. I could not have done either without the help of so many people. First, I would like to thank Bruce. You are the real champion of my adventures. Right from the get-go, I had your support one hundred percent. And it was your commitment to my goals of completing all 2,189.2 miles of the Appalachian Trail and to becoming an author that kept the dreams alive when I wanted to quit. I love you more than you will ever know. And many thanks to the rest of my family, especially Stephen and Patch, and Brittany. Thank you for letting me have a break from being "Mom" for six months. And also to Mom and Dad Leonard, my in-laws—I think you two are my biggest fans.

My support didn't stop there. Kudos to my co-workers at the Bangor L.L.Bean outlet store for being as excited about my trip as I was. And to the staff and students at All Saints Catholic School and Enfield Station School. Just knowing you were thinking and praying for me, helped me to keep clogging along when things were tough.

No thru-hike can be accomplished without the help of so many unnamed heroes—all the faces behind the Appalachian Trail Conservancy, the countless ridge runners and trail maintainers, trail angels, and hostel owners – who tirelessly give their time, talents, and love, so we can hike. Special thanks go out to Jimmy and I Believe for taking me in and showing me the ropes of how to become a competent thru-hiker.

To my "tramily." you all hold a special place in my heart. The Appalachian Trail community is unique and accepting. It is no great surprise so many people who hike its entirety are changed forever, and part of that change is because of the people we meet along the way. Whether I met you for a day and your name and face have faded from memory or if you are now part of my forever world, you are part of the reason those white blazes still call my name. Special thanks go out to Andrew for helping me get started on the hike. Then to GQ, Walking Man, Fruit Smoothie, and Pumpkin Butt, who helped ease my transition from dependence on the trail to independence. And Kilroy who saved me from the snake. I may not be here today if it wasn't for you. And Maps, Moxie, and Wye Knot, you three were the icing on the cake. Thank you for laughing, crying, and yes, even arguing the miles away. You truly are my three best A.T. friends. I will never forget our night on top of Mahoosuc Arm under the stars. My tramily wouldn't be complete without thanking Ryan for immortalizing this adventure in your documentary *Walking Home*.

Thank you to all my friends and family who I trusted with a sneak peek to help me with proofreading. Especially JoAnne, my awesome neigbhor.

A huge thanks to Paul Stutzman for sharing his Appalachian Trail thru-hike story in *Hiking Through.* Your book was the very first story I read about the trail, and it solidified my desire to hike it. And by quoting a line from your book on my *Happy Hiking* blog hosted by *The Bangor Daily News,* I caught the eye of your editor, Elaine Starner. Which brings me to the last thank you.

Elaine, I know it is trite to say words cannot express my gratitude and appreciation for what you have done to help bring this book to fruition. From first reaching out to me, introducing me to the awesome ladies in the Art and Joy of Words women's writing group, to cleaning up my mess and making this story real. Most importantly for believing in me and being my friend also.

About the Author

Emily Leonard is a devoted wife and mother of two boys. She loves the outdoors. After thru-hiking the Appalachian Trail, she became an author to share all that the trail taught her. She has published two children's books about her journey and she also writes her own blog *EmilysEscapades.com*, where she spins ordinary life into adventure with an occasional lesson hidden between the lines. When the white blazes of the Appalachian Trail are not calling her, Emily and her husband, Bruce, call Maine their home.

Meet Emily M. Leonard

at

www.EmilysEscapades.com

See her adventure photos

Follow her blog

Purchase books

Contact her

Read her 2015 AT Blog at

www.happyhiking.bdnblogs.com

www.ingramcontent.com/pod-product-compliance
Lightning Source LLC
Chambersburg PA
CBHW070327090426
42733CB00012B/2391

* 9 7 8 1 7 3 6 1 5 6 8 0 3 *